The visit to Australia by MCC in 1932–33 under Douglas Jardine's captaincy is the best-remembered and most controversial cricket tour ever to have been undertaken. The use by Larwood and Voce of fast, short-pitched bowling directed to a leg-trap of four or five (primarily to counteract the threat posed by Bradman) caused a furore that has been well documented both by the participants and subsequent commentators.

Laurence Le Quesne has written a complete re-appraisal of the circumstances surrounding the tour, the events on and off the field in Australia and England, and the continuing reverberation of the affair in the following years.

This remarkable study is based on the records of both the MCC and the Australian Board of Control and on lengthy interviews with many of the leading survivors of the series including Sir Donald Bradman, G. O. Allen and R. E. S. Wyatt. It throws new light on the origins of 'bodyline', on the changes in the nature of cricket after the First World War which provided the setting for it and on the character of Douglas Jardine, who was responsible for its use.

This extraordinary book makes it possible for the first time to see the 'bodyline' episode in true perspective and will upset many long-held ideas or prejudices.

THE
BODYLINE
CONTROVERSY

Laurence Le Quesne

With a foreword by G. O. Allen

London
UNWIN PAPERBACKS
Boston   Sydney

First published in Great Britain by Martin Secker & Warburg Limited
1983
First published by Unwin Paperbacks 1985

UNWIN® PAPERBACKS
40 Museum Street, London WC1A 1LU, UK

Unwin Paperbacks
Park Lane, Hemel Hempstead, Herts HP2 4TE, UK

George Allen & Unwin Australia Pty Ltd
8 Napier Street, North Sydney, NSW 2060, Australia

Foreword copyright © G. O. Allen 1983, 1985
Text copyright © Laurence Le Quesne 1983, 1985

*This book is dedicated, with
much gratitude and affection,
to the memory of Eric Kelly –
Australian, historian, lover
of cricket, schoolmaster
and friend.*

ISBN 0-04-796098-1

Typeset by V & M Graphics Ltd, Aylesbury, Bucks
Printed in Great Britain by Richard Clay (The Chaucer Press) Ltd
Bungay, Suffolk

Contents

Illustrations

Foreword

by G. O. Allen

'Bodyline' was an unhappy episode in the annals of cricket and in my opinion the sooner it is forgotten the better. But, having said that, I am glad this book has been written as, of all those I have read on the subject, I sincerely believe it presents by far the most impartial account of what took place and the repercussions that followed.

The author lays emphasis on two points hitherto not generally accepted and which I am convinced are fundamental to the story. The first is that the object of the discussions in advance of the tour was to consider whether ways and means could be found to contain Bradman's immense range of strokes and that what emerged was Jardine's belief that some form of leg-theory was probably the best bet. Hence, what came to be called 'Bodyline' was not a carefully hatched plot but something that developed with events. The second is that the pronounced variation in the bounce of the ball on that tour added greatly to the problems of the batsmen and thus contributed in no small degree to the success of the tactics.

The author has clearly been energetic in his research and in one respect he has been fortunate in that he has had access to certain documents until recently regarded as 'untouchable'.

For those who are interested in cricket history, of which the 1932–33 tour of Australia is sadly a prominent part, this book is a 'must' and I wish it the success it richly deserves.

Author's Note

As noted on page 14, the name of the governing body for Test Cricket in Australia in 1932–33 was the Australian Board of Control for International Cricket (now the Australian Cricket Board). Because 'ABCIC' seemed undesirably clumsy, I have abbreviated this throughout to 'ABC'; but I apologize to Australian readers for any confusion this causes with the Australian Broadcasting Commission, a body which does not figure in these pages.

Preface and Acknowledgements

This book is not the final and definitive account of the 'bodyline' controversy that I would have liked it to be – though I am immodest enough to hope that it gets some way nearer that objective than any previous account. It falls short of it partly because I am a working schoolmaster, and I have simply not had time to follow up some leads that might have proved rewarding, or to seek out all the people who might have been able to help me; partly because the surviving records are imperfect, and not all of them are available for inspection; and partly because some of the survivors of the affair still carry the scars it left and, fifty years after the event, are understandably not keen to reopen them. It is my particular regret that for this reason I was not able to interview Harold Larwood or Bill Voce; but I respect their wish not to be involved, and I hope I have done them no injustice as a result in the pages which follow.

But for all my regrets at avenues unexplored and questions unasked, my main reaction as I look back over the eighteen months I have spent in writing this book is of gratitude for a vast amount of help most generously given by a great many people who did not know me from Adam – help without which the writing of it would have been completely impossible. It is my pleasure to take this opportunity of thanking them, and in doing so one name in particular stands out – that of G. O. Allen, who has in effect been godfather to the book almost from the moment of its conception. He has been unfailingly generous in time and hospitality: his own recollections, and his scrapbooks of the tour, have been invaluable to me; and it is to his introductions and his help that I owe most of the success I have had in obtaining access to hitherto unexplored sources of information on the tour of 1932–33 and the events that followed it. In addition, he has read the entire book in typescript, and without his comments and criticisms it would contain many more errors than it in fact does. It is both inevitable and proper that my judgements have not coincided in every point with his, and for the opinions expressed in the book I alone am responsible; but his influence on it has been manifold, and my gratitude to him is deep.

R. E. S. Wyatt, Jardine's vice-captain on the tour, has also been unfailingly helpful and informative, and I stand very much in his debt. I am grateful too to Leslie Ames and Bill Bowes, both of whom made time to see me and talked to me freely about their memories of the 'bodyline' series. It is one of the great difficulties that any historian of the 'bodyline' controversy has to contend with that the one man who could have given an authoritative account of it from the pro-'bodyline' side of the fence, Douglas Jardine, died comparatively young without leaving behind him any considered version of his side of the affair. I am all the more glad accordingly to have had the opportunity of meeting his daughter, Mrs Fianach Lawry, and of hearing her account of her father and of his attitude in later life to the events of the tour of 1932–33. I am grateful to her accordingly for her help and her hospitality.

Closer home, I owe a great deal to Mark Williams, my colleague on the staff of Shrewsbury School, for the enthusiastic interest he has taken in the project from the outset, for the loan of a number of extremely helpful books from his collection, for his advice on technicalities to an enthusiastic but wholly armchair cricketer, and for his comments on the script. Of those who have willingly given me access to important source materials, or helped me to find them, I would like to thank particularly Mr Brooke Crutchley for permission to consult, and to quote from, his father's diaries, and Dr Brian Stoddart of the Canberra

College of Advanced Education for enabling me to trace Mr Crutchley and for first making me aware of the existence of the diaries by his interesting essay on the 'bodyline' tour. I am equally grateful to Lord Gowrie and to Mr E. W. Swanton for permission to quote from the letters of Lord Gowrie's father, the then Sir Alexander Hore-Ruthven, as printed by Mr Swanton in his books *Follow On* and *Sort of a Cricket Person*. I am also indebted to Mr J. D. Coldham, the editor of the *Journal of the Cricket Society*, who was kind enough to follow up a chance meeting in the Library at Lord's by sending me extracts from two interesting letters from F. R. Foster and C. J. Kortright.

The records of the MCC are obviously central to any book on this subject, and it is not the fault of their present custodians that so much has been lost and that they are in so many respects disappointing. I am grateful to the Committee and to the Secretary, Mr Jack Bailey, for giving me access to what they have; and I owe a particular debt to the Lord's librarian and archivist, Mr Stephen Green, for his unfailing helpfulness and readiness to produce records, space to work and periodic cups of tea to keep the researcher in business, as well as allowing me the run of the library, of which I have made extensive use.

In the course of my all-too-brief visit to Australia to gather material for this book, I met with a great deal of generous and courteous help from many people connected with the game. Above all, I am indebted to Sir Donald Bradman, not only for his generosity for his time and his hospitality, but also and most especially for his help in obtaining permission for me to use the records of the Australian Cricket Board in Melbourne – the most valuable single haul of primary source material on the 'bodyline' affair I came across anywhere in the course of my researches. I am further grateful in this connection to the Board itself, to its Executive Director Mr David Richards and to his deputy Mr Graham Halbish for their parts in allowing me access to the records and facilities to work on them. The Secretaries of the New South Wales, Victorian and South Australian Cricket Associations were uniformly helpful in response to my requests for information and for permission to consult the minutes of their Associations for the relevant period. I must also particularly thank the Honorary Librarian of the NSW Cricket Association, Mr Cliff Winning, for his ready and generous assistance with my researches.

Of many other friends in Australia, new and old, who helped to clarify my ideas by discussing their own memories of the events of 1932–33 and by suggesting further lines of enquiry for me to follow up, I must single out especially David Elder, formerly Oxford University Press representative in Melbourne, for the energy and enthusiasm he has devoted to helping an author who no longer belongs to his own firm.

It remains finally to complete this Preface by coming home to the most orthodox, and therefore most easily underemphasized, of all obligations. My editor, Bill Neill-Hall, has radiated cheerfulness and enthusiasm for the project from the beginning, and I am more grateful than I can say to him for his encouragement and for his invariable willingness to come three-quarters or more of the way to meet me when I have been in a mood of authorial awkwardness. It has been a pleasure to work with him, and I wish all authors could be equally fortunate in their editors.

Finally and most orthodox of all, there is my gratitude to my dear wife. I have been in her debt so long and for so much that the encouragement and interest she has contributed to this book, not to mention her willing shouldering of all the extra burdens that have come her way as a result of it, may not add much to the total account; but it has meant a lot to me, and I would like to say so now.

Shrewsbury
3 December 1982

I have taken the opportunity afforded by this paperback edition to correct one or two small errors in the original hardback edition.

January 1985

PART I

The Bodyline Tour

Introduction

The third Test Match of the 1932–33 series between Australia and England opened at the Adelaide Oval on – inauspiciously – Friday 13 January 1933.

Adelaide is a decorous city: of all the capital cities of Australia, it is probably the only one (apart from tiny Hobart) which would be likely to take pride in that particular adjective. Sydney and Melbourne have dominated the Australian urban scene for over a century, and as a matter of pride and self-respect the capitals of the less populous states (and, for that matter, the states themselves) have each had to find special qualities to credit themselves with: Adelaide has banked heavily on dignity and respectability. Its Victorian founder, Colonel William Light, planned it spaciously on the broad, featureless plain between the river Torrens and the tumbled Mount Lofty ranges, surrounding the central gridiron block of his city with a wide belt of green parkland, and the city has never lost the Regency sense of style and dignity that inspired its planning. The pace of its social life too was sedate. Adelaide was never a convict city, like Sydney, or a gold-rush city, like Melbourne: it was never brash or *nouveau riche*. Its tone was set by the wealthy squatters whose vast sheep properties dominated the state, and more than most Australian cities it retained the English sense of social hierarchy, and a social tone dictated by the respectabilities of its middle classes. There is a traditional Australian joke that, if people desire to place you socially, in Sydney they ask how much money you have, in Melbourne they ask what school you went to, and in Adelaide they ask what church you belong to. It has the nugget of truth in it that all good jokes of the kind require, and it serves neatly to summarize the air of decent, not to say prim, respectability that the inhabitants of the other Australian capital cities are accustomed to regard as typical of Adelaide. And whatever may be the case in the 1980s, in the 1930s most citizens of Adelaide were happy enough to accept this image of themselves and their behaviour.

Their cricket ground, the Adelaide Oval, mirrors the qualities of the city. Compared with the Test Match arenas of Melbourne and Sydney, it is green, gentlemanly and relaxed. There are no overpowering stands; trees grow along one side of it, the spire of the cathedral overlooks it, the river Torrens runs close by. It has something of the air of a quiet English county ground like Worcester. One cannot carry the comparison too far – Adelaide, after all, is a capital city, and the Oval has harboured Test Matches since the 1880s – but it is the sort of ground where Englishmen are apt to feel at home and relaxed, away from the great frowning stands of Melbourne and the rough democracy of the Hill at Sydney. Of all the Australian Test Match grounds of the 1930s, Adelaide was the one where one would have expected the cricketing proprieties to be most deeply entrenched; where an outbreak of bitterness on the field and fury among the crowd seemed least likely. Yet it was there that it was to happen.

CHAPTER 1

Preliminaries

(September 1932–January 1933)

Much of this book is to be about the strange and little-understood phenomena of crowd behaviour and mass emotion. This is not particularly surprising, for these are forces which have had much to do with the shaping of the history of this century; but it is a real difficulty that the understanding of them, of what exactly it is that determines how, and when, a crowd will react to a rumour, or to an event happening before their eyes, lags far behind the recognition of their importance. There have been brilliant, imaginative insights into some aspects of crowd behaviour – the way, for instance, that under the pressure of strong emotion a crowd seems to fuse into a single, synthetic personality that for the moment takes up and overrides the individual personalities of the people who make it up – and there have been men who by instinct have brilliantly exploited the possibilities that these aspects offer to a demagogue: one thinks immediately of Hitler. It is the explosion of world population, and the tendency for that population increasingly to jam itself together into vast urban antheaps, that has made the subject so urgent; and perhaps, therefore, it is not wholly accidental that a country which has one of the largest proportions in the world of its total population concentrated in its great cities – Australia – should become the scene of the first large-scale disruption of the polite world of first-class cricket by the pressures of mass emotion. For that is what 'bodyline' was: it was the failure of its creators to realize that this is what it was likely to develop into that is the most serious charge against them. The fact has not been generally recognized, but is none the less true for that. The 'bodyline' crisis has usually been thought of as a series of events which happened among the players, out in the middle, and their repercussions among the administrators of the game in Australia and England; but it was not only what happened out in the middle, but what happened among the simmering crowds in the stands and the evening-paper readers out in the streets, that turned a controversy into a crisis.

War, politics and sport have been the three great furnaces of mass popular emotion this century: in the past, religion was the greatest of them all, but in the Christian world anyway its fires have cooled. After 1918, war was unavailable: for the sophisticated societies of the western world, and especially for the victors among them, it was officially unthinkable after the horrors of the War to End All Wars. In 1928, this taboo was even made official by the Kellogg Pact, outlawing war among the signatories. Yet urbanization continued, and the experience of living together in vast urban masses breeds emotional tensions which insistently demand catharsis and release, just as its anonymity gives rise to an urgent sense of the need for identification. Add to this the fact that the Western World had just emerged from a period of prolonged emotional over-stimulation, during which partisanship and the passion for victory had been whipped up by both natural and artificial means to unheard-of heights for four years on end, and it could not be expected that public taste should adjust itself at once or easily to the humdrum pace of an ordinary life that made no demands on these emotions: a stimulus of some kind it must have. In some countries, especially the defeated, political conflict was sufficient to fill the gap in the form of fanatical parties of the right and left; but in politically more mature and stable countries like

6

the USA and the white dominions of the British Empire (as it still was), this option too was not available. What was available was sport.

Indeed, sport was more available than ever before: technical and social developments alike contributed to its growth. The mass spectator sports antedated the First World War – they originated in Britain in the last quarter of the nineteenth century, as a result of the outgrowth of improvements in public transport, the emergence of a popular daily press and a slowly rising standard of living; but after 1918, they leapt forward. Paid holidays and rising wages made them more accessible to the working man than ever before: the advent of the motor bus (and, to a lesser extent, the private car) made it easier to get to the grounds. Attendances broke all records. 'People flocked to the best county matches,' says Sir Pelham Warner, speaking of 1920, 'and where in previous years seven or eight thousand spectators had been considered a good gate, we now found twenty, twenty-five, and even thirty thousand at Lord's.' Attendances at soccer matches were, of course, much greater in England, but cricket too commanded a far wider public than ever previously, and at the other end of the social scale George V gave the final social cachet to both sports by adopting the practice of attending Cup Finals and the Lord's Test Match in person, as royalty had never done before.

Sport – especially in the form of team games – provided the opportunity for emotional release, for the engagement and identification that the average man could no longer find anywhere else, for its two tiers of followers: the spectators in the stands and the readers of the popular press. Inevitably, this release was more effective for the spectators, who had the events happening alive under their eyes and who knew that all was still to be fought for. Here again, one longs for a clearer understanding of the mechanisms of mass emotion. One knows – everyone knows – that the presence of a crowd makes a difference to a game, that the intensity of the crowd's emotions reaches

7

out and infects the players – even hardened professionals, even in a game as inherently 'cool' as cricket. The adrenalin flows more freely, and victory matters more. The larger the crowd, the more tightly packed it is, the closer its proximity to the players, the more powerful the emotion it generates.

Another important variable is obviously the strength of the crowd's commitment to their side. An impartial crowd is a cool one, and though there is no way of measuring this, there seems little doubt that post-War crowds were on the whole more committed, more closely identified with their sides, than pre-War ones had been, just as they were also larger. The pre-War spectator – and this is particularly true of cricket – was more likely to be a man of leisure, with the detachment that that brings, than his post-War successor. He was more of a connoisseur and less of a partisan. The great crowds which flocked to the cricket and football grounds of the 1920s were intensely partisan. They wanted to see their side win; and if the side in question represented not merely a local community but a national one, the identification and the passion for victory were all the stronger, given the overriding power of nationalism and the immense artificial stimulus it had received during the War. With that focus suddenly removed, the emotions it had nourished poured into sport instead, and international fixtures saw them at their hottest. If there were no longer battles to be won, there were at lest Test Matches.

Sport not only provided an opportunity for identification with a side: more than ever before, it provided an outlet for the cult of the individual hero as well. Here again the parallel with the War, and the techniques of war propaganda, is inescapable. Within the commitment to his own side's victory, the average civilian's, or spectator's, emotions find more effective release if he can identify individual heroes – both identify them, and identify with them. Sport, in fact, lends itself to this instinct of hero-worship even better than war, since the civilian cannot

8

watch the battle directly, and can only learn who his heroes are through the medium of the press, whereas the spectator of a game has his heroes and their heroisms under his eyes, and can identify with them that much more closely in consequence. The development of the sporting hero, barely perceptible before 1914, proceeded apace after the War. The spotlight that a generation before had fastened on Kitchener and the Boer War generals now swung to Hobbs and Tilden and Bobby Jones and a host of other sporting figures. A few years more, and it would fasten on Larwood and Bradman. There are few better reflections of the cult than the cigarette cards of the period – magnificent specimens of popular iconography, none of their series was more popular than the numerous sets of sporting heroes. But the chief stimulant of the cult, as of the enthusiasm for sport itself, was of course the mass media, which as usual responded with the sensitivity of mercury to this new trend of public taste.

One says 'the mass media', but 'the mass medium' would be far more accurate, for broadcasting was in its infancy and television still well in the future. The press reigned supreme – until the 1930s, it was unchallenged even by the newsreel. Originating in the 1890s, the mass circulation popular daily – made possible by the railway and universal primary education, exploiting brilliantly the tastes of the new democratic readership by its techniques of sensation, headline and photograph – was at its peak in the period between the wars. This was not only a matter of the morning papers: hot news in the 1920s and 1930s meant the latest edition of the 'evening' papers, pouring forth in edition after edition from mid-morning onwards, and for them especially – since sport was for the most part an afternoon activity – the new zest for sport was manna from heaven. The sports pages expanded ravenously, swallowing column after column and page after page. It was nothing for a Test Match to occupy two whole pages: there would be not only an over-by-over account of the play (the nearest thing yet available to a running commentary), but separate reviews of it and reflections on it by sporting critics, by famous ex-players and, by 1932, even by participants in the match itself. The sporting journalist had made his appearance – the greatest of all cricket journalists, Neville Cardus, was already writing for the *Manchester Guardian* – and rival papers competed fiercely for the privilege of putting the names of famous ex-players at the head of their columns, even if the pieces beneath them were in fact often ghosted. In 1932 the London *Star* achieved the coup of sending out the (not yet retired) Jack Hobbs as its correspondent to cover the English tour of Australia. The popular press and mass spectator sport were born for each other; and the press was to be of critical importance in the formation of English opinion on the 'bodyline' issue in particular, for whereas Australians could see it in action for themselves, Englishmen could not – their knowledge of what was happening came solely through the papers.

The growth of mass spectator sport is one of the dominant features of twentieth-century popular culture, and a sufficiently well-established one; but it might be natural to suppose at first hearing that cricket would be relatively insulated from it, and from the pressures that it brings. Football, yes – soccer especially, with its continuous action, its huge gates, and its tradition, already strongly established by the First World War, of being the working man's game. But surely cricket was different – cricket, with its powerful amateur tradition, its patrician governing body, the MCC, and its longstanding association with the aristocracy and the aristocratic code of courtesy and chivalry? Besides, as I have already said, cricket is a very cool game – the coolest of all team games. It is cerebral, and measured, and slow. Its moments of action can be beautiful and thrilling, but they are pinpoints, separated by long periods of inaction when the tension droops, when the fiction of conflict is abandoned and batsmen and fieldsmen chat cheerfully together between balls or between overs – in the average game of cricket, the ball is out of play considerably longer than it is in it: if you like, there is more peace than war. Again, the game does not involve physical contact: it is the ball, or the stumps, you are trying to hit, not the opposing player (though this idea itself was to come into dispute at Adelaide). Sheer physical strength is a relatively minor factor in it. And finally, cricket demands large grounds: seventy-five-yard boundaries are the norm, which means a minimum distance of 150 yards from side to side of the ground, and many are larger than this. The players, therefore, are remote, especially since action is heavily concentrated around the pitch, and emotional contact between them and the spectators is correspondingly harder.

All this is true; and in fact cricket *has* escaped some of the uglier consequences of the growth of mass spectator sport and passionate spectator involvement, such as violence between rival gangs of supporters. Yet in the years after the end of the First World War, cricket felt the new pressures crowding in upon it as much as any other spectator sport, and perhaps more than any. It could be argued that some of the reasons for exemption from these pressures quoted above are in fact double-edged: that, for instance, it is the moments of action that provide relief from tension, and that the repeated intervals between balls and between overs in cricket merely act as dams to the spectators' emotion, and allow it to build up again. Certainly in those moments of inaction a player is far more exposed to the emotion of a cheering, or barracking, crowd than a soccer player, caught up in continuous and demanding action, is ever likely to be – ask anyone who has fielded in the deep in front of the Hill at Sydney. But the main reason why cricket felt these pressures so strongly in the years after the War (much more strongly than it has felt them since the Second World War) is simple: the unique prestige that cricket then possessed as the national game of England and Australia.

This was primarily a matter of age and tradition: cricket as an organized and ritualized game was more than a hundred years older than any of the forms of football, and it had all the prestige of close association with the Establishment behind it. If I am right in saying that mass spectator sport in the 1920s above all provided an outlet for the emotions expressed in nationalism during the War and left unemployed after it, then it was to be expected that in these two countries they should concentrate round the game with the strongest national associations, and, moreover, the game in which international conflict was most highly developed. This point is vital. International soccer was poorly developed in the 1920s. There was no World Cup, and foreign fixtures were limited to what were essentially occasional 'friendlies'. The 'home' internationals between England, Scotland, Wales and Northern Ireland were well established, but, passionate tribal events though they could be, they did not for *Englishmen* amount to occasions for the major demonstration of patriotic emotion. Nothing in soccer in the 1920s and 1930s provided the equivalent of the trials of national *machismo* supplied by the biennial Test Match series against Australia. Nor, it will be noted, were Test Matches then devalued as they have since become. From 1921 on, each country experienced them at four-year intervals, with the regularity of doom: 1924–5, 1928–9, 1932–3, 1936–7 in Australia, where summers span the New Year, 1926, 1930, 1934, 1938 in England, which has no such complications. True, there were Tests against other comers as well, but never between the Wars did these approach equality with the struggles against the Old Enemy (though South Africa foreshadowed the shape of things to come by winning a Test series in England in 1935 – the only pre-1939 example of either of the ancestral cricketing countries losing a series at home to a third-comer). Between the series there was ample time to relish old victories, to lick the sores of old defeats, to pond up the reservoirs of enthusiasm for next time.

If this was true of England, it was far more true of Australia. Since 1945, Australia has developed an enviable reputation for prowess at several sports other than cricket: rugby, swimming, rowing and perhaps, above all, tennis. Prior to 1939, cricket was practically the only game in which Australia had a recognized existence: the only one, certainly, in which she regularly sent teams abroad, and received visiting teams at home. And this was no new thing. An English team had visited Australia as long ago as 1861. The first Test Match was played in 1877; the first Australian team came to England in 1878; in 1882 the Australians won a series in England. Since then, the two countries had run practically neck and neck in the Test series (at the beginning of the 1932–33 series, the score stood 50–47 in Australia's favour). For some years Australia too had played Test Matches against other countries – South Africa and, more recently, the West Indies – but none of these remotely approached in Australian eyes the status of the regular battles against England. In countries just developing an independent national consciousness – as Australia was doing in the first half of this century – that consciousness will sometimes be identified with a particular game, and that game cultivated with a fierceness and devotion that would be unthinkable in a country of old-established identity like England, where national pride could find more than adequate expression through dozens of outlets, from the British Empire, the Royal Navy, and the complacent contemplation of English history down to the practices of drinking beer lukewarm and tea all the time. But rugby for a New Zealander, a South African, or a Welshman, or cricket for a between-Wars Australian, was something different: it was the means by which a nation, either new or newly re-emergent, asserted its manhood and its identity, and asserted it above all against that conqueror, that repressor, that mother-country (nomenclature might vary) which denied them. Nations, like children, have to prove their independence by defying their parents, if only within the specialized confines of a game; and for Australia it was cricket which had filled this role.

13

Cricket, in fact, had become a vessel charged with fierce emotions in both England and Australia, and for an understanding of what was to follow it is important not only to grasp this fact, but also to realize that the development had taken place largely unnoticed, and in particular unreflected, in the structure of the governing bodies that controlled the game. In England, this meant the MCC – one of the most patrician offshoots of the English Establishment, wholly undemocratic, unrepresentative of everything except its own members, governed by a Committee rich in cricketing and political experience and in worldly wisdom, but symbolizing an aristocratic attitude to the game which, after 1918, was increasingly out of touch with its realities. The MCC was buttressed by two subordinate bodies it had set up over the years to assist in the administration of the game, the Advisory County Cricket Committee and the Board of Control for Test Matches at Home, but neither of these was to be involved in the exchange of cables between England and Australia which formed the climax of the 'bodyline' controversy, although the former of them was to play a part in the later stages of the affair back in England during the seasons of 1933 and 1934.

In Australia, it meant the Australian Board of Control for International Cricket, a federal body of grey administrators set up in 1912 to administer the game in Australia at international level by the constituent State Cricket Associations, which, however, continued to regard their creation with a suspicion always ready to flare into resentment if the Board made any attempt to increase its powers or enforce its decisions. With rare exceptions, the members of the Board were neither distinguished cricketers nor figures of any importance in Australian public life: bedevilled further by the interstate jealousies which have so plagued Australian history, they were no better qualified than the MCC to comprehend the changes which had come over first-class cricket in the last generation, to understand the power of the mass emotions which now flowed into this channel, or to control them once released.

Before the First World War, in spite of some famous Australian victories, the balance of the Test series had on the whole favoured England – if one looks for reasons, the mere balance of wealth and population between the two countries at this time is amply sufficient. But after 1918, that balance was dramatically upset – in 1920–21, 1921, and 1924–25, Australia won three Test series in succession, as it had never done before and has only once done since. The consequence in any case was a surge of confidence in Australia, and of despondency in an English cricketing public increasing rapidly in numbers and desperate for success. On the Australian tour of England in 1926, the balance was restored: after four draws in one of the hardest-fought Test series of modern times, England won the final Test at the Oval and regained the mythical 'Ashes' – thanks, notably, to the efforts of the veterans Hobbs and Rhodes, the Yorkshire opening batsman Sutcliffe, and the young Nottinghamshire fast bowler Larwood. In 1928–29 the victorious English captain A. P. F. Chapman, took a young and talented side to Australia, and reiterated the verdict of 1926 by winning by four matches to one. Australian morale in turn was now drooping. It was revived somewhat by a consolation victory in the final Test (there were no draws – all Tests in Australia between the War were played to a finish without time limit), and by the first appearance for them of two young batsmen of brilliant talent. One was Archie Jackson, who, due to his tragically early death, is almost a forgotten name to-day; the other was Don Bradman (as he was soon to be universally known).

When Australia came to England in 1930, the English public contemplated the prospects with blithe confidence. Chapman's 1928 side, often regarded as one of the best sides England has ever sent to Australia, was still largely intact. Chapman himself was still available to lead it and – it was hoped – inspire it by his dazzling fielding and mercurial batting. The batting available included Sutcliffe, Hendren, Woolley, the brilliant young Indian K. S. Duleepsinhji and the prodigy Hammond. There was still Duckworth to keep wicket, and if the bowling looked thinner, it nevertheless included Maurice Tate, still close to his peak, Larwood, on the summit of his youth and ferocious pace, and two highly promising young amateur leg-spinners in R. W. V. Robins and Ian Peebles. But the outcome was shattering disappointment. Bradman dominated the series as probably no other batsman has ever dominated a Test series. At Lord's, in the second Test, he scored 254, and it became unmistakably clear that a force had made itself felt in the game that promised to tilt the whole balance of Test cricket decisively in Australia's favour for twenty years to come. This was already the highest individual score in Test cricket in England: a fortnight later he bettered it in the third Test by scoring 334, and in the decisive last Test, which Australia won to take the series 2-1, he contributed 232. Single centuries no longer seemed significant: double and triple centuries were the milestones of the new kind of cricket that Bradman introduced to the world. Well as they played, Sutcliffe and Hammond paled almost to insignificance in comparison with him, while for the English bowlers, and for Larwood above all, it was a summer of martyrdom. Slow bowlers expect to be attacked – much of their skill lies in their ability to tempt aggression into folly. But for a fast bowler of great pace to be taken by the scruff of the neck and hit all over the field – as Larwood was by Bradman that summer – is the most violent rebuff possible: an experience that might shatter a man's morale, if it could not be avenged.

These successive swings of the Test Match pendulum raised the already intense public interest to fever-pitch, and the achievements of Bradman in the 1930 series concentrated it, to a degree never approached before or since, on a single man. The strains imposed upon the man himself by such a concentration were clearly colossal: it is not the least remarkable feature of Bradman's genius that, unlike a number of other much-adulated sportsmen since that time, he had the self-discipline and inward privacy never to allow himself to be mastered by it. Even in England during the tour he was subjected to a ferocity of hero-worship that would have unsettled many men, and when the Australian side returned home, the hero's welcome that awaited it seemed to many to be directed at Bradman personally rather than at the team as a whole. Throngs awaited him wherever he went: he was given a car; a cinema was named after him; newspapers fought for the privilege of publishing his articles. His autobiography – at the age of twenty-one! – had already been published in instalments in an English evening paper during the tour. His story, of the small-town boy raised by genius to the heights of international fame, had all the qualities to appeal to a mass popular audience. The instinct of hero-worship goes to the roots of human nature, and seems to be magnified in crowds and mass audiences; and it would be hard to imagine a better image of the popular hero than the young, unpretentious Bradman, who could give vicarious form to the hopeful or frustrated ambitions of so many.

It was thus under the pressure of intense public excitement and fierce emotion that the selection of the English team that was to tour Australia in 1932–33 was made. It was Australia now that had the advantage of an intact winning side, and the problems of selection for the home side seemed unlikely to be very difficult. The bowling available was certainly limited – in England in 1930 it had rested heavily on the shoulders of the leg-spinner, Grimmett. Australian fast bowling, after the passing of the great Gregory and Macdonald in the 1920s, had entered into a long period in the doldrums, and the best available was the honest and indefatigable trier Wall. But whatever the Australian selectors may have thought, the Australian public in 1932 was not worried about their bowling, nor much interested in it: they were avid to see Bradman repeat his feats of 1930 on his own wickets and in front of his own crowds, and with support for him of the calibre of

Woodfull, Ponsford, Kippax and McCabe, few doubted the Australians' ability to accumulate huge totals which England could not match. Since the Tests were timeless, it mattered little how long it took the Australian attack to bowl the Englishmen out.

For England, the problem was very different. There was an intense public desire for revenge for the humiliation of the 1930 series, but how it was to be achieved was a different matter. Since 1930, England's record in Test Matches against lesser opponents than Australia had not been especially impressive: true, two home series had been won in 1931 and 1932, but the visitors were no more formidable than New Zealand, making only their second visit to England, and India, making their first, and the series in South Africa over the winter of 1931–32 had been lost. The problem facing the selectors, when the touring party was chosen at the end of the English 1932 season, was clear-cut, but that did not make it easy: it was to find some means of checking the torrent of runs that had flowed from Bradman's bat in England in 1930, and which, on the face of it, was likely to flow even more freely on the hard, true wickets of Australia. Batting was not the problem: it was not hard to name a side which ought to make runs against the limited Australian bowling resources. Even ruling out Hobbs and Woolley as too old for another tour, there remained Hammond – whose batting performances in Australia in 1928–29 had themselves shattered all previous records, only to be eclipsed by the still more dazzling achievements of Bradman in 1930 – Sutcliffe, Leyland, the Lancastrian Paynter, the dogged and prolific R. E. S. Wyatt and, replacing Duleepsinhji, whose health had broken down after a brilliant debut in the 1930 series, another young Indian prince, who had made his name in the Oxford side, the Nawab of Pataudi; in addition, one of the two wicketkeepers, Ames, was a batsman of high class.

It was the bowling that was the difficulty, and when the cricketing public saw the final list of names it was evident that the selectors had plumped heavily for an attack based on two styles: fast and leg-spin. The side contained four fast bowlers: Larwood, whose position as the leading English fast bowler of his generation had survived his battering by Bradman in 1930 and who was familiar with Australian conditions, having toured with the 1928 side; his Nottinghamshire colleague, the left-hander Voce; the tall, bespectacled Yorkshireman Bowes; and the Middlesex amateur, G. O. Allen. Such a battery of pace was unprecedented – especially as the side also included the great fast-medium bowler Maurice Tate, though he was nearing the end of his career and, in fact, due to illness, only joined the team after its arrival in Australia. It was certain that Australia could produce no comparable array of fast bowlers to match this: what was much more doubtful was whether English fast bowling would prove any more effective against Bradman in Australia than it had done in England. The side also included two leg-spinners: T. B. Mitchell of Derbyshire and the youthful F. R. Brown, not long down from Cambridge. Neither was an established Test Match player. Leg-spin was a field in which Australia reigned supreme between the Wars, and their inclusion almost certainly owed a lot to a theory that Bradman had a chink in his armour against leg-spinners. The only other specialist bowler in the side was Verity of Yorkshire, the latest in a long line of exponents of the classic English art of slow left-hand bowling. The touring party of seventeen was made up by the Lancashire wicket-keeper Duckworth, and the captain, Douglas Jardine, of Winchester, Oxford, Surrey and England, a batsman who had been a successful junior member of the 1928 side, but who was otherwise unknown to the bulk of the Australian public.

The English team sailed from Tilbury on the Orient liner *Orontes* on 17 September and reached Fremantle on 18 October, and the pressure of public excitement under which the tour was to take place was equally evident at both ends of their journey. A huge crowd gathered at St Pancras station to see the side off on the boat-train to

19

Tilbury: there was cheering for them at every station along the line, and another large crowd of enthusiasts at Tilbury itself. Their arrival in Western Australia was – making allowance for the different size of the communities – an even bigger public event. The crew of the Australian heavy cruiser *Canberra* lined the side and sang 'For They Are Jolly Good Fellows' as the *Orontes* pulled into Fremantle: there were crowds to greet them everwhere, and a contingent of eager Australian pressmen awaited the arrival of the liner and the first opportunity of a press conference with the manager of the MCC side, Pelham Warner. Warner was, on the face of it, the ideal man for the position – one of the paladins of modern cricket. A loved and honoured figure at Lord's and throughout the English cricketing Establishment, he had captained Rugby, Middlesex and England, and had led two England touring sides in Australia before the War. Both tours had been highly successful: Warner had been an extremely popular figure, and had the fondest memories of the country and its people. In addition, few men have ever loved the game, and its traditional ethos and courtesies, as Warner did. It would have been hard to imagine a better public spokesman for the side; and he seems to have handled this conference, as he did later ones, with courtesy, tact and charm.

The issues that were to overshadow the tour were, however, audible from its beginning: the very first question put to Warner was about Bradman. On account of his activities as a journalist, Bradman was at this time in dispute with the Board of Control, who had banned current Test players from contributing to the cricket columns of the press, and there was great public excitement about the possibility of Bradman being excluded from selection in consequence. Warner refused to comment – though he later made it clear that he shared the general public anxiety in both countries that Bradman should somehow be enabled to play: a Test series without him at this time would indeed have been a *Hamlet* without the Prince of Denmark. But there was another question at the conference of interest in view of later events. One of the Australian pressmen had picked up an English criticism of Bowes' excessive use of 'bouncers', and had speculated about the possibility of Australian retaliation – what did Mr Warner think of that? Warner played it straight back to him. 'Bowes is a splendid bowler,' he said, 'and have not fast bowlers bumped the ball before?' – a question not lacking in point when addressed to a countryman of Gregory and Macdonald.

But nobody paid much attention to this at the time. The English team was received with the utmost enthusiasm: in Perth (as in Adelaide later on) all other news shrank to insignificance in comparison with their arrival. The intensity of the Australian desire for victory over the Mother Country detracted not at all from the warmth of the reception. It is not easy to recapture the atmosphere of a Test tour between the Wars – something that was an imperial embassy almost as much as a sporting venture. It was an age when the language and the emotions of Empire still came readily and without embarrassment to men's lips, and a Test tour was seen as an important means of drawing tighter the strings of Empire, of reinforcing the unity of sentiment on which the unity of Empire itself was seen to depend. Nowhere was this more true than in Australia, the most British in origin and sentiment of all the Dominions, New Zealand alone excepted. Britain was still commonly spoken of in Australia as 'home'; and the anomaly of a home the width of the world away, at a time when all regular travel between the two countries was still by sea and took no less than a month, made Australians intensely sensitive to every sign that the Mother Country had not forgotten them and still valued the intimate link that bound the two countries together. Of all such signs, the most publicly effective, short only of royal visits, were undoubtedly the four-yearly visits of English Test sides, and this gave the tours of the period – more than the relatively little-noticed early tours of the nineteenth century, more than the post-second World War ones, when the emotional link was fading and cricket had to compete with many other sports for popularity – an official, almost a diplomatic quality that comes out repeatedly in the reports of the time. As one English paper put it at the time that the team left England, 'every time England and Australia meet in friendly rivalry a valuable contribution is made to the all-vital Imperial spirit'. The link between cricket and Empire was a rhetorical commonplace (one of which the Australian captain, Woodfull, was especially fond); and wherever the team went in Australia, they were received with public honours which reflected the consciousness that their coming was a national event and not a mere sporting one.

There were six weeks between the arrival of the England team at Fremantle and the first Test Match in Sydney, with a first-class fixture over each of the five weekends, and these five matches would provide the first solid indication of the shape the tour was likely to take, of the comparative form of leading players on both sides, of selection possibilities for the Tests to come, of the kind of approach to the game that Jardine intended to adopt. All this was followed by the Australian cricketing public with avid interest; but above all there was the prospect of no less than three confrontations between the Englishmen and Bradman before the first Test, for the five preliminary games included two (against a 'Combined XI' at Perth and 'An Australian XI' at Melbourne) in which Bradman was due to appear, as well as a game against his own state, New South Wales. In these preliminary encounters, Bradman was confidently expected to resume the mastery of the English attack he had shown in England two years before. His controversy with the Australian Board of Control fanned public excitement – hysteria is hardly too strong a word – to yet greater heights. There were crowds to greet him at every station on the railway line across the continent as he travelled to Perth to take part in the match there: for the match itself an unparalleled crowd of 20,000 appeared, the equivalent of one-eighth of the population of

22

the city, many of them having come hundreds of miles for the purpose.

The outcome was a cruel anti-climax: Bradman was dismissed for 3 and 10, and though the match was a draw, the moral advantage went very decidedly to the Englishmen. To the observant, there was significance in the fact that Jardine chose to keep the strength of his fast bowling under cover. Allen alone played (with considerable success, including Bradman's wicket in the second innings), and he was not thought of at this time as a probable candidate for the Test side. Larwood, Voce and Bowes were not included in the team, and it would not have been hard to conclude that Jardine's motive was to give Bradman and other leading Australian batsmen as little chance as possible of batting practice against the bowlers who would spearhead his attack in the Tests. The disappointed Australian public found little consolation in the succeeding matches either. Bradman's four innings in them were little more successful than his first two: worse, although the dispute with the Australian Board of Control was resolved, Bradman being released from his newspaper contract and thus left free to play for Australia, it became known late in November that he was in bad health and would be unable to play in the first Test – there were even fears that his cricketing career might be at an end altogether.

During these early matches the Australian public were left little room for doubt that under Jardine's leadership the Englishmen were going to be formidable opponents. It soon became clear that Jardine had none of the ready good humour and affability that had made the last two English touring captains, Arthur Gilligan and Percy Chapman, such popular figures in Australia. Jardine was capable of being a charming companion and making a good after-dinner speech, but he was inherently a deeply reserved and private man, of clear mind and strong will. To the Australian public he rapidly took on the shape of an unbendingly patrician figure who took small pains to conceal his contemptuous indifference to what that public

23

might think of him, and who ruled his team, on and off the field, with a rod of iron.

As early as the first days of the tour in Perth, Jardine contrived to fall foul of both the local cricket authorities and the Australian popular press: the former by his appearance half an hour late on the second day of the opening match against Western Australia,* and the latter by his refusal to announce his team selections early enough for inclusion in the following morning's papers. A string of similar incidents was to follow throughout the tour, and Australians read into them (quite rightly) a contempt for the popular press and for the local cricket authorities that offended both their democratic instincts and their local patriotism. Yet it is only fair to add that the more consciously respectable Australian papers if anything lent over backwards in these early days to smooth over these incidents and to present Jardine in a favourable light – the national weekly *Australasian* was fulsome in its praise of his sportsmanship displayed in the match against South Australia at Adelaide, and unsparing in its condemnation of a small knot of spectators who jeered at him when he came into bat. In any case, it was abundantly clear that Jardine was a most skilful field tactician (he had in fact had remarkably little previous experience of captaincy, but he had learned the art under P. G. H. Fender of Surrey, widely regarded as the sharpest cricket brain in England), and that he had inspired his side with his own steely determination to win. Gay adventure was clearly not to be looked for from this side; but it came through these early games unbeaten and with great credit, and it was obviously going to be a formidable opponent in the Tests. There was also no doubt that Jardine regarded his fast bowlers as his key weapon, one which he knew that the Australians at the time could not match, nor that he intended to exploit this advantage to the limit.

* The morning was wet, and there was no possibility of play starting punctually; but protocol nevertheless required the presence of both captains at the agreed starting time.

24

What this might involve was demonstrated for the first time in the match against 'An Australian XI' in Melbourne in mid-November. This was Bradman's second encounter with the tourists: this time the full first-line battery of fast bowlers – Larwood, Voce and Bowes – played, and both the Australian batsmen and the spectators were startled and concerned by the ferocity of the attack, and by three features of it in particular: the number of short balls that was bowled, especially by Larwood and Voce; their apparent tendency to direct their attack on or just outside the leg stump, in other words at or very close to the batsman's body; and the steady reinforcement of the leg-side field. The batsmen, faced by a barrage of very fast balls rising viciously from short of a length at their chests or heads, found that any attempt at a defensive shot was likely to result in giving a catch on the leg side. Their only other resources were to duck, or to be hit. Woodfull was in fact hit hard and painfully over the heart by one such ball, and a press photograph of him reeling back in agony after the incident was widely published and did much to form the image of what the English fast bowlers were up to for the mass of the Australian cricketing public who had not seen the match.

Whether the English bowling in this match did in fact amount to a full unveiling of 'bodyline' is something that has been disputed; but it certainly left no doubt in the minds of a very large number of Australian spectators, and a considerable number of players as well, that the English tactics were based on intimidation, used more deliberately and systematically than ever before on a cricket field. Bradman at least said as much to members of the Board of Control, and made clear his fears for the future if they were allowed to continue unchecked – he seems to have sensed from the first that it was chiefly for his benefit that they were devised; but Bradman was less than *persona grata* with the Board at the time, and no action was taken. A number of Australian papers also condemned the English bowling, though their reactions were mixed, and some,

25

notably including the authoritative Melbourne *Argus*, took a scrupulously objective line.

English press reactions were also mixed. Bradman was out cheaply to Larwood in both innings, and for a number of English commentators this fact took precedence over everything else. Bruce Harris, the *Evening Standard* correspondent, said outright that 'in Larwood, assuming that he maintains his "demon" speed of the present match, lies the answer to the Bradman Problem. Bradman does not appear to like supercharged fast bowling ...'

But the most illuminating and outspoken comments were by Hobbs – who, as we have seen, was following the tour as correspondent for the *Star*. It adds irony to the situation that Hobbs himself had been subjected to an early trial of something like 'bodyline' tactics by Bowes at the Oval late in the previous season, and had protested at the time. Now he noted Bradman's vulnerability to a battery of fast bumpers: when it came to evaluation, he was brief. Hobbs as a correspondent had the rare advantage of wholly lacking the typical literary intellectual's armour of self-consciousness which ensures him against excessive honesty about his own feelings. 'Whether our bowlers overdid this kind of thing or not I am not prepared to say,' he wrote; and, even more frankly, 'I felt a lot safer in the press box, for the bowling looked very dangerous stuff. *I found it amusing, your feelings are very different when just watching*' (my italics – a comment whose naïve honesty might with advantage have been imitated by a great many of those who had so much to say about 'bodyline' in the months ahead). Other English observers countered Australian complaints by references to Gregory's and McDonald's bowling against England in the 1920s, when it was Australia that had the monopoly of great pace. None of them went so far as to condemn the English tactics.

They were, after all, successful: although the match was rained off, there could be little question that the morale, as well as the bodies, of the Australian batsmen emerged bruised from the encounter. In the following match, against New South Wales, Larwood did not play, but Voce again bowled a lot of bumpers to a close-packed leg-side field, and once more Bradman was twice out cheaply. The Sydney crowd, traditionally more outspoken than the Melbourne one, did not like it, and Voce had to endure a lot of barracking from the Hill.

By the time the first Test Match took place over the following weekend, the atmosphere was a great deal more charged and heated than it had been at the beginning of the tour. Then, it had been excited but good-spirited; above all, it had been confident. The Australian public had greeted the arrival of their English opponents with the sort of boisterous cheerfulness which comes readily when you are sure that you have the beating of them; and in Bradman they were sure that they had the man who would put the Englishmen to the sword. Since then, there had been a succession of unpleasant shocks: the possibility that Bradman's dispute with the Board of Control might keep him out of the Tests altogether; his succession of batting failures against the tourists; the grimly formidable nature of the English challenge, becoming clearer match by match, and crystallized in Jardine's austere and unsmiling style of leadership; and now, since Melbourne, the growing suspicion that English tactics were intimidatory and unsporting, if not outright unfair. On top of all, there came the news that Bradman was unfit and could not play in the first Test.

It is hard to resist the impression that, for many Australians, Bradman's absence took the heart out of the first Test from the start.English won it overwhelmingly, by ten wickets, and the match followed a pattern that was to become familiar later in the series: Woodfull winning the toss for Australia, and batting; Australia making a fair total against the English battery of fast bowling; England topping it by dint of a long-drawn-out batting performance of total dedication and unrelenting slowness (though slowness only by the standards of the 1930s, when over rates fluctuated near twenty an hour, not the standards of the 1980s); Australia collapsing in their second innings before Larwood, and England cruising home. Sutcliffe, Hammond and Pataudi all made centuries for England, but by universal consent the innings of the match was McCabe's 187 for Australia. This has often been described as the most brilliant counter-attack ever launched against 'bodyline' – but was it 'bodyline'? It was clearly a magnificent innings; but, although the English attack rested overwhelmingly on the shoulders of the fast bowlers, and especially of Larwood, who took 10 for 124 in the match, their methods seem to have been relatively orthodox. Bowes, one of the offenders at Melbourne, had not been a great success so far on the tour and was replaced by the Middlesex amateur, Allen, who had done unexpectedly well, and who throughout the tour bowled very fast, but to a full length and an orthodox line. Larwood did bowl some spells to a packed leg-side field – at one stage in the Australian second innings he was bowling to six men on the leg side, with a silly point as the only fieldsman in front of the wicket on the off – but for most of the match he too apparently preferred the traditional fast bowler's length and line, on or just outside the off stump: certainly it was these tactics that brought him most of his wickets. Voce seems to have been the only one of the fast bowlers to concentrate on the new leg-side tactics, and to have been the target for much of McCabe's dazzling hooking – he opened the bowling in Australia's first innings to a field containing five short legs and, on one occasion, having been hit for two successive fours by McCabe, bowled four bumpers in succession over his head. This was not likely to endear him to the Sydney crowd, and in fact what hostile barracking there was in this match seems to have been directed almost exclusively at Voce. But Voce was never as much of a physical danger to batsmen as Larwood, lacking his final edge of supreme pace, and in general the Hill was fairly restrained.

After the revelation of English tactics in the matches

against 'An Australian XI' and New South Wales, the Australian batsmen were clearly expecting a barrage of short-pitched fast bowling, and some of them wore body pads. But the pitch was quiescent, and although several of them were hit, none of these blows seems to have been more than waist-high – in fact, the batsman worst hurt in the match was Allen, when he was struck by the Australian pace bowler Nagel. Australian press comment was markedly restrained: there was much discussion of the new tactics, but, although there were some attacks on them as contrary to the spirit of the game, most of the criticism concentrated more on their effectiveness than on their fairness, critics like Warwick Armstrong, the old Australian captain, taking the line that they were essentially negative and a waste of a fast bowler's assets. Almost unanimously, Australian commentators agreed that England had won the match fairly on their merits.

The first Test, then, was something of an anti-climax: England had won decisively, but they had done it by relatively orthodox methods; nobody had been hurt; above all, Bradman had not played, and the Australian public could confidently hope that, when their hero was fit again, the verdict would be reversed.

Between the first and second Tests the touring side had nothing but their traditional visit to Tasmania, the midget of the Australian states. The two matches there were commonly regarded as a relaxation for touring sides, for Tasmanian cricket did not approach the standard of the big mainland states – since the total population of the island was only about 200,000, this was hardly surprising. This was clearly no arena for an exhibition of the new tactics, and none took place.

There was, however, an incident in the match at Hobart which received wide publicity in the Australian press, and which vividly crystallizes the image that Jardine was beginning to wear in Australian eyes. There had been heavy rain, but although the ground was still extremely wet the umpires declared it fit for play. Jardine appealed to the Chairman of the Tasmanian Cricket Association to overrule the umpires' decision. When he refused to do anything of the sort, Jardine threatened to refuse to lead his team out into the field, even at the cost of forfeiting the match; and when he was finally persuaded to accept the umpires' decision, he did so with the worst possible grace, limiting the bowling to himself, Paynter and Ames. No doubt his excuse would have been that he was afraid of injuring his regular bowlers; but a large crowd which had come to see the best of England's cricketers display their skills were not amused, and nor was the Chairman of the TCA, who announced his intention of reporting the incident to the Australian Board of Control. The affair, trivial in itself, nevertheless vividly highlighted Jardine's characteristics as a captain: his total concentration on the task of winning the Tests (hence his anxiety to take no risks at all with his bowlers), and his complete indifference to the desires or the reactions of the spectators. Jardine was becoming a man that the Australian public loved to hate – the Harlequin cap he commonly wore added a touch of patrician arrogance to the image that was all that was needed to round it off – and this was to be a major factor determining crowd attitudes throughout the rest of the Test series.

The English team returned to the mainland for the second Test at Melbourne, which spanned the New Year; and now at last Bradman was fit, and all Australia held its breath to see how he would fare. If there had been any doubt about the tactics England intended to employ against him, they were effectively removed by the team selection, for England again included Allen, in spite of his having achieved little in the first Test, and omitted their only slow bowler in the first Test, Verity, replacing him not merely by a fourth pace bowler, but by one – Bowes – who had a reputation for bumping the ball, and not by Tate, in spite of the latter's great reputation on previous Australian tours (and his great success in the New South Wales match before the first Test). Tate was – or had been – one of the world's greatest swingers and seamers of the ball: bumpers were completely alien to his method. He was also extremely popular in Australia. Australian crowds resented his exclusion, and read into the preference for Bowes a deliberate opting for the type of attack which was at just this time beginning to be known as 'body-line' – the hyphen still indicating the novelty of the term. Certainly there was a hostility in the air from the beginning at Melbourne that had been lacking at Sydney: the English press sensed it, and resented it, and, with the prospect of Bradman playing, there was tension among the English team too. In the dressing-room before the game began, Jardine came and sat by Allen. He wanted him, he said, to bowl more bouncers and to have a stronger leg-side field. Allen refused. It was not, he said, the way he wanted to play cricket, or thought it ought to be played. When Jardine persisted, he said, 'Well, I'm not going to, and if you don't like the way I bowl, you'd better leave me out – but I would add that if you do, every word you've said here today will be made public when I get home.' To Jardine's credit, he accepted the situation. Not only did Allen play in all the remaining Tests, but Jardine never raised the issue with him again: indeed Allen remained probably his closest friend throughout the tour.

Australia won the toss, and batted; and almost at once it became clear that the English selection committee's gamble had been a mistake. They had picked the four fast bowlers on the assumption that the wicket would be similar to the one in the 'Australian XI' match, played on this same ground. But the wicket now proved slow, and by the first afternoon it was already obvious that it was going to take a lot of spin. On top of that, Larwood, the spearhead of the attack, was virtually crippled for much of the first day by a series of exasperating troubles with his boots. He twice had to go off for considerable periods: the crowd jeered at him, Jardine lost his temper with him, and it is not surprising if

31

his own temper shortened as the match went on. Voce and Bowes bowled fast and short from the start on a leg-side line to packed leg-side fields, and Larwood increasingly followed suit. The crowd retaliated with repeated booing and barracking. Their mood was not improved by their bitter disappointment when Bradman, coming in in a crisis with the expectations of the entire country weighing on his shoulders, and cheered the whole way to the wicket, aimed a wild hook at his first ball from Bowes, less a true bumper than a gross long-hop outside the off stump, and dragged it on to his leg stump. Test Match ducks by Bradman are rare enough to stay in the memory for a lifetime – a man of my generation still remembers vividly his duck at Adelaide in the fourth Test of 1947, and the still more famous one at the Oval in his last Test innings in 1948 – and this one stunned the 63,000 Melbourne crowd into a total silence that lasted until Bradman was almost back to the pavilion.

But it was not 'bodyline' which had got him out (although it may have been the expectation of 'bodyline'), and in fact after that first day the animosity of the crowd at English tactics gradually subsided, and that for two good reasons: Australia won, and in the second innings Bradman got a century. Winning crowds, like winning teams, are rarely bad-tempered ones. Though the English fast bowlers twice bowled Australia out for small scores (228 and 191), for Australia Ironmonger and O'Reilly bowled England out for smaller ones, Australia winning on the fourth day by 111 runs and avenging the defeat at Sydney. That was enough to make any Australian crowd forget to worry about English bowling tactics; but in any case, those tactics had apparently been put to rout by Bradman in the second innings, reduced to impotence like so many other types of bowling before them.

In that innings Bradman made 103 not out out of the Australian total of 191, doing everything that the public had hoped for from their hero, and sending them into ecstasies. Typically, Bradman counter-attacked: where the rest of the Australian batting was cowed and ineffectual in

32

the face of the English attack, the speed of Bradman's footwork was such that he was never hit, that he avoided the clutching hands of the circle of short legs, and that again and again, in the face of everything that the bowlers could do, he found the gaps in the field and penetrated them. Although undoubtedly helped by the slowness of the pitch, it was a more varied and resourceful innings than McCabe's at Sydney, and it was made in spite of a much more ruthless and consistent use of fast short-pitched bowling – 'bodyline' – than England had employed in the first Test; and unlike McCabe's great innings, it won the match.

Australia rejoiced: Bradman had reasserted his dominance, and 'bodyline' was conquered – or so it was widely assumed. That Bradman alone among the Australian batsmen had shown any degree of mastery over it, and that the wickets on which the other Tests were to be played were likely to suit it better – all this was overlooked. Even in England some commentators thought that 'leg-theory' (for so it was still called in England) had been decisively refuted. In Australia, euphoria reigned. Spectators used knives and pins to dig out tiny pieces of the Melbourne turf and carried them away wrapped in handkerchiefs 'as though they were diamonds', and a shilling fund was opened by the Melbourne Cricket Club to present Bradman's wife with a memento of his performance. Hostility to the Englishmen was forgotten: now that 'bodyline' had been defeated, resentment was no longer necessary; chivalry was the order of the day. When Jardine came out at the end of the game to make the traditional losing captain's speech, he received a rousing cheer – a very different kind of treatment from that accorded to him by the crowd on the first day, when he had been formidable.

The moment was crucial, for it is clear in retrospect that if a public protest was ever to be made about English bowling methods, it should have been then, in Australia's moment of victory, and not in the midst of Australian defeat later on. The Board had a meeting in Melbourne immediately before the second Test, and there is some evidence (though there is nothing in the minutes to bear it out) that there was some discussion of the English fast bowlers' methods; but if so, it was decided to take no action. After the match, in the light of the Australian victory, protest seemed still less necessary, and in any case the Board would not meet again for weeks to come.

The mood of public euphoria still held at the beginning of the third Test at Adelaide a fortnight later. The teams were one-all in the series: there was everything to play for. But the crowds flocking to the Adelaide Oval had had their confidence restored. If the Englishmen bowled 'bodyline', Bradman had the answer to them. The crowd expected excitement, but they expected victory. The day was fine and hot. The turnstiles opened.

CHAPTER 2

Flashpoint
(January 1933)

It was plain enough that Friday morning that excitement was running high in Adelaide. If one wants some measure of the level of excitement at the opening of the Third Test – and some measure of what cricket meant to Australians in 1933 – one has only to look at the gate. 39,300 people paid to enter the Adelaide Oval that day. In a city of a mere half-million people, this was considerably more than any English cricket ground of the date could have accommodated – the equivalent on the same scale for a Test Match in London at the time would have been around 350,000. It was also a record for the ground, and that on the first day, a Friday, and not on a public holiday.

There had, it is true, been an unseemly incident two days earlier, when even the chance of watching the English team practise in the nets had been sufficient to attract over 3000 spectators to the ground. Some of them had, unfortunately, misbehaved themselves: the appearance of Jardine had given rise to an outburst of jeering, and on his protest the public had been excluded on the following day, when the Englishmen were again in the nets. Taken together with the incident already mentioned in the MCC's earlier match against South Australia on the ground, it was a clear sign that Jardine was already unpopular with a section of the Adelaide cricket-going public, and his action on this later occasion can have done nothing to endear him to them; but their conduct was roundly condemned by Adelaide's leading paper, the *Advertiser*, and the bulk of local opinion was clearly looking for no repetition of this unseemly incident when the match began.

The crowd were packed in the enclosures, the sun shone with the fierceness of the Australian summer, a south-west breeze tempered the heat. Jardine won the toss, and inevitably chose to bat on what promised to be a beautiful batting wicket. The stage was set; and the play ran magnificently, ecstatically true to the crowd's eager expectations.

On the face of it, there was little enough in the Australian attack that should have troubled the English batsmen in those conditions. Certainly it included three slow bowlers of the highest class in the leg-spinners Grimmett and O'Reilly and the left-hander Ironmonger, but on the first day of an Adelaide wicket they would have enough to be proud of if they could get the ball to deviate from the straight at all. Apart from them there was only Wall, a fast bowler of something markedly below top pace, and McCabe (whose bowling figures for the entire series were 3 for 215) to turn an innocent medium-paced arm when the others tired. But there was more life than usual in the Adelaide wicket that morning, and Wall, bowling before his home crowd cheering him on, by all accounts bowled his heart out. In the first hour and a half four England wickets went down for 30 runs. Throughout the series, England never found a satisfactory opening partner for Sutcliffe. In the first two Tests, Wyatt had filled the role; at Adelaide Jardine, a fine player of fast bowling, with typical moral courage took on the responsibility himself. Wall bowled him, to the accompaniment of a great roar from the crowd, with only 4 on the board, and at 16 he also had Hammond caught at the wicket by Oldfield. Sutcliffe went to O'Reilly at the same score, and at 30 Ironmonger bowled Ames. Leyland and Wyatt held on by their fingernails and eyelids until the interval; but England were tottering on the edge of complete and catastrophic collapse, and with the wicket quietening down, the crowd could take lunch in the happy expectation of soon seeing their own batsmen going in in ideal conditions to take full advantage of a quite inadequate English total.

For the rest of the day, the English middle order batsmen slowly and doggedly, in the fashion of all the English batting during the series, fought their way back into the game. Leyland (83) and Wyatt (78) added 156 for the fifth wicket; but both they and Allen were out in the last hour and a quarter, and England ended the day at 236 for 7, with only one recognized batsman, Paynter, still in, and only the bowlers, Verity, Larwood and Voce, to hold up the other end for him. It had been a brave recovery, generously and chivalrously appreciated by the crowd; but their spirits remained high, for it was still unquestionably Australia's day. On this wicket, nothing less than 400 could be considered a satisfactory total, and 600 would not have been surprising: to most observers on that Friday evening, it seemed that England would be lucky to top 300, with the second new ball still young and the necessity of facing a refreshed Australian attack on the Saturday morning. But on Saturday everything went wrong.

The weather was again perfect, and over 50,000 people watched the day's play, far and away the biggest crowd the ground had ever seen. But the English innings, instead of ending quickly, lasted until half-way through the afternoon, Paynter, the quick-footed little Lancashire lefthander, making 77 and Verity doing his studious imitation of Sutcliffe to help him add 96 for the eighth wicket. The wicket offered no help at all to the Australian spinners and O'Reilly, Grimmett and Ironmonger, all turning the ball primarily from the leg, came kindly on to the lefthander's bat. In the end the English total reached 341 – still far from a match-winning score, but an infinitely better one than had seemed likely on the Friday morning. And, when Australia went in to bat, the atmosphere of the game was instantly and chillingly different: different in the way it usually is when one side has fast bowlers of the highest class and the other has not.

All fast bowling is menacing, and is meant to be, and it is best to be clear about that from the start: that is, it works not only on the batsman's reflexes, but on his fear of pain. But Wall was an honest run-of-the-mill Test Match fast bowler, not of extreme pace, and, what matters more, not supported by another bowler of comparable pace from the other end. It is a commonplace nowadays that two fast bowlers are worth much more than twice one. With O'Reilly or Grimmett on at the other end to Wall, there might be no relaxation for the batsmen's concentration, but for his nerves there certainly was; and this would have been true even if Wall had been a good deal faster than he was. It is important to remember that the idea of opening an attack with a pair of fast bowlers, even with a pair of pace bowlers of any sort, was still a novelty in 1933. Gregory and McDonald had set the fashion, and in 1932–33 Australia for the first time had the experience that England had had then, of facing fierce pace from both ends with nothing comparable of their own with which to reply.

The England attack was opened by Larwood and Allen, the Middlesex amateur. Allen had been given a chance to show what he could do with the new ball at Melbourne, when, put on for an over to enable Larwood to change ends, he had shown his ability to move the ball away from the bat and had got Fingleton, the young New South Wales opener, cheaply. Now Jardine gave him the chance to do it again, and in his first over Fingleton was caught at the wicket. This was a bad enough start, but it was an orthodox opening bowler's wicket. Allen, who was Australian-born, was a popular figure in Australia: as he did throughout the tour, he was bowling a full length on the off stump to a slip field – bowling, that is, in the traditional style of a fast bowler, which contemporaries called 'off-theory'. His refusal to use leg-theory was not public knowledge, but the contrasts between his bowling methods and those of

Larwood and Voce had already been noted and marked by the Australian press and public. There was no resentment, therefore, at the fall of Fingleton's wicket: even the disappointment had its compensations, for his dismissal brought Bradman to the wicket, the one man whom the crowd wished to see above all others. But the bowler at the other end was Larwood; and Larwood's next over – his second – gave the crowd something else to think about than what Bradman might do, and set the entire cricketing world ringing with a controversy whose echoes have even today not been wholly stilled.

Larwood was a bowler of the most thrilling and beautiful menace: one of the very greatest fast bowlers, in the opinions of almost all competent judges. In that season of 1932–33, he was on the narrow ultimate summit of a fast bowler's peak. He himself thought he was bowling faster than ever before – why, he could not say: he thought it might be because of some work he had lately had done on his teeth, and so finely tuned does the body of a fast bowler at the peak of his form have to be that the explanation may be the right one. I myself never had the good fortune to see Larwood bowl, but I have seen film clips of him, and they were enough for memories of that glorious action to have fixed themselves ineradicably in my mind – a gallop to the wicket that was all rhythm and freedom, gathering itself for the final pounding down of the left leg and the perfect co-ordination of muscle in the final release of the ball. Even on film, Larwood bowling looks like windblown fire. There will never be any end to the arguments about the relative pace of the great fast bowlers of different ages, but Larwood's bowling that season is said to have been timed at over 90 m.p.h., and the batsmen who had to play him were almost unanimous in their judgement that they never saw or played against anyone faster.

There was no trouble at first. Larwood was a natural outswinger, and he opened that day, as he commonly did as long as the ball was moving, to an orthodox slip field, bowling an off-stump line. The last ball of his second over was pitched on the wicket, by most accounts not a lot short of a length, but it got up fiercely, and Woodfull, moving across as was his habit to cover his stumps, was hit plumb over the heart, just as he had been in Melbourne. Woodfull dropped his bat and staggered away from the wicket, clutching his chest in pain. A number of English fieldsmen gathered round him, as a storm of hooting went up all round the ground. It was plain that the temperature of the crowd was dangerously high; for the incident in itself, up to this point, was slight enough. If it was not common for a fast bowler to hit a Test batsman on the body, it was very far from unknown: at Manchester in 1921 McDonald had hit Ernest Tyldesley on the head, and back in the nineteenth century occasional knocks of this sort were an occupational hazard of playing fast bowling on the pitches of the time and seem to have been taken for granted in the game. Moreover, and more to the point, by any definition Larwood was not bowling 'bodyline' at the time: he was bowling to an off-side field, and the ball had pitched on the stumps, and not much short of a length at that. But in the tension of the moment these distinctions were lost on the crowd. They knew that Larwood had a reputation for bowling short at the batsman, and here he was doing it again, and if the crowd were unfair on him in hooting him for that particular ball, they might well have felt themselves justified if they had heard what Jardine, walking up to Larwood, said to him: 'Well bowled, Harold.' This is a remark which may seem inexcusable in the circumstances – though it is important to remember that the circumstances were a moment of great tension in a Test Match, with the sides standing one-all in the series, and that the pressures on a captain at such a moment are very great. Some of those who heard him thought that Jardine meant to reassure Larwood, in the face of the crowd's hostility, that he had done nothing which needed apology, for an incident such as this can shake a bowler's confidence as well as a batsman's; others thought that the remark was deliberately intended to unsettle Bradman,

40

who had just come in and was standing at the bowler's end within easy earshot, by intimating to him that he could expect the same treatment when his turn came to face Larwood. Nobody who knew Jardine doubted that there was a calculated purpose of some sort in it.

When Woodfull had recovered enough to play on, Allen resumed bowling from the other end. The crowd simmered throughout his over. Then, as Larwood ran up for the first ball of his third over, again to Woodfull, Jardine stopped him in his run and called up the leg trap – in effect, moved his slip field across to the leg side, so that Larwood was now bowling to four or five short legs close up round the batsman, an outer ring of two or three more men on the leg side, and a mere two or three patrolling the wide open spaces of the off side.

To the crowd, the implication was unmistakable: having 'softened up' Woodfull with that fearful blow over the heart, Jardine was now trying to finish him off by adopting a directly intimidatory field setting and style of attack. A storm of hooting and booing broke out, not confined to the crowd in the outer enclosures but extending even to the members in the pavilion. When Woodfull faced up to the next ball, he was 'as white as a sheet of notepaper', and when Larwood, with the second ball of the new over, knocked the understandably shaken Australian captain's bat out of his hand, the storm of noise mounted to such a peak that more than one observer, and more than one of the English players, began to wonder whether the crowd would come over the fence at the players, and what would happen then if so. One of the English fieldsmen said to the umpire, Hele, 'George, if they come over the fence, leave me a stump.' 'Not on your life,' replied Hele, 'I'll need all three myself.'

The best that can be said for Jardine's switching of the field at that moment is that it revealed an extraordinarily insensitive misjudgement of the situation and the crowd's reaction, which it should not have been hard for anyone to foresee. Jardine was to say afterwards that there was nothing sinister in his action at all, since it had become common form for Larwood to switch from 'off theory' to 'leg theory' when the ball lost its first shine and ceased to swing, because beyond that point there was no reasonable prospect of obtaining catches in the slips from edged shots outside the off stump, and that it was pure coincidence that he made the change immediately after Woodfull had been hit: he simply failed to foresee that the crowd would read it as deliberate intimidation of the crudest kind, and if he had foreseen it, he would not have made the change. There may indeed be no more to it than this: certainly nobody would ever have claimed that sensitivity to crowd reactions was a feature of Jardine's captaincy. But it has to be said that the ball was only four overs old at the time, and that Larwood himself had not anticipated the change, and was apparently taken by surprise by it – as has already been said, Jardine stopped him in the middle of his run-up for the first ball of the over. Years afterwards Larwood himself said that the ball *was* still swinging at that stage, so that there was no apparent necessity for the change.

It is impossible to be sure of Jardine's motives, although it does not seem too impossible to imagine him taking the line that if a front-line Test batsman allowed himself to be intimidated by a knock from a fast bowler, he deserved what he got; but it is possible to be very sure indeed of the consequences of his action. If there was one incident that can be identified as the moral turning-point of the 1932–33 series, the point at which Australian public opinion swung finally and overwhelmingly over to condemnation of the English bowling tactics, it was that moment in the fifth over of Australia's first innings at Adelaide, when Jardine stopped Larwood in his run-up and called up his leg trap.

The weekend of 14–15 January marks unmistakably the point at which almost all Australian opinion set firm against 'bodyline' – the conversion of the highly responsible and respectable *Australian Cricketer*, the leading Australian cricket journal, is typical. Up to that point it had defended Larwood's, Voce's and Bowes' use of 'headers' (one of the early attempts at finding a name for this new phenomenon), but in its next monthly number it came out in firm condemnation and insistence on the necessity for immediate action against this type of bowling. There was room for argument about the ball which actually hit Woodfull – though a great many of the spectators on the ground were certainly in no mood to make distinctions, and to them the fact that he had been hit was itself a sufficient indictment of the English tactics – but about the setting of the leg trap immediately afterwards, there was no room for discussion at all. This, to the vast majority of Australians, was plain malice; and its author was Jardine.

The point is worth noting. It was Larwood's bowling that heated the crowd's resentment to frenzy – the booing and the hooting were at their height during his walk back and run up, and during the latter the crowd repeatedly 'counted him out' ('one, two, three, four, five, six, seven, eight, nine, ten, OUT!') – but it was always clear that the real target of it all was Jardine, with his stiff, crane-like, contemptuous bearing, his silk choker and his Harlequin cap, the model of the overbearing English arrogance that of all the mother country's qualities was the most intolerable to a young country striving to assert its independence and its identity. In Larwood they saw only his instrument, at worst his willing instrument; and broadly they were right about this. Australia is a country that thinks well of the common man, and Larwood, the Nottinghamshire coal-miner's son, offended no Australian susceptibilities – as his own successful emigration to Australia after the War was to prove. He was also a professional cricketer, with the professional's usual hard-bitten view of the job by which he makes his living. He had taken a battering from Bradman, and from other Australian batsmen, in 1930, and he was out to ensure that that did not happen again. He himself stated the case as he saw it with admirable straightness years later: 'I wouldn't say I was told to bowl leg theory. I was asked to do it, and I complied.' But the choice of tactics, and the responsibility for them, was, fundamentally, Jardine's – Jardine himself would have been the last man to deny it – and to that extent the Australian crowds were right to make him, not Larwood, the object of their hatred. Jardine did revisit Australia after the War, but he certainly never contemplated settling there; and it seems unlikely that he would have been welcomed as readily as Larwood was if he had.

Woodfull survived Larwood's spell of leg theory, battling on with the dour stoicism which was his public response to English tactics throughout the series. But just as it was Jardine, and not Larwood, who was the prime target for the crowd's hostility, so it was against Bradman, and not Woodfull, that leg theory was primarily directed; and we have already noted the possibility that Jardine's handling of the Woodfull incident was dominated by his preoccupation with the problem of how he was going to get Bradman out. It was, anyway, Bradman who went. He was not hit – which, given the temper of the crowd, was just as well: there is no saying how they might have reacted if Australia's national hero had received the sort of blow that Woodfull did. Now, as throughout the series, his marvellous quickness of foot protected him against physical injury; but he was manifestly ill at ease against Larwood bowling leg theory at that terrific pace, and with the score at 18 he was out, caught in the leg trap fending off a ball that lifted. McCabe followed him at 34, likewise caught off Larwood in the leg trap, and Australia went into tea in the direst kind of trouble, compounded when Allen bowled Woodfull soon after the interval. That was 51 for 4, but Ponsford (badly dropped at first slip by Hammond off Allen before he had scored) and Vic Richardson, the South Australian captain, saw them through to the close of play without further loss. Their styles were contrasting: Ponsford wore massive bodypadding and, like Woodfull, stoically took a series of nasty knocks about the body, whereas Richardson, like McCabe, believed that counter-attack was the best means of defence against 'bodyline' and went for his shots, particularly the hook. He lived dangerously, although no doubt Larwood (who in any case was only bowled in short spells) tired as the evening went on: in any case, he and Ponsford survived, and at the close of play Australia were 109 for 4.

Their position was nevertheless close to desperate, for they were still 222 runs behind, and the Australian tail in 1932–33 was alarmingly long: after Richardson, only Oldfield could be considered any kind of accredited batsman. The crowd went home in that knowledge, and in a mood in which anger and disappointment were explosively mingled: anger at the ferocity of the English tactics and at Jardine's apparent callousness, disappointment at the pricking of the bubble of high expectations with which they had gone to the Oval that morning – the failure to finish off the English innings quickly, the fall of so many Australian wickets, above all perhaps the cheap dismissal of Bradman. Obviously there is no chance of calculating the proportions of the mixture, which will have been different in every individual; but it does not take much insight into human nature to recognize how the humiliation of failure can be released and made respectable by any suggestion that your opponent isn't playing fair. The public mood in Adelaide over that weekend was explosive.

It had, too, natural focuses for both its hostility and its sympathy in the two captains, Jardine and Woodfull. The comments of the cricket correspondents in the Adelaide evening papers that Saturday were remarkably restrained and objective; but the kind of public hush that this imposed for the moment was sensationally shattered by the news of a confrontation in the Australian dressing-room on Saturday evening, news that flew round the ranks of the numerous press corps attendant on the Test on Sunday, and which would be in all the papers on Monday. Warner, the English manager, had been to the Australian dressing-room after Woodfull was out to enquire about his injury, and Woodfull had snubbed him, answering Warner's enquiry by saying, 'I don't want to speak to you, Mr

Warner. Of two teams out there, one is playing cricket, the other is making no effort to play the game of cricket. It is too great a game for spoiling by the tactics your team are adopting. I don't approve of them and never will. If they are persevered with it may be better if I do not play the game. The matter is in your hands. I have nothing further to say. Good afternoon.'* Beyond answering Warner's enquiry about his injury, he would say no more; and Warner left the dressing-room.

This confrontation epitomized the Australian reaction to 'bodyline' so vividly and sharply that it resounded throughout the Australian press – and soon throughout the English press as well. Woodfull had said what almost all Australians felt: he had been courteous, he had been firm, he had shown Warner the door. Whether he would have said quite what he did if he had realized that it was to be all over the front pages of Australia on Monday morning may be open to doubt. Technically, the words were spoken in private, but most of the members of the Australian side heard them, and looking back on it it seems obvious that with feelings running as high as they were running that afternoon, somebody was bound to leak the incident to the press. There was indeed a pressman in the room – Fingleton, the opening batsman, was himself a professional journalist, and it was widely assumed that it was he who had passed the story on. Warner himself thought so, and, according to Fingleton's own story, so much resented it that he offered a sovereign to anyone who got Fingleton out cheaply in Australia's second innings. Fingleton, however, always denied that it was in fact he who revealed the incident to the press. He claimed that it was Bradman – who, as has been seen, also had connections with the press, which had been the subject of conflict between him and the Australian Board of Control at the beginning of the

* Versions of what exactly Woodfull said vary slightly – which is not surprising in view of the length of the speech, and the improbability that anyone on the spot took it down in shorthand – but not substantially. I have quoted the version given by Bruce Harris in his book *Jardine Justified*.

English tour; but this in turn is emphatically denied by Bradman himself. Perhaps the exact source of the leak does not matter very much in any case, when the leak was bound to come somewhere.

Unintentionally, Woodfull had provided the much-needed expression and release for the tension of the moment; and obviously nobody was in a position to do it as well as he, Australia's captain and himself the chief victim of the English tactics. If it was Jardine's switching to the leg trap field immediately after Woodfull had been hit on Saturday afternoon that finally convinced most Australians that the basis of the English tactics was naked intimidation, it was Woodfull's confrontation with Warner, and the press revelation of it on Monday, that turned the affair into a controversy between the two nations, in which the pride of both was deeply invested and which was bound to be long and bitter accordingly.

Warner's own position in the affair must have been acutely painful. His two pre-1914 tours of Australia had been huge successes on both the team and the personal level, and his memories of them were bathed in a golden glow which suffuses all his references to them, and to Australia itself. He had been chosen for the job of manager mainly for this reason: on the face of it he was an ideal sporting ambassador, and up to this point he had been accepted as such in Australia. His reception in the Australian dressing-room that day was a shattering personal experience for him. Bill Bowes remembers him returning to the English dressing-room like a broken man, repeating incredulously, 'They turned their backs on me – they wouldn't speak to me.' For Warner wholly disapproved of 'bodyline', which to him as to Woodfull was completely contrary to the game's traditional ethic, and whose use threatened to open an unbridgeable gap between the English team of which he was manager and the Australia he loved. As early as the first Test he had written to Findlay, the Secretary of the MCC, in terms which made quite clear his unhappiness at Jardine's tactics.

Yet Warner's position prevented him stating his opposition to 'bodyline' in public, and inevitably therefore in Australian eyes he was tainted with the responsibility for it – as Woodfull had plainly implied.

The manager's role in touring sides was a good deal less influential between the Wars than it has since become. It was exclusively an off-the-field public relations job – Warner in fact was one of the first English managers who had himself played international cricket. As he himself saw it, his role did not entitle him to interfere with the captain's conduct of the tour on the field: he could at most protest privately to him, and this Warner did to Jardine on several occasions. But Warner was not the man to break down Jardine's flint-like resolution; and if Jardine persisted with his tactics, Warner's conventional sense of loyalty to the side and to the MCC – his whole upbringing, in fact – forbade him to make his disapproval of Jardine's tactics public.

Warner is the most pathetic of the leading actors in the 'bodyline' controversy. He held his tongue on 'bodyline' for the remainder of the tour – held it so completely that he has been accused of a tacit collusion with Jardine, of trying to salve his popularity with the Australian public while conniving at the tactics which were winning England the Ashes. To my understanding, this is a complete misreading of the man. The rest of the tour was a prolonged agony to him: when he got home, he spoke his mind on 'bodyline' to the MCC with no hedging at all. 'When he sees a cricket field with an Australian on it, he goes mad,' was his later rueful verdict on Jardine, the man he had helped to promote to the English captaincy.

On Monday morning, then, the news of the incident broke sensationally throughout the Australian press; and inevitably this had its effect on the atmosphere in which the rest of the game was played. Up to this point, the official decencies had been observed. There had been indignation at the English tactics on the terraces, in the Australian dressing-room, and in some portions of the

Australian press, but it had received no official expression. Neither Woodfull nor the Australian cricketing authorities had made any public protest, and most of the leading Australian papers had been at great pains to maintain their objectivity in their coverage of the tour and to avoid outright condemnation – it is significant that most of them had so far avoided use of the emotive term 'bodyline'. Equally significantly, the same appearance of objectivity, and the same abstention from condemnation, had been observed in the commentaries on the day's play that had been broadcast each evening from the local radio stations by several of the leading Australian players, including Woodfull and Bradman. Until the scene in the Australian dressing-room on Saturday afternoon it was, therefore, still possible to maintain that, whatever the Australian public might feel, there was no breach between the two sides and that as far as they were concerned the ethic of traditional cricketing sportsmanship still held. But once Woodfull's condemnation of the English tactics became public knowledge, the whole situation was changed. The issue was no longer which side was going to win, especially as it soon became increasingly obvious that England were going to: to put it baldly, the point was that in the eyes of the vast majority of Australians, England were cheating. A game is only possible on condition that there is agreement between the players on the rules and the conventions defining it, and Woodfull had accused England precisely of breaching the conventions that define cricket. He had said that Australia were playing cricket and England were not; and if that was true, there was no game to be either won or lost, and the only logical thing to do was to stop playing – as Woodfull had said he might.

From Monday onwards, therefore, there was a sense in which the crowd were less concerned to cheer their own side on than to protest at England's methods. Of course, this is an oversimplification. Strictly speaking, there had still been no official protest. The game went on, and there was no further suggestion that the Australians might withdraw from it. Not all Australians, after all, were agreed in condemning the Englishmen's methods. And when play resumed on the Monday morning, the game was not yet a foregone conclusion. Allen bowled Richardson at 131, but Ponsford, his body bulging with padding, played Larwood with confidence, and received stout support from Oldfield, a highly competent middle-order batsman. With the wicket now playing very easily, and the English attack limited by an ankle injury to Voce, these two took the score to 185 at lunch, at which point it still seemed possible that Australia might make a fight of it. This prospect did not long survive the interval. At 194 Ponsford was out in the same way as both of his dismissals in the first Test: he walked across his wicket to Voce and was bowled behind his legs for 85. With the new ball due at 200 and only tail-enders to come, it was a bad moment for him to go. Up to this point, though, there had been little call for barracking: Voce had scarcely bowled, and although Ponsford had taken one or two blows on the body during Larwood's two brief spells the episodes had been minor, and there had been nothing to blow the crowd's simmering resentment into flame. The lull was not to last. Larwood and Allen took the new ball: Grimmett was out to Allen at 212, and then at 218 Oldfield, attempting to hook Larwood, was hit on the head and so badly injured that he had to retire and took no further part in the match.

This was the second crisis of the match, and the second time Larwood had badly hurt an Australian batsman; and it is small wonder if the crowd's fury boiled over. Not content with the injury he had done to the Australian captain on the Saturday, Larwood had now disabled the quiet, modest, and universally popular Australian wicketkeeper: obviously, if he could not bowl them out, he was determined to knock them out – so the crowd read it. Yet, although Larwood bowled much leg-theory during the Australian innings, he was not in fact bowling it when either Woodfull or Oldfield received their injuries, and there is unanimity among observers that both were hit by balls that were pitched on the wicket, though obviously short of a length.

Oldfield himself said immediately that it was his own fault. He had taken the risk implicit in all good hooking, which requires that the batsman get his head behind the ball's line of flight, the risk of being hit on the head if he misses; and against a bowler of Larwood's pace, it was all too easy to make the fractional misjudgement of timing which was all that was required. Nor could it well be argued that Larwood had no right to be bowling short stuff at tail-enders: Oldfield, batting at 7, had made 41 in good style. It would have been hard to fault that particular ball of Larwood's by even the most exacting standards of cricketing ethics (certainly no fast bowler of the 1980s would think twice about bowling a bouncer in similar circumstances, for whatever that may be thought worth); but in the prevailing atmosphere, that was not the point. After the events of Saturday and the revelations of the weekend, it was the sort of bushfire atmosphere in which the slightest spark could set off a conflagration. If Jardine had been bent on conciliation, no doubt the spark might have been avoided, but he was not: he simply went on playing the game in the way in which he had determined to play it, and it was a way which involved the chance of the completely accidental injury to Oldfield.

The spark, anyway, had been struck, and the ground went up in fury – yelling, booing, counting Larwood out. The anger and frustration of the crowd was even more intense than when Woodfull had been hit, and O'Reilly, the next batsman, had to use his bat to force his way through the crowd of members of the South Australian Cricket Association in front of the pavilion 'standing on the steps and yelling'.

Looking back on it, it is a remarkable tribute to the strength of the conventional taboos in the 1930s that more did not happen. Irruptions on to the field – streakers, garland-hangers, embracers of century-makers – have become commonplace, even on quite trivial occasions, by

51

the 1980s: in an enormously more powerful emotional situation at Adelaide in 1933, not one spectator appears to have come over the pickets and not one missile to have been thrown. Probably there were few places in the British Empire where the code of good behaviour imposed its disciplines more rigidly than in Adelaide; but certainly they never showed their strength more impressively than at that moment.

There are two sides to this, of course. Discipline is repressive: it was *because* the crowd's anger was allowed no form of expression more effective than hooting, because they were inhibited from *doing* anything, that that anger was so formidable, and was felt as such in the middle. It also made it more dangerous, for the same reason as the explosion of a boiler is more dangerous than the explosion of a toy balloon. All disciplines have their limits: if the crowd's anger *had* boiled over that day, and they *had* come over the pickets, the consequences might have been very ugly indeed – at least for Jardine and Larwood. Almost certainly the match, and the tour, would have ended there and then – with incalculable consequences for the future of Anglo-Australian cricket. One of the more remarkable features of the 'bodyline' controversy is that 'bodyline' was introduced against the Australians, not in England, but in front of hostile Australian crowds – a fact that says volumes for the absolute complacency of the assurance with which it was assumed in the 1930s that spectators did not interfere with the game, or for Jardine's insensitivity, or both. But it is clear that the authorities in Adelaide were aware of the dangers – they showed it by sending out a hurried call to Adelaide police headquarters for police reinforcements at the ground – and it is important to bear this in mind in passing judgement on their actions in the next couple of days.

After Oldfield had been helped off, the game did eventually go on; but the crowd's anger did not subside, and certainly from this point onward the outcome of the game was both a foregone conclusion and a secondary issue. Australia were all out for 222, and England in their second innings ground their remorseless way to a total of 412 – since all Tests in Australia between the Wars were timeless, there was no thought of declaring. Jardine, unbending as ever in the face of intense crowd hostility, opened the innings and set the tone with 56 in four and a quarter hours. The entire innings took twice that long – not bad going by the standards of the 1980s, but funereal for the 1930s, and so far had interest drained away from the game itself by this stage that only some 8000 spectators watched England bat on the Tuesday. But the calculated effect of setting Australia an impossible target was achieved: in the end they needed 523, and Larwood immediately bowled Fingleton for a duck (thereby winning his sovereign from Warner) and had Ponsford caught in the gully for 3 in his opening spell, before resorting to leg-theory. Woodfull carried his bat through the innings for a brave 73 not out, taking some further knocks from Larwood in the process, and Bradman played a brief but hectically brilliant innings of 66 until, unsettled by Larwood's leg-theory, he threw caution to the winds against Verity, hit him for one magnificent 6, and was then caught and bowled; but of the remaining Australian batsmen only Richardson reached double figures, and by the Thursday afternoon it was all over, England winning by 338 runs, and Larwood and Allen taking 15 wickets between them.

The match indeed appears to have ended in a mood of comparative reconciliation, if the account of the leading Adelaide daily (which had played down the bitterness throughout) is to be trusted, with cheers for Jardine and highly characteristic speeches by both captains. Jardine was brusque: 'What I have to say is not worth listening to. Those of you who had seats got your money's worth – and then some. Thank you.' Woodfull was moralistic – 'This great Empire game of ours teaches us to hope in defeat and congratulate the winners if they manage to pull off the victory. I want you to remember that it is not the individual but the team that wins the match.'

But by then everyone's interest had shifted to a different drama being played on a wider stage.

The events of the weekend had confronted the Australian cricket authorities with the most intractable of dilemmas – whether to take any action about the English 'leg-theory', or 'bodyline', tactics, and if so, what action to take. There was no precedent for the official body controlling cricket in any country protesting about the tactics employed by a side representing another country in the course of a Test series. And to whom should such a protest be made? To the captain of the English side? To its managers? Or to the ultimate authority responsible for sending it, the august MCC, half the world away in London? What prospect was there that a protest to any of these would be effective? Yet what else could the Australian authorities do? A change of the Laws to outlaw 'bodyline' was far too slow and heavy-handed an expedient to be appropriate – apart from the fact that according to all tradition such a change could only be made by the MCC, and that to make it unilaterally in the middle of a series would be certain to lead to the withdrawal of the English side from the rest of the tour.*

But to do nothing – or, rather, to rely entirely on what could be achieved by private representations behind the scenes – clearly looked even more unthinkable to the members of the Australian Board of Control present at Adelaide. The mood of the crowd on Saturday and on Monday had been so ugly that they had some reason to feel

* It made things no easier that an undercurrent of friction had existed between the two controlling bodies even before the MCC party left England, due to the MCC's insistence that at the end of the tour of Australia they should go on to New Zealand, which necessitated abandoning several of the minor country matches which England teams had been accustomed to play in Australia – an unpopular change which the Board had been extremely reluctant to sanction. There had been some very tough exchanges by cable between the two bodies before the Board had grudgingly conceded the point.

that some form of official condemnation of 'bodyline' on their part was essential to release some of the pent-up popular emotion, and if the danger of uncontrollable crowd action on the field of play itself was to be avoided. Inevitably, they were keenly aware too of how high feeling was running in the Australian team itself and in its captain; and that also was their responsibility. And, finally, they were Australians themselves, and there is every reason to suppose that they resented the English tactics, and the injuries caused already to Woodfull and Oldfield, as much as anyone on the field. The task of identifying the precisely correct course of action, that which would do most to reduce bitterness and restore mutual understanding when emotions were running so high, and action (if any) had to be taken so quickly, might have tested the most experienced diplomats. The position was made much more difficult for the members of the Australian Board of Control by the fact that only five of them were present at Adelaide† (the other nine were scattered throughout the vast distances of Australia, some of them more than a thousand miles away), and that none of them were experienced diplomats: indeed, none of them were even very distinguished cricketers – only two of them, J. S. Hutcheon and R. J. Hartigan, the Queensland represent-atives, had had any experience of the first-class game. The ABC, as we have seen, has always been a body very different from the MCC, lacking both its social prestige and the authority the MCC derives from the power wielded within it by the leading amateur cricketers of their generation. The MCC Committee had on it men who knew Test cricket at first hand, including past captains of England like F. S. Jackson; the ABC, a body of adminis-trators pure and simple, had nobody remotely of this calibre.

† The three South Australian members, B. V. Scrymgeour, H. W. Hodgetts and R. F. Middleton; W. H. Jeanes, the Secretary, also a South Australian; and W. L. Kelly of Victoria.

It appears to have been the Secretary of the Board, W. H. Jeanes, who had most to do with the course of action eventually followed (the Chairman, Dr Allen Robertson, was in Melbourne), and the injury to Oldfield was the catalyst that drove the Board to action. On the Monday afternoon, after the Oldfield incident had occurred, the little enclosure where players, pressmen and committee offices were grouped closely together was red-hot with rumour, argument and expostulation. Even before the Oldfield incident, the pot had been further stirred by an exacerbation of Saturday's confrontation between Woodfull and Warner. Following a further meeting with Woodfull, Warner happily announced to several journalists that Woodfull had apologized, and that they were now the best of friends. He had been the victim of his own intensely wishful thinking. A few hours later his statement was directly contradicted by a statement from Woodfull, read out to the assembled Press contingent by Jeanes. All Woodfull had said, it seemed, was that the difference was not a personal one between Warner and himself – he retracted nothing of what he had previously said, and had neither made nor intended any apology. In other words, his condemnation of the English 'bodyline' tactics stood intact; at most, he had recognized that Warner did not bear the responsibility for them. This denial of the apology reported earlier was blazoned all over the Australian evening papers; and, as usual, an apology denied or withdrawn left the breach more naked than before.

During that Monday afternoon or evening, the Board – or, rather, the minority of its members present at Adelaide – finally acted, in the first place with commendable tact. They sought out the English managers, Warner and Palairet, and asked them to abandon the use of 'bodyline' tactics. It was the last point at which the dispute might have been settled as between friends, by a gracious concession on England's part; but the failure of the attempt was predictable. Warner would undoubtedly have liked to accede to the Australian request,* but he knew he had no hope of persuading Jardine, who was not present, and on whom a request emanating from the ABC to modify his successful tactics would undoubtedly have acted like a red rag on a bull. The English managers could only reply that they were not responsible for the control of tactics on the field.†

The members of the Board present in Adelaide therefore contacted the Chairman, Dr Allen Robertson, in Melbourne (presumably by telephone), and Robertson thereupon instructed Jeanes to submit to all the members of the Board a proposal to send to the MCC immediately a telegram of protest which had been drafted by Scrymgeour, Hodgetts, Middleton and Kelly, and approved by Robertson himself. The process of consultation was necessarily hurried and unsatisfactory. It had to take place by cable, and the actual text of the protest was not included in the cables: the absent members were merely asked to approve the sending of a telegram of protest that they had not seen – those responsible for the draft were later to excuse the omission on the grounds that it was essential to act quickly. It does not seem a very convincing plea, and it is not surprising that it gave rise to some heated debate at the special meeting of the Board that was summoned to discuss

* Palairet's position is obscure: his main responsibility was oversight of the financial side of the tour, and in the course of the 'bodyline' debate he seems consistently to have kept his head well below the parapet.

† It should be added that Jardine, in his book on the tour, was later to claim that he 'had been at pains on more than one occasion to let it be known in certain quarters that in the event of there being any desire for a friendly conference, whether formal or informal, the managers of the team and its captain would be only too willing to co-operate'. On the face of it, such a conference should have been the ideal way of resolving the 'bodyline' issue; and it is not surprising that the statement on its publication in July 1933 caused some consternation in Australia, particularly among those members of the ABC who had not been present at Adelaide and who had disapproved of the action the Board had taken in their name. But Robertson and Jeanes both denied that any such approaches had been made to them 'early in the tour' – which in context presumably means up to the time of the sending of the cable. The matter must be left unresolved.

the developing controversy at the end of January. Nevertheless, the consent of eight members was duly obtained – one assumes the four present at Adelaide, the other two Victorian delegates, and the solitary representatives of Western Australia and Tasmania, for at the special meeting the New South Wales and Queensland delegates made their disapproval of what had been done very clear indeed, pressing Jeanes with a series of hostile questions. This was the narrowest possible majority, but it was enough. The protest cable was dispatched on the afternoon of Wednesday the 18th, the fifth day of the match. Warner was given a copy and, at the same time, on the authority of the Chairman, Jeanes read out to the clamorous Press not merely an announcement that a protest had been made, but the actual text of the cable itself.

These transactions were to be the subject of much controversy. The decision to raise the issue with the MCC in London, given the state of public feeling in Adelaide and the refusal or inability of the English managers to take any action, was perhaps inevitable – indeed, according to Fingleton, the English managers (Warner, surely, must have been the principal one involved) themselves suggested telegraphing Lord's. Warner also suggested that the ABC should seek his opinion on the draft wording before the cable was sent, a sensible suggestion that was unfortunately not followed. The decision was nevertheless controversial. The Australian team themselves were divided on it. Woodfull had said that he thought the Board should take action, after the injuries to himself and Oldfield, and apparently approved of the cable; but – according to Fingleton, anyway – both he and Bradman refused to put their names to it when asked to do so by the Board. Why Bradman in particular should have been asked to do so is not clear; but Richardson, the vice-captain, was certainly opposed to the sending of any protest. He thought the proper course was for Australia to keep its mouth shut and look round for fast bowlers of its own who could retaliate in kind. The rest of the players were not consulted. When the news of the protest broke in the Wednesday evening papers, many Australians, including a number of leader writers, agreed with Richardson, and condemned the sending of the cable as undignified and humiliating.

The timing of the protest was admittedly unhappy. Any querying of English tactics would have come with a better grace when the Test was over (and the members of the Board may well have reflected in retrospect that it would have come best of all after the Australian victory in the second Test rather than in the course of Australian defeat in the third, and that they should have paid more attention to Bradman's misgivings expressed to them earlier). Since on the face of it there was nothing to be gained by acting immediately, rather than allowing time for tempers to cool during the next few days – no action that the MCC might take could be quick enough to affect Jardine's conduct of the third Test itself – one can only suppose that the Board, or those of its members present in Adelaide, allowed their judgements to be swayed by the high emotional temperatures prevailing there, or else that they thought there was a serious danger of crowd violence on the field unless a safety valve was provided for the popular anger.

The release of the protest telegram to the press strongly suggests that the second of these explanations is the correct one: it is impossible to assess its validity at this distance of time, and one can only say that on this point the Board's judgement may well have been right. This may have been a persuasive reason for releasing the text of the cable, but if the object was conciliation – or even to make the abandonment of 'bodyline' tactics by England as easy as possible – it was a strange error of judgement which published the text without seeking the opinion of the English managers on it, and which released it to the press before it could even have been received, let alone considered, by the MCC to whom it was sent. These considerations were presumably overlooked in the heat of the moment, but they must have contributed a good deal to the harshness of the English reaction. The text itself contributed even more. The telegram read:

> 'Bodyline' bowling has assumed such proportions as to menace the best interests of the game, making protection of the body by the batsman the main consideration.
> This is causing intensely bitter feeling between the players as well as injury. In our opinion it is unsportsmanlike.
> Unless stopped at once it is likely to upset the friendly relations existing between Australia and England.

The telegram was succinct – perhaps excessively so. It assumed – wrongly, as the succeeding controversy was to demonstrate – that 'bodyline bowling' was something that the MCC (not to mention the British public) would find it easy to recognise and to define. But it was the last two sentences that were to cause the most trouble. The last sentence at least looked like an exercise in fantastic hyperbole that at once cast the gravest doubts on the judgement of the men who had composed it – was a question of ethics on the cricket field really likely to imperil the relations between two closely related and intimately linked nations like Australia and England?* And finally, and worst of all, the telegram accused the England side of 'unsportsmanlike' tactics. The thoughtless choice of that word – even though it probably represented accurately enough what most Australian observers present in Adelaide thought – was to loose a nest of hornets in England, and to embitter the resultant controversy beyond all calculation. It is to England that we must now turn.

---

* Though it may be that it was only *cricketing* relations that the members of the ABC had in mind in drafting the telegram; and even if this was not the case, the events of the coming year make the sentence look a good deal less fantastic.

CHAPTER 3

Conflict

(January–February 1933)

Up to the weekend 14–15 January 1933, it is fair to regard 'bodyline' as nothing more than a novel technique – a matter of bowling and fieldplacing tactics – something that happened out in the middle and that concerned the players alone. It was certainly thus that its creator, Douglas Jardine, always saw it; and as such, 'bodyline' had a history, a logic and a technique of its own, and these are things that we shall look at in due course. But over that weekend, 'bodyline' assumed a new dimension. As a result of the injuries to Woodfull and Oldfield and the crowd's reactions to these incidents, of the confrontation between Woodfull and Warner and the revelation of it in the press, and, above all, as a result of the ABC's protest telegram to the MCC, 'bodyline' became the matter of a public controversy and the cause of a deep division between the cricketing publics and the cricketing Establishments of England and Australia. Maybe this development was always inevitable once England adopted 'bodyline' tactics in the first place; but this is not now the point. The important point to grasp is that this controversy, once launched, soon developed a logic and a dynamic of its own, at best loosely connected to 'bodyline' as an actual technique on the field of play. They have to be understood in their own terms; and that understanding requires first a recognition of the fundamental asymmetry of the controversy.

In absolute terms, the size of the cricketing public and the degree of its commitment were as great in England as they were in Australia – as had been amply demonstrated in recent Test series, in the interest taken in the selection of the touring side, and in the immense enthusiasm of the team's send-off from Tilbury. The difference lay not here, but in the way in which 'bodyline' was experienced in the two countries: directly in Australia, indirectly in England. To Australians, 'bodyline' was an outrage which they saw happening under their eyes. The crowd at Adelaide had *seen* Woodfull hit – and Jardine's immediate switch to a packed leg-side field – and *seen* Oldfield felled, and *seen* Fingleton, Ponsford and the other Australian batsmen taking blow after blow from Larwood's and Voce's rearing, chest-high bumpers, while the shark-like short legs crowded near: every Australian paper was full of the accounts of eye-witness correspondents and denunciations by past Test cricketers. Australians knew what 'bodyline' meant, knew that it was like no bowling they had ever seen before, and in the vast majority of cases knew precisely where they stood on it.

None of this was true in England. It is hard to realize how minutely thin the channel of communications between Australia and England was in 1932–33. Because play in Australia ended about 9 o'clock in the morning by English time, first news of the Tests was the perquisite of the evening papers, which were then in their heyday. None of the national dailies, in consequence, had thought it worth while to send out a correspondent with the team, and of the three British press correspondents accompanying it, two represented London evening papers and the third Reuter's – most of the morning papers relied on these Reuter's reports, backed up by what comments their own cricket correspondents ten thousand miles distant from the events could provide on the strength of them. Accounts of events in Australia were thus filtered through a very narrow channel on their way to England. Above all, the vital *visual* experience of 'bodyline' was lacking. There was, of course, no television. The only substitutes were the newsreels and press photographs. Flown to England, these sometimes appeared within days of the events, but never simultaneously with the news of them. The static quality of press photographs made it impossible for them to give any exact notion of 'bodyline': they could show Woodfull reeling from his blow over the heart at Melbourne (but many Englishmen could recall seeing English batsmen hit just as badly by Gregory and McDonald), and they could show the ring of short legs, but they could give no impression of the cumulative effect of Larwood and Voce bowling two or three bumpers an over, for over after over, and of the batsmen taking blow after blow on the body. The newsreels were not much better adapted for the purpose: true, they had the dynamic quality that the press photographs lacked, but in practice they were restricted to clips a few seconds long that rarely (if ever) showed two balls consecutively, and consequently again failed to give any coherent impression of 'bodyline' as an entity.

As far as voice communication was concerned, broadcasting of course existed. Sports commentating was in its youth, if not its infancy: Australian broadcasting companies had transmitted short wave ball-by-ball commentaries to appreciative audiences down under during the 1930 series in England, and in 1932–33 the BBC broadcast similar commentaries on some, if not all, of the last four Tests by the Australian Test batsman Alan Kippax (who had himself played in the first Test). Kippax, however, seems to have observed a diplomatic reticence in his references to 'bodyline', and there is nothing to show that the medium did anything to bring home the realities of 'bodyline' to those who heard the programmes. A radio-telephone link also existed, which was certainly used by the press on occasions; but it seems very doubtful if it was ever used for direct communication between Lord's and the touring party. Apart from this, when it came to the war of cables with the ABC, the MCC had no information to go on other than telegrams and month-old letters from Warner and Jardine. There was no regular air service to Australia until the end of 1934, and hence no air mail. As for the possibility of going out to Australia to see what was happening for oneself, the sea passage took a month: so if an MCC representative, or anybody else for that matter, had set out for Australia when the 'bodyline' storm burst in its full fury in mid-January, he could scarcely have hoped to be in time to see anything of the last Test at Sydney.

The state of communications between Britain and Australia in 1932–33 is critical for a proper understanding of the 'bodyline' controversy; and the upshot of it was that the sole effective interpreters of what was happening in Australia to the cricket-following public of Britain were the three correspondents representing British newspapers and agencies accompanying the team – plus, one must add, the Australian ex-captain Warwick Armstrong, who was covering the tour for the third of the big London evening papers, the *Evening News*. It is correspondingly important to know something of who they were, and of the qualifications and attitudes they brought to their job.

The representative of the *Evening Standard* was Bruce Harris. Harris was not primarily a cricket correspondent at all: his real game was tennis. The *Standard* had recently recruited the young E. W. Swanton as their cricket correspondent; but he was still in his first year with the paper and was apparently considered too junior to be sent to Australia, a decision much to be regretted. It is clear that Harris' knowledge of the game was limited – Leslie Ames still remembers him asking on the voyage out what kind of a bowler Verity was. This necessarily meant that in writing his reports he leaned heavily on the opinions and advice of other members of the touring party, and since from the first he seems to have struck up a close relationship with Jardine – an unusual feat for a pressman – it is not surprising that the *Standard*'s reports were wholly uncritical of Jardine's tactics. After the team's return to England,

Harris was to write an account of the tour under the significant title of *Jardine Justified*, to which Jardine himself wrote a foreword.

The *Star*, on the other hand, scored a considerable coup by sending out Jack Hobbs, the doyen of English batsmen, as its correspondent. I have already referred to the growing frequency in the 1920s of this practice of papers recruiting well-known first-class cricketers to add the prestige of their names to their cricket reports. The practice was commoner in Australia than in England, and we have seen that there was trouble when the ABC forbade Bradman to write for the press during the 1932–33 series while he was a member of the Australian side. But in England also leading players like Percy Fender had made a considerable reputation for themselves as cricket journalists. The *Star*, though, seems to have scored a genuine first in sending out to Australia a leading professional cricketer who was still playing the game. No English cricketer of that generation commanded more respect on both personal and professional grounds than Jack Hobbs, and his verdict on 'bodyline' could have been uniquely authoritative: we have seen, too, that he had already registered his own protest at the excessive bowling of bumpers during the Surrey *v* Yorkshire match at the Oval in the previous August. But in fact his verdict was effectively muffled for two good reasons. Hobbs was a professional to the backbone, and this for him involved a very strong sense of loyalty to his side. He had toured Australia no less than five times (there were those who thought he should have been included in the 1932 party), and he inevitably identified with the English team, with whom he was travelling, and whose members were his fellow-cricketers and in many cases his friends, while Jardine himself was his county captain.

All this tended to make him play down his own unquestionable hostility to 'bodyline'; and there was another factor which may have been equally important. Not surprisingly, Hobbs was not a fluent writer. His contributions accordingly passed through the hands of a ghost writer, Jack Ingham – although even after this process they retained a laconic, and naïve, quality which makes it clear that they are not the work of a professional writer – and the combined effect of the ghosting and Hobbs' limitations as a writer did much to blunt the point of such comments as he made on 'bodyline'. I have already quoted some of his comments on the 'Australian XI' match at Melbourne; they made it clear that England's tactics were controversial, but nothing like a clear condemnation of 'bodyline' emerged from them, and this was true of his later reporting of the Tests themselves. It is significant that in his account of the third day's play at Adelaide – i.e., after Oldfield's injury but before the sending of the ABC's cable – Hobbs made no comment at all on England's methods of attack, but appealed to the public at home for loyalty to Jardine: 'There is enough to put up with playing in Australia [this is probably a covert reference to Australian barracking] without a feeling that your own people at home are against you.' Hobbs presumably had in mind the criticisms of Larwood's and Voce's 'leg theory' that were beginning to appear here and there in the English press, some of them over the names of famous cricketers of the past; but, given Hobbs' own hostility to 'bodyline', the comment says volumes about his attitude and sense of priorities during the affair. There was too the additional point that, whatever his opinions of 'bodyline', Hobbs was convinced that (to quote from another of his reports two days later) 'only leg theory can stop Bradman' – and believing that, it was clearly difficult for him to condemn it outright.

The English morning papers relied overwhelmingly on the reports of Reuter's agent with the side, Gilbert Mant. Mant was a knowledgeable follower of the game: he was himself an Australian, and from the first he strongly disliked all that he saw of 'bodyline'. But the tradition of Reuter's reporting is spare and factual, and this was scrupulously observed by Mant, who excluded his personal opinion of English bowling tactics from his reports altogether – it may well be that, as an Australian working for an English agency serving English newspapers, he felt additionally inhibited from speaking out.*

This left only the *Evening News* correspondent, Warwick Armstrong – only one of a number of distinguished Australian ex-Test players to cover the series for the press, but the only one to do so for an English paper. The situation as it developed was not without piquancy, for as Australia's captain in the two series of 1920 and 1921 Armstrong had won a reputation as a hard man who gave no quarter, and at times sailed pretty close to the Laws, and, in Jardine, England had arguably sent to Australia a captain who approximated more closely to the Armstrong mould than any other English captain of modern times. Whether or not Armstrong was aware of the kinship, his contributions to the *News* are distinguished for their restraint and realism. His descriptions of the English bowling were dispassionate and objective, and although he was critical of 'bodyline', he never questioned its sportsmanship – whether because he was never himself one of the great ethical idealists, the Woodrow Wilsons, of cricket (as, for instance, both Woodfull and Warner were), or because he realized that this would be a sure way of antagonizing his English readers.

Armstrong's hostility to 'bodyline' was based partly on the trouble he foresaw it was bound to cause, but mainly on the fact that he saw it as an impoverishment of cricket, reducing the game to an intolerably tedious spectacle of batsmen ducking, weaving and sometimes being hit, while being quite unable to play any strokes – except, at peril, the hook. He argued that the public would lose interest and refuse to pay to watch such cricket, and found justification for his view in the derisory total of 8000 spectators who turned up for the fourth day's play at Adelaide (though one

* He contemplated writing a book to make his real opinions known on his return to England after the tour was over, but was dissuaded from doing so by his employers.

detects a loophole in his logic here, for England batted all that day, and there was no 'bodyline' to be bored by). Moreover, he saw 'bodyline' as a prostitution of Voce's, and especially Larwood's, great gifts, since, in complete contradiction to Hobbs, he held consistently that England were the better side anyway and could have won without resorting to it. But as far as the enlightenment of the British cricketing public was concerned, the important fact was that Armstrong consistently played down the ethical objections to 'bodyline', which were the real core of the Australian case against it, and instead stressed an aspect of it which most of his English readers probably regarded as fairly unimportant as long as it was keeping Bradman's run-flow in check and winning Test Matches for England – and which was anyway dubious; another famous Australian ex-player, Arthur Mailey, found 'bodyline' a thrilling spectacle, and maintained that the crowds did too.

What all this amounts to is that the avid cricket-following public of England were reduced, by the imperfection of communications between England and Australia, to seeing events in Australia through a slit so narrow that it was almost impossible for them to see 'bodyline' in any kind of broad perspective; and this was hardly less true of the committeemen of the MCC than of the average cricket follower in the street. From the beginning of the tour, before anyone had heard of 'bodyline', the picture that emerged from the English press accounts was one of the English pace attack achieving a moral and technical superiority over the Australian batsmen. This impression dated back to the early matches in Western Australia and the crushing victories over South Australia and Victoria: it was reinforced by the match against the 'Australian XI' in Melbourne, in which Larwood first showed his full potential (up to this point, the great success among the fast bowlers had been the widely disparaged Allen) and Australian voices were first raised in criticism of the bowling of him and Voce. Bruce Harris' comment on that match in the *Evening Standard* is typical and revealing: 'In Larwood, assuming that he maintains his "demon" speed of the present match, lies the answer to the Bradman Problem. Bradman does not appear to like supercharged fast bowling ...' English pride and pleasure in the triumphs of their fast bowlers were not shadowed by any suspicion of the tactics they were employing. The accounts published in the English press certainly made it clear that Larwood and Voce were disquieting the Australian batsmen with a lot of short balls – this was particularly true of Hobbs' account of the 'Australian XI' match – but there was little or no suggestion that their methods were open to legitimate criticism. In consequence, when they also reported, as they sometimes did, the hostile crowd reactions that these methods were evoking, the implication necessarily was that this Australian indignation was *not* legitimate.

By the time of the first Test, and still more by the time of the Third, two impressions were already fixed so fast in most English minds that for the rest of the tour nothing could move them. The first was that there was nothing essentially novel in the methods of their fast bowlers – Larwood and Voce were merely bowling as top class fast bowlers had always bowled, but faster and more effectively. The bumper had always been part of the fast bowler's stock in trade, and first-class batsmen should be prepared to defend themselves against it – there was indeed already audible in much English comment a discernible undertone of satisfaction that the Australians were now receiving what they had themselves dished out a decade earlier. As one typical English press comment put it after the 'Australian XI' match, 'Australia, who in the twenties begot those incomparable terrorists, Gregory and McDonald, must not complain of Larwood and Voce in the thirties.' Equally typical is the way this comment ignored the all-important fact that Gregory and McDonald did *not* bowl to packed leg-side fields.

The second impression was that Australian crowd protests were evidence not of anything properly questionable in English tactics, but of the partisanship, unfairness and inability to take defeat with good grace of the Australian crowds. It was at this point that a major red herring was drawn across the central track of the controversy, confusing the English public still further – the red herring of 'barracking'. Australian conventions of crowd behaviour were different from English ones: they probably still are. That there was such a difference is not in question: on this, all those who knew the game in both countries were agreed. The question was how the difference should be evaluated. Australian crowds were, by and large, noisier and more outspoken than English ones. This no doubt owed something to the fact that they tended to be bigger (since there was more accommodation for them); but there was more to it than that. The behaviour of English cricket crowds – at least of southern English ones – between the Wars was still bound by conventions so strict as to look in retrospect positively Victorian: traditionally, they applauded, and on occasion they cheered, but they did not shout, they did not criticize, and certainly they did not boo. The further from London, and especially the further north, you went, the less this was true: Yorkshire and Lancashire crowds had a longstanding reputation for apt and salty comment on incidents in the field. But even in the heat of the Roses matches, booing seems to have been unheard of; and in any case, it was Lord's rather than Headingley or Old Trafford that set the official standards of good behaviour.*

In the less inhibited and more democratic society of Australia, they ordered things differently. Crowds there

* The Australian satirical weekly *Bulletin* hit off the Australian view of this attitude nicely in verse:

> At 'Ome, of course, we Play the Game,
>   The crowd behave decorously;
> They never criticize or blame,
>   But say 'Bravo!' sonorously;
> 'Played, sir!' they chirp, or cry 'Well run!',
>   But barrack, haw! – it isn't done.

were accustomed to keeping up a running commentary on what went on before them, and to venting their sense of humour, and their approbation and disapprobation of individual players, with a freedom unheard of in England. Individual players reacted to this differently. Some never liked it – the stiffly correct Jardine is a classic example of this reaction: his experience of Australian crowds during the 1928 tour seems to have been a major source of his enduring antipathy to Australia and Australian behaviour – and these included some Australians: the Test all-rounder Alan Fairfax objected to it so strongly that he walked out of first-class cricket altogether. No doubt, according to a widely-recognized rule of human behaviour, those who showed their dislike of it got the worst of it as a result. Others, those who took the crowd's ribaldry in good part and showed that they had a sense of humour themselves, found that the crowd too were equally capable of enjoying a joke at their own expense: 'Gawd, I could have caught that one with my mouth!'; 'So could I, if I had a mouth as big as yours' – that sort of thing went down very well in the outfield. Similarly, not even Jardine minded when a flight of pigeons flew over the Oval at Adelaide during the third Test, and somebody shouted, 'Don't go away – there he is at mid-on.' But when it was a matter of a crowd expressing mass disapproval of the way one side was playing the game – of unduly slow batting, for example – obviously not much could be achieved by individual repartee.

In the great anti-'bodyline' demonstrations of 1933, this was the case in an extreme degree; and there is no question that such demonstrations could be unpleasant and on occasion frightening things. A crowd of 40,000 booing, hooting, catcalling, counting bowlers out, throwing orange peel (though never apparently anything more dangerous than that) at outfielders, and so on, is not a pleasant spectacle. But was this outrageous partisanship, or fair comment on one side's tactics? The Australian defence was that the barrackers were not partisan, that they applauded good play and condemned bad, irrespective of which side produced it, and if most barracking on the tour of 1932–33 was anti-English, this was because the Australian crowds were genuinely outraged by 'bodyline', and with good reason. A point that was often and fairly made was that when Larwood scored 98 in the last Test at Sydney, he was received on his return to the pavilion with a public ovation.

This, though, was not the picture of barracking that the average English cricket follower formed from his reading of the newspapers. The impression he got from them, from the 'Australian XI' match onwards, was of a grossly partisan Australian public doing its best to make up for the failures of its cricketing heroes by the hostility of its demonstrations against the Englishmen – in other words, by an attempt at intimidation, ironically enough the very offence of which the Australian public was at that moment accusing the English bowlers! Since the English newspaper reader had no notion that his bowlers were doing anything questionable, and since the conventions of crowd behaviour in the two countries were so different, it is not surprising if he soon came to see the real source of the trouble that was going on in Australia not as English bowling, but as Australian bad sportsmanship and bad manners – the conduct of what a *Times* correspondent summed up as 'larrikins, habitual loafers, deadbeats ... and irresponsible youths who will always follow the lead of rowdy seniors'. This did not conduce to a swift and friendly settlement of the dispute.

The truth probably lies somewhere in the middle, and anyway is now irrecoverable. Jardine, in the book that he wrote after the tour was over, claimed that Australian barracking had been growing worse ever since the Great War – it probably had been growing noisier, if only because crowds had been growing larger – and referred, legitimately enough, to an occasion in the MCC *v* Victoria match in 1929 when Chapman led his side off the field in protest at the barracking. He also referred to outbreaks of crowd hostility in the more distant past, including an incident from one of the Tests on Warner's first tour of 1903–4, when the Sydney crowd took such violent exception to an umpire's decision against one of the Australians that their groaning and hissing went on all the afternoon, and – greatest scandal of all – was supported by the members in the pavilion. To Jardine this was a sign of the fundamental degeneracy of the Australian character – English crowds, like English cricketers, were supposed to take umpiring decisions in good part and in silence. Nor is there any question that Jardine himself was singled out on the field for a great deal of crowd hostility in which humour played no part at all, and he was made all the more aware of it by the fact that his pride would not permit him to shelter himself from it – by avoiding service on the boundary, for example. The crowd may have given Larwood an ovation at Sydney, but Jardine received no ovations: the hostility to him was deep-felt and genuine.

Certainly Australian crowds could be demanding and difficult – Fingleton, for instance, has borne testimony to the problems of opening the batting for New South Wales before a Sydney crowd whose only real wish was to see the Don get among the runs, and had little patience with opening batsmen who delayed their pleasure by sticking around for too long. You have to take into consideration the cultural gap between a basically aristocratic and disciplined society, as England still largely was, and a much more democratic and spontaneous one in which both crowds and individuals felt much freer to speak their minds forcefully and frankly: perhaps, indeed, one can trace it deeper, to the difference between a tradition of cricket in which the game was still fundamentally an aristocratic recreation, to which spectators were admitted on sufferance, and a tradition in which cricket was a form of mass entertainment in which the spectators expected and enforced their right to call the tune.

For all these reasons, the chances of the ABC's cable of protest being received with sympathy, or even with comprehension, were slim from the start. To the average

Englishman, the Australians had been beaten and were squealing – and the English had themselves lost too many Test Matches to Australia since 1918 to be very sympathetic with their predicament. The *Daily Herald*'s dismissal of the Australian protests as 'undignified snivelling' was not untypical. The arrival of the cable made the headlines in all the evening papers on Wednesday the 18th – coming as the sequel to the reports of the injuries to Woodfull and Oldfield, the crowd demonstrations that followed them, and the scene between Woodfull and Warner in the Australian dressing-room, this was exactly the sort of sensational material in which they delighted.

For the next few days, the press was agog with the issue. *The Times*' first reaction, on 19 January, was more moderate than most: it was 'unthinkable' that Jardine would permit a form of attack that 'was not cricket': the trouble was the two-eyed stance (of which more anon), the crowd's irritation at the failure of their idols, and the craving for sensational news stories. Recurring to the topic the next day, it went over to counter-attack, in a way characteristic of much of the English reaction – 'It is permissible to suggest that there has been a form of interference quite as serious as the alleged unfairness of "leg-theory" bowling. Larwood has had to bowl under the disability that, if a batsman as the result of his own negligence were hit, the blame would be assumed by the mass of spectators to lie with the bowler.' The *Star* reported that 'the cheapest possible insults are daily levelled at Jardine and the English team … The remarkable fact is that the England bowling was described at Melbourne as excellent. Now it is labelled as a menace to life, although there is one fast bowler fewer – Bowes – and methods have not changed.' This comment failed to take note of the very considerable difference between the wickets on which the two Tests were played, and did a good deal less than justice to the degree of crowd protest that the English bowling at Melbourne had nevertheless evoked; but its defensive tone was typical. The unfortunate word 'unsportsmanlike' in particular was

74

like a red rag to the bull of British public opinion. The dispassionate discussion of the fairness or unfairness of 'bodyline' which the occasion demanded – and which would have been difficult enough to achieve anyway when 'bodyline' had scarcely, if ever, been seen in England, and the events that were the cause of dispute were taking place ten thousand miles and a month's travel away – never took place. In its place there arose a bitter dispute between the two cricketing nations, in which national pride and partisanship were the fuelling emotions, and what was sought after was not agreement, but victory.

There was, naturally, a rush by the newspapers to the leading figures of the game for their reactions; and these varied interestingly – and hardly surprisingly, given the very imperfect appreciation in England of the nature of 'bodyline'.* Current players for the most part tended to dismiss the Australian protests as absurd: again and again one comes across the argument that Larwood and Voce were bowling nothing that fast bowlers, especially the Australians Gregory and McDonald, had not bowled in the past without arousing protest, and that there were no grounds for objection now. In some cases these views may have been something less than impartial. When the *Star* asked Larwood's and Voce's county colleague George Gunn for his views, it can scarcely have expected a ringing condemnation of 'bodyline' (and didn't get it: Gunn's comment was, 'They have a bat in their hand, and should take care of themselves'), and still less when they asked his county captain, the rumbustious Arthur Carr, who had himself been responsible for encouraging his two fast bowlers to make several experiments in the direction of 'bodyline' during the previous English season and is sometimes regarded as its real begetter. His reply was,

* The term itself seems never to have been used in England at the time, except in half-ironic quotation of the Australian criticisms of Larwood and Voce, since it was itself becoming a shot in the battle: almost invariably, English sources referred to Larwood's and Voce's tactics by the less emotive term 'leg theory'.

'There is no law in cricket against bowling the leg theory, and if a fast bowler is to be told how to bowl the sooner we give up the game the better.' One might also suspect ulterior motive in the *Evening Standard*'s approach to Lionel Tennyson. Tennyson had captained England for the last three Tests of the disastrous home series of 1921, when Gregory and McDonald had spread havoc among the English batsmen, dealing some pretty nasty knocks in the process. Tennyson took more than a fair share of the knocks himself, but he was an old-fashioned aggressive front-foot driver of unbounded physical courage. In the third Test he played two heroic innings of 63 and 36 against the fast bowlers practically one-handed, having very badly injured his right hand, and in the final Test he took a dreadful crack over the heart from McDonald, which must by all accounts have been fully comparable to Woodfull's injury at Adelaide, but 'shook himself like a great collie dog and promptly drove the fast bowler to the ring'. With those memories and that character, Tennyson was not likely to have very much patience with Australian complaints about English fast bowlers. His column was headed 'We owe no apology', and its theme was that the Australians had brought their trouble on themselves by adopting the two-eyed stance and a fundamentally back-foot style of batting, and were now squealing because they were losing.*

There is little doubt that this was the prevailing view among English cricketers at the time – always remembering that they had not seen Larwood and Voce bowling in Australia, that all their instincts must have been against condemning the tactics of a touring England side in the middle of a Test series against Australia, and perhaps that the best of the current players were not available for comment since they were themselves members of the

* Another notable figure of the past who took this view (though only in private correspondence) and might be thought to have known something about fast bowling was the legendary C. J. Kortright – the fastest of all time, they say.

touring party. But it is worth noting – and it is a fact that may have carried some weight with English public opinion as time went by and the controversy continued – that some distinguished voices were raised on the other side, and that almost all of them were those of men who had played the game in what is generally regarded as its golden age, before the Great War. Ranjitsinhji led the way in the *Sketch*. Even more significant was a weighty and cogently argued piece by Sir Stanley Jackson, an ex-captain of England and current member of the MCC Committee, in the *Telegraph*, in which he drew the vital, and up to that point generally neglected, distinction between conventional 'leg theory', which to him depended for its effect on swing and hence on bowling a full length, and the use of fast bumpers – he maintained that the possibilities of the latter were well known to the great fast bowlers of the Golden Age, but they forbore from exploiting them. Most indignant of all was F. R. Foster, one of the greatest of English fast left-handers, who had been consulted about field placings for Voce by Jardine before the side left England, but now, when he heard what use was being made of them, vehemently rejected Voce's bowling methods as contrary to the spirit of the game. It is probably not too much to read into these views a change that had come over the nature of cricket since the War – a greater ruthlessness and readiness to pursue victory at all costs, reflecting the declining control of the pedigreed amateur and the increasing influence of the press and the crowd. At least one England captain of more recent vintage also took a critical view of 'bodyline', however: Arthur Gilligan, the very popular captain of the 1924 touring side to Australia and himself a fast bowler, who, consulted by an enterprising Australian journalist by radiotelephone, said that it 'did not savour of fairness in the slightest', and should be abandoned as contrary to the spirit of the game.

These more critical views of 'bodyline' came to assume greater significance in the course of the next twelve months; but for the moment they were the views of a small minority, and were almost drowned out by the far greater volume of support for Jardine and his bowlers, and of rejection of the Australian protest, which dominated the discussion of the issue in leaders, on sports pages, and in correspondence columns for the rest of the week. To some extent, of course, what the public thought and the press said mattered comparatively little: the ABC's cable had been addressed to the MCC, and the crucial question was how the MCC would react, and how they would reply. But the executive body of the MCC, its Main Committee, did not meet until Monday 23 January, five days after the arrival of the cable and the publication of its text in both countries, and by then their response had been largely pre-empted by the strength of the public and press reaction. Certainly the MCC's task was made immensely more difficult by the fact that the text of the ABC's cable had been public property and the matter of intense public debate for five days before the Committee met to consider it: they were acting under the same sort of pressures as those which had driven the ABC to take action in Adelaide in the first instance, even if in England the pressures were somewhat less intense.

It is a major handicap that the historian of 'bodyline' has to put up with that no detailed MCC Committee minutes for the period appear to survive, and that almost all the leading protagonists in its discussions of the issue in the course of the next twelve months are now dead. It is therefore impossible to give any account of the Committee's proceedings on that Monday morning. They apparently had before them cables from Jardine and Warner commenting on the Australian protests. These cables do not survive, but it is safe to assume that Jardine's was dismissive and that even Warner's would have had no truck with the charge of lack of sportsmanship, since there is other evidence to show that he regarded the ABC's cable as both foolish and offensive, and that he strongly approved of the MCC's reply. That reply itself is the only certain evidence of the Committee's views: beyond that, one can only speculate. However, it does not seem to be a case in which speculation is very difficult or very dangerous. It was almost unthinkable that the MCC, confronted by a challenge to the sportsmanship of their side in the midst of a tour of Australia, would do anything but support the captain and the team they had chosen to represent them – especially when the exact nature of the offence charged against them was so unclear. The ABC's complaint was about 'bodyline bowling'. What was 'bodyline bowling'? The term was certainly not in the vocabulary of any member of the MCC Committee – as a neologism coined in Australia only a month earlier, it scarcely could be. It was a vague, emotive term which conveyed no precise picture, and it was all too easy to interpret it as a blanket condemnation of any form of bowling which might even occasionally and accidentally threaten a batsman with injury or pain. Composed in haste and under pressure as it had been, the ABC's cable made no attempt to list the characteristics (at least four of them, as we shall see in due course) which, taken together, might be held to define 'bodyline'. Nor did the cable make it clear what action the ABC were asking the MCC to take: they were left to draw the conclusion that they were being asked to instruct Jardine, at a distance of ten thousand miles, to abandon a form of attack which they had never seen.

The Main Committee of the MCC was a very different body from the Australian Board of Control. They were rich alike in social prestige, in wisdom of the world, and in cricketing experience. They included half a dozen members of the peerage and four other titled gentlemen – a Speaker of the House of Commons, a Chairman of the Unionist Party and ex-Governor of Bengal, a cabinet minister and a Lord Mayor of London – a former captain of England (Sir Stanley Jackson – not to mention the absent Warner), and half a dozen other men who had played first-class cricket, though it is fair enough to add that only Jackson had done so with any great distinction, and that none of them had any personal experience of the first-class game since 1918. As a body, and even without the considerable pressure of public opinion behind them, they were extremely unlikely to make concessions to so crudely formulated a protest without the showing of far more reason to do so than they could in fact see before them; and they were undoubtedly aware that the ABC's cable had come in for much hostile criticism in Australia as well as in England. They must have known that they were on impregnable ground; and their reply, based apparently on a draft by Lord Lewisham, the President, and Sir Kynaston Studd, was in fact unyielding. It read:

> We, Marylebone Cricket Club, deplore your cable. We deprecate your opinion that there has been unsportsmanlike play. We have fullest confidence in captain, team and managers and are convinced that they would do nothing to infringe either the Laws of Cricket or the spirit of the game. We have no evidence that our confidence has been misplaced. Much as we regret accidents to Woodfull and Oldfield, we understand that in neither case was the bowler to blame. If the Australian Board of Control wish to propose a new Law or Rule, it shall receive our careful consideration in due course.
>
> We hope the situation is not now as serious as your cable would seem to indicate, but if it is such as to jeopardize the good relations between English and Australian cricketers and you consider it desirable to cancel remainder of programme we would consent, but with great reluctance.

This was a far clearer piece of drafting than the ABC's protest. It made clear the MCC's substantial refusal to accept the criticism of their team's tactics, still more to interfere in Jardine's direction of them; and it presented the ABC starkly with the only alternatives if they refused to modify their stand: amendment of the Laws of Cricket (which must, of course, take months) or abandonment of the tour. At the same time, it cannot be called a conciliatory piece of drafting, as was clear enough from the bristling tone of the first two sentences. Perhaps conciliation was hardly to be looked for; but it would have been at least possible for the MCC not merely to express their readiness to consider a new Law if the ABC felt like drafting one, but to ask the Australians for a precise definition of what exactly they meant by 'bodyline'. Their failure to do so suggests fairly strongly that the majority of the MCC Committee, like the bulk of English public opinion, thought that there was nothing fundamentally new about the English tactics, and that the Australians had no real cause for complaint.

It is at this point that one would most value a detailed account of the Committee's discussion and of the vote that presumably must have been taken (on the strength of his article in the *Telegraph*, one would expect Jackson at least to have preferred a more conciliatory reply); but apparently no such record exists.

In any case, this first exchange of telegrams had not defined the main lines which the controversy was to follow during the succeeding weeks; and defined them, one may well feel, not very happily, and in a way which left unresolved the formidable misunderstandings between the two sides. Regarded as a contest, there was little doubt that the MCC had so far had the best of it. Their reply to the Australian cable was received with general approval in Britain (the MCC released the text to the public immediately, no doubt inevitably once the ABC had set the precedent), and in Australia also its effectiveness was generally admitted. In fact, by the time it reached the ABC a week had elapsed from the sending of their original cable, giving time for second thoughts, and the position there had changed considerably. The Adelaide Test and all its unpleasantnesses were now past history and, although the immediate effect of the ABC's cable may have been to provide a much-needed outlet for the strength of public indignation in Adelaide, in the following days it had become clear that it was having two other, and quite unlooked-for, effects. It was drawing the England side together in united indignation at the slur on their sportsmanship; and it was arousing strong criticism in Australia itself.

As far as the England side were concerned, they were stirred to action in the first place by a report which appeared in an Adelaide paper on 11 January, the day of the dispatch of the ABC's cable, alleging deep divisions on 'bodyline' and widespread resentment of Jardine's methods of captaincy among the touring party. This seems to have been little more than a piece of journalistic trouble-making. Jardine as a captain was abrupt, authoritarian, and uncommunicative, and no doubt this was not always appreciated by his players. Bowes still remembers his exasperation when Jardine rejected his repeated requests for another leg-side fieldsman in the match against South Australia, and then, when Bowes asked yet once more if he could not have a man moved across, suddenly replied, 'No, but you can have five,' and only then initiated Bowes into his ideas on 'leg theory'. Nor was his habit of delaying team selection until the last moment, and requiring the entire touring party to change into flannels on the first day of Test Matches before telling them which of them were to play, very popular. There were, too – as there are apt to be in touring teams – one or two players who might with some reason have felt resentment at being passed over for selection: this applies particularly to Duckworth, still widely regarded as a better wicketkeeper than Ames (who had been his understudy throughout the 1928–29 and 1930 series), and to Tate. The Australian press lavished a lot of unsolicited sympathy on Tate, who was extremely popular in Australia and had bowled magnificently there in the 1924–25 and 1928–29 series, but who played in very few first-class matches on the 1932–33 tour: the truth seems to be that he was past his peak and not properly fit, and probably should not have been selected for the tour.

But whatever private resentments there may have been,

there was no question that the side had complete confidence in Jardine's powers of captaincy and more than enough *esprit de corps* to resent the attempt to make public capital of differences between them. A meeting of the touring party was held to discuss their position, in view of the newspaper report and the ABC's cable – a meeting at which Jardine was not present. The lead was taken by Sutcliffe, the senior professional. It was agreed to issue a statement, though the terms of it might have presented some difficulty, as Allen at least was not prepared to put his name to anything that implied approval of Larwood's and Voce's bowling, and a statement that was not supported by all the members of the party would obviously have been worse than no statement at all; but as it was he agreed to join the rest of the team in signing the actual draft, emphasizing that he did so because it involved no reference to the bowling tactics being employed. As released to the press the following day, the 19th, it read:

> Members of the MCC and the England team do not desire to enter into public controversy, for they deplore the introduction of any personal feeling into the records of a great game.
>   In view, however, of statements which have been given space in some sections of the press to the effect that there has been dissension and disloyalty in their team, they desire to deny this definitely and absolutely.
>   They are, and always have been, utterly loyal to their captain, under whose leadership they hope to achieve an honourable victory.

This statement was received by the Australian papers which had published the original accounts of conflict within the English camp with a good deal of sarcastic incredulity ('OH WE'RE ALL SO HAPPY TOGETHER'), but it seems to have been the literal truth. The Australian press was understandably eager to snap up any crumb of English support for the Australian side of the controversy (hence the radiotelephone conversation with Gilligan, and the extensive Australian reporting of the views of Ranjitsinhji and F. R. Foster), and anything that looked like open conflict within the MCC touring party on the issue would have been instant grist to their mill.

But although reports of divisions between them and of personal resentments of Jardine's leadership continued to appear, they never got beyond the gossip columns, and apparently no member of the party ever let fall a word which could be used to substantiate them. Considering the intense pressures to which they were subjected, and the fact that differences on the ethics of 'bodyline' could scarcely be denied, given Warner's public denunciations of Bowes' 'direct attack' methods before the tour began and Allen's unmistakably significant persistence in traditional 'off theory' methods, this says a good deal for the cohesion of the side. Strange man though he was, Jardine did have the essential captain's knack of commanding loyalty – no doubt largely because of his own complete and selfless dedication to the success of the tour (meaning by that the only thing that he did mean by it, the winning of the Test series) and the team. Twice, before the third Test in view of his own poor batting form, and after it in view of the Australian public's outcry against him, he offered to stand down from the Test side and allow Wyatt to lead the team instead of him. The rest of the selection committee (Warner, Wyatt and Sutcliffe) would not hear a word of it, though both Warner and Wyatt were personally opposed to 'bodyline'. *Esprit de corps*, loyalty to the corporate whole, was of course a much more fashionable virtue between the Wars than it is today: it may be doubted whether a similar standard of team discipline would stand up under similar pressures nowadays.

If the insinuations of the Australian press worked only to reinforce the unity of the touring side, a direct accusation of unsporting conduct by the official body controlling Australian cricket worked far more powerfully in the same direction. There was an interval of three weeks between the end of the ill-starred third Test in Adelaide and the start of the fourth in Brisbane. The cricket played by the touring side during this period was in the main inconsequential. There was a two-day country game at Ballarat – there had been some talk in the press beforehand of the selectors including in the country side a pair of fast bowlers who would give the MCC some of their own 'leg theory' medicine, but although Alexander, the Victorian opening bowler, was included, nothing came of it – a rain-damaged and rather low-key return match against New South Wales at Sydney, in which neither Jardine, Larwood nor Voce played, another country game at Toowoomba in Queensland, chiefly remarkable for a row about the gate money, and a crushing victory in the State game against Queensland on the eve of the fourth Test. But interest in the cricket by now was secondary: all attention centred on the developing controversy between the ABC and the MCC, and the rapidly looming question of whether the fourth Test was going to be played at all. The MCC's suggestion in their cable that the tour might be abandoned had thrown the ABC thoroughly on the defensive. It seems fairly clear that this at least was not a possibility they had envisaged when drafting their original cable: certainly by the time the Board gathered in their special meeting at Sydney on 30 January to consider their response to the MCC reply, it had become amply clear that both among its own members and among the Australian public at large there was a great deal of criticism of the terms of the original cable and a great deal of concern at the prospect of the cancellation of the remainder of the tour.

In the week after the end of the Adelaide Test, the controversy over 'bodyline' was at its furious height, and amid the whirlpools and boiling eddies of conflicting opinion it was by no means easy to detect the main currents. Denunciations of 'bodyline' were as passionate as ever, from quarters as diverse as the bench of bishops and the more lurid extremes of the Australian popular press. In

Sydney, a judge wrote to the highly reputable *Sydney Morning Herald* suggesting that a bowler who injured a batsman might be liable to prosecution at law. The news that Jardine had sent a telegram of sympathy to Oldfield's wife after her husband's injury at Adelaide was the subject of particularly savage satire. Of the breadth and genuineness of the sense of outrage felt among Australians at Jardine's tactics there was never any doubt; but by the ABC's meeting, more than a week had elapsed since the end of the third Test, and a different tone was beginning to become audible amid the uproar of controversy. There was a growing tendency to emphasize the absurdity of allowing a dispute over a point of sporting ethics to develop into a controversy of such bitterness that it threatened the harmony between two nations as closely related as Britain and Australia; and even among those otherwise opposed to 'bodyline', there was an increasing feeling that the ABC's cable had been injudicious and had deserved the rebuff it had received from the MCC. We have already seen that this view had supporters within the ABC itself. It was strongly shared by several members of the Anglo-Australian Establishment, who felt that they had a foot in both camps.

The day after the dispatch of the ABC's original cable, the Board were made aware of this school of thought by a telegram from Kent Hughes, an ex-Rhodes Scholar, an Olympic athlete, and a current member of the Victorian government, objecting to the 'boorish, bitter, and insulting' wording of the cable, drawing unflattering comparisons between the behaviour of Australian crowds in 1933 and that of English crowds in 1921, when English batsmen were taking a battering from Australian fast bowlers, and suggesting a conference between leading cricketers of both nations to resolve the issue. On a more populist level, the highly sensational Melbourne weekly *Truth* – the rough equivalent of the British *News of the World* – pursued a similar theme to a different conclusion, claiming that the cable was a stupid blunder which had made the ABC look ridiculous and Australians a pack of squealers, when the truth was that the English bowlers were just too good: the right answer was for Australia to keep its mouth shut and retaliate in kind. As *Truth* had previously been well to the front of the field in the savagery of its denunciations of 'bodyline', this attitude was interesting (even making allowance for the fact that consistency was not always one of *Truth*'s most conspicuous features) in showing that hostility to 'bodyline' and to the ABC's cable were quite compatible.

Against this background, the ABC's second cable, drafted this time not in the heat of the fray at Adelaide, but in the measured calm of their committee room in Sydney, was a very different document from their first – it was, significantly, the work of a special sub-committee appointed for the purpose, on which the influence of the Chairman and Scrymgeour, who had helped to draft the original protest, was balanced by that of R. A. Oxlade and Hutcheon, the senior representatives of New South Wales and Queensland respectively, who had opposed it. Sent on 30 January, while the MCC party were on their way north to Queensland, it read:

We, Australian Board of Control, appreciate your difficulty in dealing with the matter raised in our cable without having seen the actual play. We unanimously regard 'bodyline' bowling, as adopted in some of the games in the present tour, as being opposed to the spirit of cricket, and unnecessarily dangerous to the players.

We are deeply concerned that the ideals of the game shall be protected and have, therefore, appointed a committee to report on the action necessary to eliminate such bowling from Australian cricket as from beginning of the 1933–34 season.

We will forward a copy of the Committee's recommendations for your consideration, and it is hoped co-operation as to its application to all cricket. We do not consider it necessary to cancel remainder of programme.

It was another sign of the wisdom that comes with experience that this time it was agreed not to release the text to the press until twenty-four hours after its dispatch – i.e., until it had been received by the MCC.

By this cable the ABC succeeded in closing the gaps in their own ranks that had been opened by their original intemperate protest, since on the basic issue of the acceptability of 'bodyline' there was no conflict between New South Wales and Queensland and the other states. They also went a long way to meet the MCC. The cable preserved the essentials of the ABC's position – that 'bodyline' was incompatible with the spirit of the game, and must be eliminated from it; but it now recognized that the MCC could hardly be expected to condemn it without seeing it, and it tacitly accepted that, that being so, no action could be taken to halt it immediately. Taken in conjunction with the last sentence, this in effect meant that the ABC also accepted that the England side would continue to use 'bodyline' tactics for the remainder of the tour – saving an unlikely change of heart on Jardine's part. The threat of unilateral 'anti-bodyline' legislation might make trouble in the future, but time could be left to look after that. As for the explosive word 'unsportsmanlike', it was neither reiterated nor repudiated. The cable bears all the marks of having been the result of a tug-of-war between men of peace who wanted to back out of an untenable position, and men of pride who did not want to eat their words in public.

This cable was received in England with qualified satisfaction. Several papers regarded the ABC's stated intention to legislate unilaterally against 'bodyline' as provocative. *The Times* stiffly remarked, in a leader on 1 February, that the phrase 'contrary to the spirit of the game' in the cable was synonymous with 'unsportsmanlike' – which indeed seems difficult to deny – and that 'in the matches still to be played it will be the duty of the English captain, with the full support of the MCC, to employ such methods, allowed by the laws of cricket, as he considers most likely to win the game' – which certainly made it clear enough what England expected – and went on to suggest that the ABC should do something on their part to check barracking. There was indeed an increasing tendency in England to see barracking as the root of the problem, and to go over from a mere defence of England's bowling methods to vigorous counter-attack on this issue, and *The Times* was particularly prominent in it. The ABC's partial retreat from their original position may well have reinforced this English conviction that if anyone was sinning against the ethics of the game, it was the Australian barrackers rather than the English bowlers; but at the same time the placatory note of the ABC's second cable was not without its effect. The *Evening Standard*, on the last day of January, while regretting the ABC's pre-emption of the 'bodyline' issue by their stated intention to appoint their own committee to prepare legislation on the subject, agreed that some authoritative enquiry into 'leg theory' bowling was required, and that a strong section of English opinion too was unhappy about it – though not, the paper hastened to explain, because it presented any danger to life and limb, but because of the dull cricket it produced.

Two days later the *Daily Mail* published a contribution which was an almost exact counterpart of Kent Hughes' telegram to the ABC. Its author was R. H. Bettington, like Kent Hughes a member of that Anglo-Australian Establishment which between the Wars still felt equally at home in either country. English by origin, he had played cricket for Oxford and Middlesex, but was now a doctor in Australia, where he had represented New South Wales. Bettington brushed aside the suggestion that 'bodyline' was unsportsmanlike, but nevertheless deprecated Jardine's use of it, both because of the bad feeling it aroused and because, like Armstrong, he thought England were good enough to win without it. He demonstrated his even-handedness further by criticizing the ABC's original cable as intemperate, and by hoping that Jardine would see his way open to employing less controversial methods of attack in the two remaining Tests. Voices of peace like this were becoming more and more audible by the end of the month, the counterparts of the growing doubts being expressed in Australia about the wisdom of the original cable.

In both countries there is reason to think that higher authority may by this time have been exerting its influence in favour of moderation. It is clear that the last thing either the British or the Australian government can have wanted is to have their customary good relations interrupted by a burst of uncontrollable and irrational popular frenzy originating in nothing more important than a row on a cricket field; and by the last days of January they were becoming increasingly aware that such a thing was not impossible. We come at this point to a man who was to play a continuing and significant role in the development of the controversy and its eventual pacification. It was still the invariable convention between the Wars in Australia that Governors-General and State Governors should be selected from the upper ranks of the British Establishment. The Governor of South Australia at the time of the Adelaide Test was Sir Alexander Hore-Ruthven, the scion of an ancient Scottish noble family, a soldier with a distinguished military record. Hore-Ruthven, like some other British governors of Australian states, had found it no easy task to keep out of political controversy during the bitter years of the Depression: he was nevertheless very well liked and widely respected in his State and elsewhere in Australia, going on from Government House at Adelaide to become successively Governor of New South Wales and a highly successful Governor-General of Australia for almost the whole of the Second World War. In early 1933 Hore-Ruthven (as he then was: he was promoted to the peerage as Lord Gowrie in 1935, after he became Governor-General) was in England on leave. Himself a member of the MCC, he was an ideal intermediary to put the Australian case before the English cricketing authorities in a more sympathetic light than the ABC's cable had succeeded in doing.

During the controversial Adelaide Test, Hore-Ruthven's deputy was approached by three highly influential members of local society – the editor and manager of the *Adelaide Advertiser* and the general manager of the important shipping firm Elder Smith – and at their insistence got in touch with Hore-Ruthven and suggested that he should intervene in the developing dispute. As a result of this, and of numerous similar suggestions from other Australian sources, it appears that Hore-Ruthven went to the Dominions Office and suggested to his chief, who was none other than the egregious National Labour cabinet minister and former railwayman J. H. Thomas, that he should get in touch with the MCC and presumably try to take some of the heat out of the controversy. As a result, an MCC deputation of four – Lewisham (the President), Jackson, Studd and Lord Bridgeman – called at the Dominions Office on 1 February at Thomas' invitation, and a meeting, at which Hore-Ruthven and Sir Thomas Inskip (the Attorney-General and himself a keen cricketer) were also present, was held which lasted over an hour.*

No report of what transpired at that meeting is available, but it is reasonable to suppose that Thomas, Inskip and Hore-Ruthven urged the advisability of moderation. The meeting was supposedly secret, and when news of it leaked out to the press Thomas was at great pains to play down its significance; but there seems no doubt that in reality he was deeply concerned over the issue. He is credibly reported as having said that he had more trouble over it than over any other issue that arose during his tenure of the Dominions Secretaryship, and in August he was to speak out strongly against 'bodyline' at a lunch held at Claridge's for Sir Julien Cahn's MCC side then about to

---

* I suspect that this meeting was the origin of the frequently repeated rumour that 'bodyline' was discussed in the British Cabinet. If it was, it has left no trace in the Cabinet minutes of the period.

depart for Canada, and is reported to have said to Cahn himself, 'All I can say is, don't take Larwood with you to Canada.'

Although the departmental files concerned with the 'bodyline' controversy have been destroyed (like all too many other records of it), it is significant that they were apparently very bulky. Taken together with similar evidence from Australia that we shall come to shortly, it seems clear from this that during the week of 29 January–5 February official weight was being brought to bear in both Australia and England to soften the attitudes of the embattled cricket authorities and reach a quick compromise settlement of the controversy, and that this weight must have influenced the MCC's deliberations in particular, when the Committee met on the day after the deputation's visit to the Dominions Office to draft a reply to the ABC's cable of 30 January.

By this time, though, the pot had been further stirred by developments in Australia. When the English party, in Queensland by this time, had had time to digest the ABC's second cable, they felt strongly that in one vital respect it was inadequate: it had failed to make an unequivocal withdrawal of the accusation of unsportsmanlike conduct against them. Sportsmanship is a highly elusive quality, but it is one which stirs feelings, perhaps particularly British feelings, to the depths: is it unfair to add that this is most of all the case when the accused is aware that perhaps his defences against the charge are not quite watertight? Perhaps it is unfair; but the side anyway felt strongly enough about the issue to make another demonstration of solidarity and take a strong line on it. The MCC had already made the threat of cancelling the remainder of the tour, and the ABC had obviously recoiled from it: now the players themselves made the threat more concrete.

It so happened that a fellow-traveller with the MCC party on the *Orontes* on the way out to Australia had been E. T. Crutchley, the head of the British Mission at Canberra –

in effect, though not in formal title, High Commissioner. Crutchley had been returning from leave: himself a keen follower of cricket, he had seen a good deal of Warner and the rest of the party during the voyage, and Warner now made use of this contact. On 1 February, while the MCC were playing their country game at Toowoomba, Warner sent Crutchley a telegram, warning him that there was a strong possibility of cancelling the remainder of the tour unless the charge of lack of sportsmanship was unequivocally withdrawn, and begging him to use his influence with J. A. Lyons, the Australian Prime Minister, to obtain the required retraction. Clearly, to the MCC party the equivocal terms of the ABC's second cable were not sufficient; but Warner was doing his best to keep this further exacerbation of the crisis secret, and to avoid driving the ABC into a corner by making the touring party's threat to cancel the rest of the tour public. His good intentions were partly frustrated by a breach of confidence by a telegraph clerk in the Post Office at Toowoomba who told the press of it – a revealing indication of the heat of the crisis at that juncture, and the inducements that the press was prepared to offer for inside information. Within twenty-four hours the news was all over the papers in both countries. Crutchley, in Canberra, was inundated by calls from journalists seeking information, but he nevertheless got in touch with Lyons by phone, and passed on Warner's message. Lyons had been a Labour politician, but in Australia as in Britain in the early 1930s the Depression had brought about the fall of a Labour government and a split in the Labour Party, and he was now heading a right-wing coalition which strongly supported the traditional British connection. He was therefore at one with Crutchley in feeling that abandonment of the tour would be a disaster, but, before using his influence with the ABC, he asked Crutchley to see if there was any chance of a *quid pro quo* for the withdrawal of the offending word 'unsportsmanlike' – perhaps (it was Crutchley's suggestion) a modification of the leg trap in subsequent matches.

But Crutchley's consequent phone call to Toowoomba found Warner resolute, no doubt reflecting the opinion of the rest of the party: the withdrawal of the word must be unconditional.

Increasingly, though no doubt reluctantly, officialdom was finding itself involved in the dispute; and it must be regarded as a striking demonstration of the completeness of the breakdown of relations between the touring side and the Australian cricket authorities that Warner and Palairet felt unable to approach the ABC directly, but instead made this clumsy and roundabout approach through Canberra and the British Mission there. This approach to Crutchley was known in England by the time the MCC met to draft their second reply to the ABC on 2 February. Whether the two managers had consulted Lord's before making the approach is unclear. They could have done, for – as we have seen – a radiotelephone link between Britain and Australia already existed in 1933, but, apart from one very doubtful press reference, there is nothing to suggest that either they or Jardine ever did so. However this may be, knowledge of the team's action, together with the representations of Thomas, Inskip and Hore-Ruthven the previous day, must have indicted clearly enough the main lines that the MCC's reply to the ABC's second cable should follow. The reply, sent on the 2nd, read:

We, the Committee of the Marylebone Cricket Club, note with pleasure that you do not consider it necessary to cancel the remainder of programme, and that you are postponing the whole issue involved until after the present tour is completed. May we accept this as a clear indication that the good sportsmanship of our team is not in question?

We are sure you will appreciate how impossible it would be to play any Test Match in the spirit we all desire unless both sides were satisfied there was no reflection upon their sportsmanship.

When your recommendation reaches us it shall

94

receive our most careful consideration and will be submitted to the Imperial Cricket Conference.

The MCC thus accepted the olive branch – with one reservation. Their reply observed the time-honoured tactic of seizing on the most conciliatory point of the ABC's cable and interpreting it in the most positive, not to say hopeful, sense; and, the ABC having tacitly abandoned the extreme demands of its first cable, it made broad promises of co-operation for the future. The issue of sportsmanship, however, remained; and now that the MCC's own team in Australia had taken so strong a stand on the issue (there is some evidence that some members of the MCC Committee regretted that they had done so), and that the next Test was only a week off, there was little alternative to requiring the ABC to swallow their pride publicly and withdraw the offending word.

By the time this reached Australia, it was sufficiently clear to everybody that the rest of the Test series had to be saved. The Board by now was under formidable pressures from above. It was reported in the Australian press – with considerable confidence and some circumstantial detail – tht while the Adelaide Test was still in progress, Bruce, the Australian representative in London, had got in touch with Lyons and urged him 'to use his influence to bring about a better feeling between the governing cricket bodies in England and Australia'. Crutchley's approach of course pointed in the same direction, and on the very day it was made – 1 February – Lyons acted upon it. He saw Robertson, the Board's Chairman, personally, and put strong pressure on him to withdraw the accusation of bad sportsmanship, expressing his confidence that if this was done, the English fast bowling attack would be modified (this was before he had heard from Crutchley that the MCC side were not prepared to make concessions on this issue), and warning Robertson that if the word was not withdrawn and the MCC refused to continue with the tour as a result, there was a real danger that the conversion of an Australian loan in London, then at a delicate stage, would be imperilled. The Board could hardly be expected to resist pressures of this kind; and moreover, the atmosphere of public opinion in Australia was by now very different from what it had been a fortnight before.

It is a remarkable fact that the tempest of anger which had burst over the Adelaide Test seems to have subsided as rapidly as it had arisen. This was not because the fundamental Australian rejection of 'bodyline' had been abandoned, or even modified: it remained as strong as ever. But from the beginning of February onward, as we have seen from the wording of the ABC's second telegram, it increasingly came to be seen as a long-term problem. The demand for immediate action, which had been implicit in the crowd's anger at Adelaide, for instant abandonment of 'bodyline', or, perhaps, failing that, for instant retaliation – and equally implicit in the ABC's original, and ill-considered, cable – had been dropped: it had been tacitly conceded that Jardine and his team would persist in the use of it at least for the rest of the tour.

There is probably more than one explanation of this change of front. One important point, obviously, is that the MCC's resolute stand in defence of their team, and the team's own demand for the withdrawal of the charge of bad sportsmanship, swiftly made it clear that the demand for instant satisfaction, persisted in, would mean the premature end of the tour; and for financial and other reasons, that was unthinkable. In particular, it became increasingly clear that Brisbane did not intend to be done out of its Test Match by the whims of an Adelaide crowd. The obstinate and admirable regionalism of the Australian states played, I think, a real part in the controversy at this point.

The image of Queensland has always been of a rough, tough, bare-chested, outback state, as far removed as one can well conceive from the slightly prissy Victorian moralism of South Australia, and especially of Adelaide.

Deserting analysis altogether for the impressionist realm of caricature, perhaps it is not altogether misleading to suggest that Queenslanders were the sort of people who liked to think of themselves as not minding a few hard knocks, and who were prepared to take 'bodyline' as all part of the game. But Queensland also, together with Western Australia and Tasmania, shared the consciousness of Australia's underprivileged outback states, forever resentful and suspicious that they are not getting a fair deal from the metropolitan south-east of the country, whose great cities and big battalions always carried the electoral weight. The State had been admitted to full membership of the Sheffield Shield as recently as 1926–27, and only one MCC touring party, that of 1928–29, had so far played a Test Match there. Now, in 1933, Queensland would get its Test Match, or it would know the reason why: that note is audible in the local press in the early days of February. It gives it a tone quite different from that of the Adelaide papers a fortnight earlier, and it immensely reinforced the leverage of the MCC side's insistence on the withdrawal of that hideous word 'unsportsmanlike' before the Brisbane Test could be played.

This was not, of course, the only explanation of the growing will to compromise that is so evident in the controversy from the beginning of February onwards: another comes from the realm of social psychology. It seems to me likely that the much maligned – and in a sense justly maligned – cable sent by the ABC representatives during the Adelaide Test had in fact fulfilled its essential function: it had acted as a lightning conductor. By giving it official expression, it had discharged the pent-up volume of Australian popular wrath that had been gathering about the subject ever since the 'Australian XI' match at Melbourne: the explosion past, the air cleared. No doubt on a baser level one could also argue that the sensationalist popular press of the two countries had now had its field day, and, in the absence of further dramatic incidents, went off in search of new sensation elsewhere.

Certainly the atmosphere of the MCC's visit to Queensland seems to have been – comparatively, at least – friendly from the outset. Even the wrangle over the gate money at Toowoomba,* which would have been grist to the press mill in the atmosphere of the Adelaide Test, was brushed aside as the triviality it clearly was. There was some excitement before the State game which immediately preceded the Test, because of a rumour that Gilbert, Queensland's Aboriginal fast bowler, was to experiment with 'bodyline' tactics against the MCC; but in the event Gilbert kept to orthodox methods and came in for some rough treatment from the English batsmen, while he was entirely cast into the shade by the performance of Larwood, who found no need to resort to 'bodyline' and took 6 for 38 in the Queensland second innings, the MCC winning by an innings and 61 runs.

There was one moment of tension in Queensland's first innings, when the all-rounder Oxenham was (to judge from most accounts) straightforwardly caught at short leg off Larwood, but stood his ground and was given 'not out' by the umpire. Such things happen occasionally, but not for choice when the bowler is Larwood. Larwood had sat down and turned away, assuming that Oxenham was on the way out: when the truth dawned on him, he was furious. 'Give me that bloody ball,' he said, 'I'll show him'; and I have heard some of the fieldsmen say that they never in their lives saw a batsman more frightened when he realized what he had done. The rest of the over consisted of a series of Larwood's most ferocious bumpers, to the accompaniment of hostile barracking from the crowd; but, perhaps wisely, Oxenham threw his wicket away to Allen in the next over, and the trouble subsided at once. It is significant too, after the trouble there had been over it at Adelaide, that at Brisbane spectators were admitted

* Which seems to have been remarkably petty: it concerned the ground authorities' right to deduct £4 from the MCC's share of the takings in payment of the state entertainment tax.

without question to see the MCC practising in the nets before the Test, and there was no trouble at all: evidently the will to peace was present on both sides.

By this time, the outstanding issue had been settled. Essentially, peace seems to have been made at a private conference, untroubled by press releases, between Warner on the one side and the two Queensland members of the ABC, J. S. Hutcheon and R. J. Hartigan, who had been given discretionary powers to reach agreement by the Board as a whole, on the other. As we have seen, neither Hutcheon nor Hartigan had been present at Adelaide: neither had been privy to the wording of the ABC's original cable, and both had disapproved of its use of the word 'unsportsmanlike'. They were, therefore, ideal intermediaries, and although details of their discussions with Warner have never been made public, it seems overwhelmingly probable that they specifically withdrew the offending word.* The ABC themselves, when they came on 8 February to reply to the MCC's second cable, were a shade more evasive, but with the issue already settled privately in Brisbane, they could afford to be; and their cable in any case conceded just enough to pacify ruffled feelings in England. It read:

> We do not regard the sportsmanship of your team as being in question.
> Our position was fully considered at the recent meeting in Sydney and is as indicated in our cable of January 30.
> It is the particular class of bowling referred to therein which we consider is not in the best interests of cricket, and in this view we understand we are supported by many eminent English cricketers.

* That they did not do so publicly may well have been an offset for the MCC's refusal to make any reciprocal concessions about their future tactics.

99

We join heartily with you in hoping that the remaining Tests will be played with the traditional good feeling.

The last sentence, perhaps, was a shade double-edged. But 'bodyline', which had been 'unsportsmanlike' in the ABC's original cable, then 'opposed to the spirit of cricket' in the second, was now only 'not in the best interests of cricket' – a considerably less damning charge; and the first sentence of the cable came about as close to an outright retraction as anyone could reasonably expect the ABC to give. So it seems to have been felt in England. An (anonymous) 'prominent member of the MCC Committee' was grudgingly satisfied – 'It is put in the way an Australian would express himself,' was his barbed comment. Still, for himself he would accept it, though he could not say what the other members of the Committee would do. They decided to let relatively well alone. There were no more telegrams, and the fourth Test began on time.

CHAPTER 4

Aftermath

(February–May 1933)

The fourth Test should, by rights, have been the tensest of the 1932–33 series. After Adelaide, England led 2-1, but the result of the series was still open: Australia could still reverse the verdict. Remembering that all Tests in Australia were played to a finish, this was much more than a merely theoretical possibility: in fact, on England's next visit to Australia, in 1936–37, Australia succeeded in reversing a 2-0 deficit to win the series 3-2. So if England won at Brisbane, the series was theirs: if Australia won, it was 2-all, and Australia would go to the final Test at Sydney with their tails up and every chance of winning it.

There was a great deal of tension and excitement in that Test; and yet, reading the accounts of that game played fifty years ago, one does seem to sense a certain air of anti-climax in the atmosphere of it.* As far as the Australian public at large were concerned – though perhaps not the Queensland spectators – so much emotion had already been spent at Adelaide that not much was left to invest at Brisbane. More important than that, it had been tacitly conceded that England would persist with their 'bodyline' tactics, at any rate for the rest of the tour, and there was a widespread feeling that, if England were going to play the

---

* The total gate was less than 100,000, although the match lasted into the sixth day.

game that way, Australia did not have the means of beating them (there is even a sense in which it would have weakened the Australian case against 'bodyline' if they had). Since Adelaide, nobody thought that even Bradman had the answer to 'bodyline'; and if Bradman hadn't, none of the other Australian batsmen had much chance against it. Such at least seems to have been the widespread Australian impression, and it must clearly have infected the Australian team as well. Moreover, one of the most powerful effects of 'bodyline' was cumulative. In the last two Tests the Australian batsmen went out to face Larwood and Voce conscious of previous failures against them, but, more than that, with the memory of repeated physical batterings that must have made it physically almost impossible to face them with the confidence and determination that had come much more easily at the beginning of the season. In the circumstances, it does very great credit to them, and to the qualify of Woodfull's leadership, that Australia did so well in the earlier stages of both Tests.

Two, or perhaps three, other circumstances also contributed to take the sharp edge off the 'bodyline' issue at Brisbane. Voce was still not fit, after his ankle injury at Adelaide, and did not play. Voce seems always to have bowled more 'bodyline' than Larwood (if less menacingly, since he lacked Larwood's pace), since his natural method was more akin to it, and this in itself made a significant difference to the nature of the English attack – all the more so since he was replaced not by Bowes (who had achieved little in the only Test in which he had played), but by the Derbyshire leg-spinner Mitchell. For the only time in the series, the English attack contained two slow bowlers. Secondly, the Brisbane wicket was so easy-paced that even when he dropped the ball short, Larwood had great difficulty in making it get up more than waist-high. And thirdly, the first two days of the match at least were played in tremendous heat, which inevitably took its toll of the fast bowlers, bravely though Larwood and Allen stuck to their task. Larwood remained the spearhead of the English attack, and he continued to bowl spells of 'bodyline' to the familiar packed leg-side field; but on the first day he failed to take a wicket, and at the end of it Australia were 251 for 3.

Once more, as after the second Test, the columnists began to speculate that the answer to 'bodyline' had been found, and found not in any alteration of the Laws, but in the evolution of new batting techniques – this (which would have been a very satisfactory outcome from all points of view) was Mailey's view in particular. In fact, the Australian batsmen do seem to have gone some way to working out a technical answer to 'bodyline' in the period between the two Tests. Part of their response lay in the evolution of new forms of bodypadding, including cork heart-protectors; but they had also obviously worked out their individual tactics in the face of it, and these differed interestingly from man to man. Woodfull and Richardson opened the innings with a stand of 133, but their methods were quite different, Woodfull consistently ducking the bumpers and moving inside the line of anything outside the leg stump, Richardson standing up to it and hooking hard and often – playing it, in fact, as McCabe had played it at Sydney in the first Test. By all accounts, his 83 must have been one of the best attacking innings played for Australia during the series. Bradman also attacked, and was 71 not out at the close of play, but in a quite different way: he used his phenomenal speed of footwork and eye to make himself room on the leg side and force the ball to the wide unguarded spaces on the off. Intellectually, so to speak, it was the right answer to 'bodyline'. Richardson, in a sense, was doing what Larwood wanted him to do: he was prepared for batsmen to go for the hook, and had fieldsmen back on the leg boundary – always two, sometimes three – for the catches: though on this occasion Richardson escaped them, thanks to a combination of skill, good luck and a benign wicket. Bradman, on the other hand, was forcing the ball away from the fieldsmen, the gist of all good attacking batting: doing what the bowler wants to make impossible. Against a bowler of Larwood's pace and accuracy, even on a kindly wicket, there was probably no batsman in the world but Bradman who could have done it; but done it was, and the day ended with Australia in a far better position than most of their spectators can have dared to hope for.

By the standards of the 1932–33 series – perhaps by any standards – the first day of the fourth Test was a day of fine cricket, and almost entirely free of incidents which had so scarred the Adelaide Test. There were no injuries: thanks to the easy-paced wicket, even the comparatively slow-footed Woodfull, who had taken such a battering at Adelaide, was able to keep out of the way of anything that Larwood pitched short, and was hit only once, and then not by a bumper. The only outburst of barracking occurred when McCabe was hit once, on the upper arm, and it was short-lived at that.

So far, so good. But this was not the end of the matter; and next day Larwood showed it, coming back into the game like a great bowler with a reputation to live up to. His first ball of the day was hit to the leg boundary by Ponsford, and it is some sign of the emotion invested in these Test Matches that the crowd 'stood and cheered wildly for a considerable period'; but it was the last liberty that anyone took with Larwood that day. At 264 he bowled Bradman, leg stump, as Bradman once more made room and tried to force him through the covers, the classic reply to Larwood's tactics. Given the chances of variable bounce, especially on a wicket with so little bounce in it, sooner or later attempts to force balls short of a length on the wicket through the covers with a cross bat were bound to end this way. Three runs later he bowled Ponsford too, in a way Ponsford was repeatedly out during the series: bowled behind his legs playing no stroke, as he moved across his wicket to a ball just short of a length which he judged wrongly would bounce more than stump-high. Both Bradman and Ponsford were in the purest sense victims of leg theory, even though both were out bowled – the classic and most annihilating form of dismissal there is – and after that, there was not much left of the Australian batting. To counter the leg theory, the Australian selectors had introduced two young left-handers into the side, Darling and Bromley. They fought bravely for the sixth wicket for a while, but once they were parted the Australian tail proved as long and vulnerable as it did throughout the series, and the side was all out for 340, Larwood 4 for 101: not enough, as – one suspects – Woodfull in his heart of hearts, and the rest of the Australian side, must have known.

Nor was it: although England, in their endeavour to eliminate all risk from their batting and to pile up a winning score by sheer accumulation, came close to losing their way in a fashion sadly familiar to followers of their fortunes in more recent years. This, however, is a book about the 'bodyline' controversy, not about the English tour of 1932–33, and an account of the England innings in any detail would be out of place. Suffice it to say that just after tea on the third day England were 225 for 7, and that the little Lancashire left-hander Eddie Paynter then appeared from a hospital bed, where he had been recovering from tonsilitis, to play the innings of his life. He made 83. Verity helped him to add 92 for the ninth wicket, and in the end England just topped the Australian total, making 356.

A lead of 16 in itself meant nothing, particularly with England having to face the prospect of batting last against O'Reilly and Ironmonger. But in what was left of the fourth day Australia lost their first four wickets for 108, and were never really back in the hunt. It was the pattern that had been established in the first Test: it was as though the moral and physical effort of battling their way to 340 in the face of Larwood's onslaught in the first innings, followed by the disappointment of seeing England, after their early setbacks, struggling into the lead, left the Australian batsmen with nothing to give in the second innings. Larwood in fact took only three wickets in this innings, two of them those of tail-enders, but the third was again

Bradman's – the wicket which of all Australian wickets England most desired – and the way that he went symbolized to perfection the effect that exposure to 'bodyline' had had on his batting. Significantly, Woodfull, battling stoically away at the other end, tried to shield him from Larwood – the notion that Woodfull would ever need to shield Bradman from any bowler would have seemed ludicrous at the beginning of the season. When their actual encounter came, it was brief and hectic. Bradman took 10 off Larwood in an over, including two square cuts for 4 off straight balls; in the next over he dodged two roaring bumpers, then got another short straight ball and cut it hard to deep cover, the only fieldsman in front of the wicket on the off side. It was typical not only of Bradman's response to Larwood, but of the way that 'bodyline' got most of its victims, intimidation unsettling batsmen into reckless indiscretion, whether against Larwood himself or against other bowlers. It was the shadow of Larwood that lay dark across the rest of the Australian batting – Mailey noted the evident sense of inferiority with which several of them faced him – even though it was in fact Verity and Allen who took most of the wickets. Australia were all out for 175; and although O'Reilly and Ironmonger made England fight long and hard for the 160 they needed to win, they always looked like getting them, which they duly did, for the loss of four wickets, shortly before lunch on the sixth day. The Ashes were once more theirs.

The public decencies were very fully observed on this occasion – another token of the atmosphere of comparative reconciliation in which the Brisbane Test was played, at least on the official level. Friendly relations between the two teams were never properly restored after Adelaide; but at Brisbane, Woodfull was the first visitor to the English dressing-room to congratulate Jardine on his side's victory, and the tone of the speeches to the crowd gathered in front of the pavilion was similarly chivalrous. J. S. Hutcheon, the President of the Queensland Cricket Association, was particularly gracious, going out of his way to congratulate not only the MCC team as a whole, but 'their great captain' in particular – significant words, especially as Hutcheon was also one of the Queensland members of the ABC and, as we have seen, had played a major role in persuading the Board to withdraw their charge of unsportsmanlike behaviour in order that the fourth Test might take place.

The match was followed by a Governor's reception at which also good feeling, or at least the appearance of it, seems to have been the order of the day; according to the report in the London *Evening News*, Woodfull made a polite and appropriate speech, 'the teams drank each other's health with three hearty cheers', and both Jardine and Warner paid just tributes to the loyal co-operation that Jardine had received from his side.

It is perhaps not remarkable that the English papers should have been full of praise for Jardine's captaincy – both Hobbs and Armstrong wrote in this sense, for all their individual disapproval of 'bodyline' – but the same note was widely echoed in the Australian press too. Mailey in the Brisbane *Mail* paid a high tribute to his leadership, and a columnist in the same paper summed up what seems to have been the feeling of many Australians at the time: 'Much has been written that is derogatory to Jardine, but whether the body theory is right or wrong (and I consider it totally wrong) one must admire Jardine [for his tactical abilities] and for his ability to adhere to his purpose through a storm of abuse.' As a leader on the field, Jardine's qualities were never challenged – as a skilled tactician, an acute analyst of opposing batsmen's weaknesses, and an exceptionally clear thinker about the game, he can have had very few equals among England's captains – but the note of admiration, even reluctant admiration, for his moral qualities in this last tribute is more notable. It was not unique: Jardine himself referred to the 'hosts' of letters of goodwill he had received from Australians (even if one suspects that the other sort were a good deal more numerous!).

Not only had England regained the Ashes at Brisbane: official good relations had been restored. Even at the spontaneous and uncontrollable level of crowd reactions, there had been very little that could be called barracking and little other evidence of serious bad feeling at Brisbane. Several of the English batsmen had reportedly not liked the umpires' decisions by which they were given out, but as their dissent seems to have been confined to the English dressing-room, only to be overheard through the windows by members outside and relayed to eager press ears, it seems more reasonable to blame the troublemakers who reported the remarks than the batsmen who made them: things will have come to a pretty pass if players are not to be allowed to say what they think of the umpires in the privacy of their dressing-rooms.* A generation which has become sadly accustomed to far more flamboyant forms of dissent is unlikely to take this incident very seriously – indeed, considering the explosively controversial nature of the tour, it is a very high tribute both to the cricketing etiquette of the period and to the quality of the work of the two umpires who stood throughout the series, G. Hele and G. E. Borwick, that this is the only mention of dissent during the series that I have come across. For the rest, their umpiring seems to have commanded the confidence of both sides so completely that it went wholly unremarked. Anyway, apart from this storm in a teacup, the contrast with the atmosphere in which the Adelaide Test had been played could hardly have been more striking; and certainly none of those present seem to have been in any doubt that the better team had won.

After this, the remainder of the tour was even more inevitably an anti-climax. There was still another Test Match to be played, at Sydney, but for the tour party and their Australian opponents as well as for the cricketing public of the two countries, the essential issue was already settled, and nothing that happened in the final Test could

* I speak as an umpire.

matter much. All those who have been on one bear testimony that the strain of a prolonged tour, and of a prolonged series, is tremendous, and for most men it is hardly possible to maintain the exacting strain of total commitment and concentration once the main object is achieved, or lost beyond recall. It is on the whole remarkable that the final Test was still contested as keenly as it in fact was; but in the other fixtures that still remained some relaxation seems certainly to have been perceptible among the MCC party, and on occasion to have provided some ammunition for the more relentlessly critical portions of the Australian press.

The only fixture that intervened between the fourth and fifth Tests was a three-day game against the Northern Districts of New South Wales, played at Newcastle. Even today the long train journey from Brisbane to Newcastle does not rank high among the luxurious travel experiences of the world, and it is not very surprising that in 1933 several members of the MCC party were seduced by what was then the alternative method of travel, the slower but more comfortable trip by sea to Sydney. In the end, only Wyatt, Leyland and Mitchell of those who had played in the Brisbane Test made the journey to Newcastle – Wyatt, as vice-captain, obviously had to go, if Jardine didn't, and Mitchell would not be required for the last Test: maybe Leyland was a railway enthusiast, or a bad sailor, or maybe he tossed up for it and lost. With the six members of the touring party who had not played in the Test, this still left the MCC two men short, and the numbers were made up by Hobbs and Warner. The Newcastle fixture, however, was not one of the two-day country games, but a full three-day match. The Northern Districts of New South Wales (which have for decades had aspirations to independent statehood) were little below full State standard,* and their pride was hurt (fairly reasonably, one feels, in the case of

* On this occasion they included the later Australian Test player Chipperfield, who made 152.

Warner, who was fifty-nine and had played no first-class cricket for ten years or more; a good deal less so in the case of Hobbs, one of the great batsmen of the world, who was still playing the first-class game, and in fact opened the MCC innings and scored 44). It was again a storm in a teacup, no doubt, but Jardine's contemptuous attitude towards the minor fixtures of the tour was by this time notorious and widely resented, and it was typical of the small frictions which cropped up repeatedly during the tour* – perhaps no more of them than occur on all tours, but with the thunder of the 'bodyline' controversy muttering in the background all the time they were seized upon by the papers, blown up to a magnitude that would never normally have been attached to them, and woven together to support a generalized indictment of contempt for Australians and Australian opinion – of which 'bodyline' was, of course, the culminating example.

MCC, anyway, escaped from the match with perceptibly the worse of a draw. At Sydney the party were reunited, and there two days later the final Test began. At Brisbane the inclusion of the left-handers Bromley and Darling to counter Larwood's leg theory (since none of the established batsmen in the side were left-handers) had been successful enough to induce the Australian selectors to repeat it at Sydney, though this time they brought in the Victorian O'Brien in place of Bromley. For England, Voce was once more fit and replaced Mitchell, so the full 'bodyline' battery from both ends was once more available.

But the fifth Test was a muted affair, although Larwood and Voce bowled a lot of 'bodyline' on a wicket considerably more receptive to it than the wicket at Brisbane had been. Ruthlessly consistent to the last, Jardine had adamantly refused to listen to Warner's pleas that 'bodyline' should at least be dropped for this match, now that the rubber had been safely won. Indeed one sees the point that to drop it

* The local Cricket Association went so far as to ask the Board of Control to claim compensation from the MCC for loss of gate money.

now would have been to acknowledge tacitly the justice of the Australian criticisms of it, although it is impossible to resist the suspicion that for Jardine this consideration counted for less than his determination to rub in the Australian defeat to the uttermost – as he himself said, 'We've got the bastards down there, and we'll keep them there.'

A number of Australian batsmen were hit, notably McCabe, and also, for the only time on the tour, Bradman himself, hit on the upper arm by Larwood: it says volumes for the speed of his footwork that he, for whose destruction the weapon of leg theory had primarily been fashioned, and who had made more runs in the series than any other Australian batsman, had never been hit hitherto. Again, as at Brisbane, it was clearly 'bodyline' that was responsible for the downfall of a number of the leading Australian batsmen. Although Bradman made 48 in the first innings, his uneasiness against Larwood was manifest, and in the end Larwood again bowled him leg stump as he tried to glance a straight ball – another very good example of the way leg theory often achieved its successes indirectly. Woodfull, shaken by one short-pitched ball from Larwood that 'whizzed past his chin', backed away from the next and played on.* Yet all this took place in front of the notorious Hill apparently almost without serious protest from the crowd (which was indeed much smaller than it had been for the first Test, played on this same ground). Even more than at Brisbane, the basic crowd attitude at Sydney by this time seems to have been one of resignation: several of the English commentators remarked on their placidity. In any case, up to a point Australia did quite well, much aided by the fact that the English close catching, which had previously been one of the features of the tour, with Jardine himself setting the example, on this

* Though it is worth mentioning that when Oldfield, now recovered from the blow he had received at Adelaide, came in to bad late in the day, Larwood was at pains to bowl a full length at him. Oldfield went on to make 52.

occasion lapsed badly from grace, at least seven catches going down – no doubt another token of waning concentration. Australia's young left-handers also did well, O'Brien getting 61 and Darling 85, and Australia, 296 for 5 at the end of the first day (and that with three fast bowlers bearing the brunt of the English attack! – as often in reading the records of the 1932–33 tour, the jaded follower of Test cricket 1980s-style blinks in incredulity), in the end reached 435, their highest total of the series.

England in reply also batted far faster than they had done at Brisbane, Sutcliffe and Hammond setting the tone by adding 122 for the second wicket in roughly even time. Hammond went on to make a century; but by universal consent, the innings of the third day was played by Larwood, who had been sent in the previous evening at no. 4 as night-watchman. Larwood was always a good hard-hitting batsman at no. 7 or so, but so strong was the England batting on this tour that he had not previously batted higher than 9; however he averaged over 24 for the series. On this occasion he thrashed the Australian bowling to the tune of 98 in two and a quarter hours, before being caught off a skier going for a big hit for his century – caught by the ageing Australian slow left-hander and notable character Bert Ironmonger, an unusual achievement in itself. It was a brilliant innings, and it gives an important and unexpected insight into the attitudes of the Australian crowds on this tour that he was received on his return to the pavilion with a great popular ovation. It does indeed seem that the Australian crowds never held 'bodyline' against Larwood personally: they might boo while he was bowling it (though in this Test they had shown little sign even of doing that), but if the booing had a personal target, it was always Jardine rather than Larwood. It would have been interesting to see the crowd's reaction if it had been Jardine who had scored a brilliant near-century at Sydney.

The rest of the England batting was much more laborious, but once more they grimly struggled into the lead, reaching 454; and once more the Australian batsmen, finding themselves back at square one again and facing the prospect of going out to face Larwood and Voce (not to mention Allen) yet once more, cracked in the second innings. One has indeed in that Australian second innings the sense of two weary boxers staggering out for the umpteenth round, one already on the ropes, the other so tired that he can barely find strength for the knock-out punch. Australia made a dreadful start, Richardson completing a classic 'pair of spectacles' by being caught off Larwood for 0 without a run on the board for the second time in the match, but Woodfull and Bradman then added 115 for the second wicket.

The news that Bradman was batting brought the spectators pouring in as it always did in Sydney, so that the crowd on this fourth afternoon, a Monday at that, was actually bigger than at any other stage of the match – it reached 40,000. Both met Larwood's and Voce's spells of 'bodyline' with the techniques they had devised for the purpose in the course of the series. Woodfull moving inside the ball when he could and letting it pass down the leg side or over the stumps, stoically taking it on the body when his footwork was not fast enough, Bradman consistently moving the other way and forcing the ball to the off with a cross bat from a position well outside the leg stump. It was thrillingly risky but highly profitable batting, and it was successful to the extent that Jardine for the first time in the series was forced to weaken his leg-side field and set two gullies for Bradman in the attempt to counter his tactics. It was a critical moment: Allen, who had strained his side and had not wanted to play in the match at all, was limited to half-pace, and Larwood by this time was nearly dead on his feet. He had borne the role of spearhead of the English attack throughout the series with unflagging dedication and hostility, and to that responsibility was added the enormous physical strain of bowling for long periods at his terrific pace, often in great heat and on very hard grounds. In particular, in the final stride of his classic action his body pivoted on his left leg, which was raised high and then pounded down with tremendous force into the ground. Sooner or later there was bound to be a physical price to pay for this, and by the time of the last Test Larwood was having a lot of trouble with his feet, which were badly bruised, and in particular with his big toe (it later proved to be broken).

By the middle of the Monday afternoon he was in great pain and could barely hobble. He had bowled thirty-two overs in the first innings and taken 4 for 98, and given his last ounce in the second. Now, after ten more overs, he broke down in the middle of an over. Jardine insisted that he must finish it: he simply stood at the stumps and swung his arm over for the last five balls, and Woodfull, gentleman to the last, patted them back to him. He asked Jardine if he could go off; but Jardine would not let him go. Bradman was still in full flow, and Jardine would not run the risk of lifting his morale still further by letting him see his chief and most deadly opponent leaving the field. Even if Larwood in fact could not bowl, he must stay on the field so that Bradman would have to bat with the awareness that, for all he knew, Larwood might return to the attack at any moment. In its unsparing clarity it was a typical bit of Jardine's thinking; and it worked, though it was not Larwood who got the wicket. One of the dangers that 'bodyline' posed to batsmen was the risk of allowing one's concentration to slip when Larwood was out of the attack and less obviously menacing bowlers came on. In this sense, Verity, the Yorkshire slow left-hander with his immaculate length and teasing flight, made the perfect foil to Larwood and Voce. He had bowled well, in a primarily defensive role, at both Adelaide and Brisbane, keeping the scoring down to a minimum while the fast bowlers recruited their strength, and picking up a useful wicket here and there when batsmen, too eager to make at least a little hay while for a moment the sun was not obscured by the thunder-cloud of 'bodyline', took excessive liberties against him. At Adelaide he had already once got

Bradman's wicket in this way: now at Sydney, on a wicket which for the time was beginning to give him the chance of a bit of turn, he did it again – at 115 Bradman, going for another attacking shot against him, was beaten through the air and bowled.

With Bradman gone, Jardine had no further fears: Larwood could go off now. They were the two great opposites of 'bodyline', though neither was responsible for it, and it was fitting that they left the field together now, in silence. They were, arguably, the greatest batsman and the greatest fast bowler the game has ever seen. Larwood had done what he had set out to do. Jardine's plan had worked, superbly: for all his 396 runs in four Tests at an average of 56.57, the Bradman threat had been defeated, and as he had dominated the series in England in 1930, so it had been Larwood, with his 33 wickets in the Tests at 19.51 apiece, who had dominated the 1932–33 series and won it for England. Yet Bradman was to dominate five more Test series against England, four of them as captain, all of them successful, two of them overwhelmingly triumphant. In them he was to score another triple century, four more double and seven more single centuries. He was to rise to the highest pinnacles that the game in his time had to offer, as captain, as administrator, as the acknowledged greatest player of his time, and perhaps of all time. He was to receive the first knighthood ever awarded to a cricketer, or to any sportsman, purely for his achievements on the field. What awaited Larwood was what awaited most professional cricketers in the 1930s: five years going down the hill, and then obscurity so total that by the 1960s followers of the game were often surprised to hear that he was still alive. He would never play in a Test Match or walk on to an Australian cricket field again.

The rest of the game was a formality: once more, Jardine's calculations were perfectly justified by events. O'Brien and McCabe both fell to catches in Voce's leg trap before tea: after it, Verity was irresistible. Allen bowled Woodfull for 67, and Verity finished with 5 for 33 off 19 overs. Australia were all out for 182, only Lee apart from Woodfull and Bradman reaching double figures. It was a débâcle, and England needed only 164 to win, a task which nobody doubted was well within their compass.

So it proved: O'Reilly and Ironmonger made them work hard for it, but they won by eight wickets midway through the Tuesday afternoon, Hammond finishing it in style with a huge lofted drive for 6. But the game did not end without a last, and characteristic, flare-up of controversy. Wall did not play in this last Test because of an injured heel. He was replaced by the Victorian fast bowler H. H. Alexander – who, it may be remembered, had been included in the country game at Ballarat after the Adelaide Test, supposedly to give the MCC a taste of their own 'bodyline' medicine. Nothing had come of it on that occasion, nor in the last Test did Alexander bowl anything resembling systematic 'bodyline' – Woodfull always set his face adamantly against any suggestion of retaliation, for all the considerable support that the idea received in some sections of the Australian press. Nevertheless, he clearly bowled at least the traditional fast bowler's ration of short ones, and made some of them fly a bit, as Larwood had done to more formidable effect. In the first innings, one of these deliveries hit Jardine, who was again playing an obdurate innings as a substitute opening batsman, on the elbow, and for all the general quiescence of the Hill during the match, this was enough to bring out their underlying attitude to the English captain – according at least to the London *Evening Standard*, the blow was received with 'yells of derisive satisfaction'. There was no English complaint about Alexander's length – clearly there scarcely could be – but on this same Friday afternoon, Sutcliffe complained about his running on the pitch. This is not of course a very uncommon cause of complaint against fast bowlers, and from England's point of view on this occasion the issue might be serious, for England had to bat last, and the Australian attack, built round three spin bowlers (O'Reilly, Ironmonger and Lee), was obviously well qualified to take

116

advantage of a damaged wicket (we have seen that Verity was already getting some help from it by the fourth day).

The incident passed off for the moment; but at the beginning of England's second innings on the Monday evening, Jardine, again opening the innings, complained again about Alexander's follow-through, and this time there was uproar. There was an outburst of hooting and booing from the crowd, which was at its largest that day. The idea of Jardine of all people complaining about the tactics of other people's fast bowlers was clearly more than they were prepared to take. The umpires spoke to Woodfull, and Alexander retaliated by bowling several bumpers at Jardine: when one of them hit him on the hip, there was loud cheering. Jardine was in obvious pain – when he returned to the pavilion at the end of the day, there was blood running down his leg – but when some of the close fieldsmen moved towards him to see if he needed help he waved them away and resumed his innings. He was not going to give a derisive Australian crowd the satisfaction of knowing that he was hurt. He had expected his opponents to take the knocks of 'bodyline' without complaint, and he was not going to complain himself. It was a very typical Jardine episode.

But the incident was, on the whole, untypical of the atmosphere in which the last Test was played, and it is significant that both the leading Australian papers, and the old Australian captain M. A. Noble on the air, condemned the crowd's reaction. It would be misrepresenting the Australian attitude to say that it was one of 'forgive and forget': with England defiantly flaunting 'bodyline' tactics to the last, that was hardly to be expected. The tone was much more than that that had been set by the ABC's last cable: the 'bodyline' issue would be raised again, but for the moment it had been agreed to put it on file, and for the rest to observe the traditional sporting courtesies. There were some exceptions to this – crowd reactions could not always be controlled, and between the two teams themselves the alienation was so deep that genuinely friendly relations

117

were never restored to the end of the tour (in spite of optimistic statements to the contrary by some English papers). But from the establishments both of politics and the game itself there was an urgent emphasis on conciliation, and this evidently had a marked effect on press reporting and even on crowd behaviour. Most Australian papers, when the series was over, agreed that the better side had won, and were united in praising Larwood's bowling and Jardine's captaincy, even while deprecating the use they had made of their skills.

Perhaps, though, the most revealing evidence is to be found in the reports of the dinner given by the New South Wales government for the MCC party while the last Test was still in progress. The mere fact that such a function should take place is evidence enough of the semi-diplomatic nature of MCC tours between the Wars, as is the list of guests, who included the Mayor of Sydney and the Speaker of the NSW Legislative Assembly as well as representatives of the Board of Control and most of the Australian team. It was probably the grandest social occasion of the tour, as it was also the last considerable one, and the reports of the speeches leave no doubt of the anxiety of all concerned to paper over the cracks that the tour had opened in Anglo-Australian relations. The Governor, Sir Philip Game (who sounds as though he came perilously close to caricature of the sort of thing expected of the likes of him on this sort of occasion), reportedly 'likened the Ministry to the cricket team, and said that in politics, as in cricket, it was for all members of the team to play the game'.* More directly, he went on to say that

* New South Wales politics during the Depression had not been uniformly characterized by harmony and unity, to put it mildly, and one suspects here an attempt to pour oil simultaneously on more than one troubled pool. Space forbids any discussion in this book of the party political reverberations of the 'bodyline' controversy; but in Australia at least they certainly existed, and at this point they are so obvious that it seems impossible to pass over them entirely without notice. I have already noted that the fact that Lyons and the United Australian Party were in office in Canberra at the time of the 'bodyline' troubles strengthened the

'they all admired the skill, stamina, and good fellowship which permeated the English team'. Perhaps I have done less than justice to the Governor's subtlety: few could withhold admiration of the precise qualities he enumerated, and one wonders if the choice of 'fellowship' rather than 'sportsmanship' was altogether accidental.

The State Premier, B. S. Stevens, however, left nothing to be inferred from *doubles entendres*, but played very straight down the line indeed. He said that 'the function was primarily to mark their respect for the members of the visiting team and to show their appreciation of the sportsmanlike manner in which they had played the game throughout the Tests' (applause – though one suspects that the ABC representatives and the Australian players may have swallowed fairly hard at this juncture). 'He would like to emphasize that in Australia, as in England, cricket was looked upon as a national game, and one which represented the best aspects of the national character. When they said a thing was "not cricket", they expressed an attitude of mind that was common to both Australia and England' (applause, maybe a shade two-edged in some cases). 'The visitors had played cricket in the best traditions

---

bargaining position of the MCC, because they put much more stress on good relations with Great Britain than the Labour Opposition. Nationalism has generally been a left-wing cause in Australia, and the main root of it has generally been Anglophobia. To that extent, the anti-'bodyline' agitation had obvious affinities with it; and I have in fact no doubt at all that when the history of Australian nationalism comes to be written, the 'bodyline' controversy will make an interesting section in it.

In New South Wales, the Labour government of J. T. Lang, which had bitterly resisted the deflationary policies urged upon it by the banks and the Commonwealth government, had revealed its traditional Anglophobic instincts by suspending payments of dividends to British bondholders. In 1931 Lang was dismissed from office on constitutional grounds by the English Governor, Sir Philip Game, who installed in his place B. S. Stevens as leader of the United Australia Party, i.e. a right-wing coalition of the same complexion as Lyons' federal government in Canberra. Game and Stevens, therefore, both stood for the British connection, and with a realization of this the political and Anglophile overtones of their speeches at the dinner are obvious enough.

of the British people. The visiting team, like the Australians, had come from all walks of life, so that cricket was not only a national game, but also a democratic game. They met in common on the cricket field as they met in common on the battlefields in the Great War.' It is difficult to see what more he could have said short of an open commendation of 'bodyline' to justify Jardine and to repudiate the ABC, but his remarks seem to have gone down well.

Jardine and Warner replied in highly characteristic fashions. Jardine's emphasis was all on the loyalty of the team, though he did also pay a tribute to the 'sportsmanlike manner in which his team had been received throughout Australia': he said not a word to imply that their tactics had ever been impugned. Warner, who believed that they had been impugned rightly, was one diplomatic step nearer to frankness. He said that 'there had been little ruffles on the surface during the progress of the contests' – well, yes, you could say that; and you would never have known as much from anything else that was said on this occasion. 'He sincerely hoped these would now be forgotten and everything unpleasant relegated to the dustheap of oblivion' ('Hear, hear, and applause' – there unmistakably speaks the voice of the occasion). 'He congratulated Mr Jardine on his resourcefulness' (what a choice of word!) 'and the fighting spirit which he had shown throughout the contests, but in all the matches the spirit of cricket and sportsmanship had not been forgotten' (applause). 'He was an old man, but he greatly loved cricket, and was gratified to see the matches contested in a spirit that reflected all that was best in the character of both the Australian and the English people.' There is no doubt that Warner was speaking from the heart: he was not in fact an old man yet, but there was both the pathos and the illusions of old age in that last sentence.

The tour was not yet over – MCC still had two first-class matches to play after the fifth Test. It was not a good arrangement, and especially not after a series as traumatic as this one had been: if anti-climax had already been in the air before the last Test, it was overwhelming after it. It was still more unfortunate that these last two matches involved revisiting the abandoned battlegrounds of Melbourne and Adelaide; and it is not surprising that the team did themselves scant justice in either. Neither Larwood nor Allen played in either, and the games at least served to indicate the extent to which the side's bowling depended on them. At Melbourne, Victoria came within a hair's breadth of victory: set 178 in two hours, they ended at 177 for 3. Back, finally, on the scarred battlefield of the Adelaide Oval, MCC had overwhelmingly the better of their last game but failed to bowl out South Australia, who ended up 165 behind with two wickets standing.

There was incident to the last. Jardine's Harlequin cap, which he wore regularly on the field, had always been a source of irritation and a subject of satire for the Australian crowds: it symbolized so perfectly the angular awkwardness of the man, his refusal to give an inch to what the crowds demanded of him. It is very unusual for a player in a Test Match to wear any cap but the cap of his country, and the Harlequin cap seemed to sum up in itself the patrician disdain that so offended the democratic egalitarianism of Australia. At Adelaide on the last day the MCC side came out to field in a dazzling array of Harlequin and other club caps of every hue of the rainbow – all except Jardine, who alone wore the sober blue England cap with the lion and the unicorn. It was a harmless enough jest at the crowd's expense, and no doubt the great majority of them took it in good part, but some of the commentators found cause for offence even in this. There was still a lot of heat under the embers at Adelaide.

The MCC team returned overland to Sydney, and sailed from there for New Zealand a day or two later. Most of them, no doubt, had enjoyed the tour. Australia had been as beautiful, and its hospitality as warm, as ever: the moments of rancour on the field had never infected ordinary social contacts off the ground.* They were a close-knit side, and they had the sense of intense satisfaction that winning a Test series in Australia must always bring. Yet, uniquely, none of the Australian side were on the quay to see off their departing visitors. However great the satisfactions of victory, and however soothing the platitudes of the official speeches and the end-of-tour editorials had been, their absence was a chilling proof that something about the tour had been a failure and that the wound was still open and would not easily be healed. It was a jarring reminder of the bitterness that had marred the tour, and it can have left the minds of few of the MCC party entirely at peace.

Although the team had always been loyal to Jardine, and although the hostility of the Australian press and the stigma placed upon their sportsmanship by the Board of Control's original cable had tended to drive them into closer unity, there had always been divisions between them on the 'bodyline' tactics. Allen, as we have seen, had flatly refused to bowl 'bodyline': he had discussed the issue with his close friend Wyatt, who shared his views, and they had agreed never to discuss it with the team or with anyone else, English or Australian, at any rate until the tour was over. Pataudi (who does not seem to have enjoyed himself in Australia) also disliked it – in the first match against New South Wales he is said to have refused to field in the leg trap, and to have been dismissed by Jardine as a

* This is a remarkable fact, but there seems to be no doubt of its truth. Even Larwood, by his own account, apart from one or two minor encounters, experienced nothing but kindness away from the ground. If anyone encountered unpleasantness on the street, it must surely have been Jardine, but he, tight-lipped to the last, has left no record of it. All this may well say something about the generosity of the Australian temperament: I suspect, though, that it says more about the extent to which sportsmen, and public entertainers in general, become artificial personalities when the spotlights are on them. Met on the street in the flesh, they are simply not the same people as the ones you cheered or booed out in the middle yesterday. As Larwood once heard a small boy say to his mother, 'Mummy, he doesn't *look* like a killer.'

'conscientious objector'. Brown, the youngest member of the side, played in none of the Tests and was scarcely involved, but apparently also disapproved. These were all amateurs, who could afford to refuse their support to Jardine's tactics, and it was of course the amateur code of cricketing values that was at stake.

The professionals were in a substantially different position: in the 1930s, they were not expected to criticize their captain's tactics, or to ask the reason why, and in any case they were probably likely to take a harder view of the game and to give mere victory a higher priority – after all, to an extent their livelihood depended on it. It does seem to have been among the professionals that Jardine found most support, notably from Sutcliffe, the senior professional and a member of the selection committee for the Tests, who clearly carried considerable influence. Sutcliffe seems never to have wavered in his support for 'bodyline' (though, according to Victor Richardson, even Sutcliffe said that he 'would not play for five minutes against "bodyline"').

Yet even among the professionals, Hammond and Ames at least seem to have disliked 'bodyline', though they were not in a position to speak out about it: most of the rest never gave any indication of their opinion one way or another. Duckworth, a wholehearted supporter of 'bodyline' in Australia, was later to undergo a dramatic conversion. He was not the only one of the party to become nervously aware, as time went by, that they might soon find themselves on the *receiving* end of 'bodyline', and to find his opinion of it changing accordingly. 'Bodyline' was not something that could be left behind and forgotten as the Australian coast faded from sight: it had a future as well as a past.

A coda to the tour still remained. For the first time, the MCC had agreed that after the Australian itinerary was completed the team should go on to New Zealand and play two Test Matches and one other match there. No full-strength English team had ever visited New Zealand before, and it was only in 1931 that New Zealand had first been admitted to the dignity of playing official Tests against England, so there was great local enthusiasm for the visit – an enthusiasm that, as we have seen, was markedly not shared by the Australian Board of Control. There was, accordingly, something of an anti-Australian overtone to the New Zealand tour. After the strains and stresses they had been through in Australia, the England players came to New Zealand prepared to relax, with the comforting knowledge that the opposition on the field was unlikely to be too formidable, and ready to enjoy what they found.

They did enjoy it a lot. As it turned out, all three matches were interrupted by rain and ended as draws, but England had enormously the better of the two Tests, Hammond scoring 227 and 336 not out (at the time the highest score ever made in a Test Match, though not seriously to be considered beside Bradman's 334 at Headingley in 1930), and doing much as he pleased. The New Zealand crowds were very appreciative, and no bad feeling of any sort marred the success of the short tour.

The contrast with the course events had taken in Australia was obvious – not unrelished in New Zealand, which has always felt the need to defend its identity by emphasizing the distance in manners as well as miles between itself and big brother over the Tasman Sea, and had often found asserting the closeness of its ties with the Old Country (as the Mayor of Wellington actually called it when welcoming the MCC party to his Town Hall) a highly effective way of doing this. When the Prime Minister (G. W. Forbes) said, at a reception for the team at Parliament House, 'We in New Zealand want to follow the British tradition – that the spirit of the game counts more than the game itself,' there is not much doubt that this was intended not as a warning to Jardine as one might think (perhaps the Prime Minister was a little hazy as to what exactly the 'bodyline' controversy was all about), but as a contrast with Australia. Jardine's own awareness of the contrast is apparent in the wry comments on the party's experiences in Australia that punctuated his reply to the Mayor, and which obviously appealed to his audience. He quoted (or, rather, misquoted) some hackneyed lines of Arnold Wall on cricket: 'A time will come when they will sit watching the game, orderly, at peace, calm, serene,' adding barbedly, 'Australian papers please copy,' and was met with 'a roar of laughter' – New Zealanders liked that sort of thing – and he referred appreciatively to the many letters of support he had received from New Zealand when the controversy in Australia was at its height.

But of course the real point was that the cause of the conflict which had so embittered the series in Australia was wholly absent in New Zealand. The Sydney *Referee* had remarked that: 'New Zealanders are not likely to see the "bodyline" in action. It is reserved for special occasions and special batsmen.' This was quite true; and although Jardine, asked on the team's arrival in New Zealand whether he intended to use leg theory there (the questioner's deliberate avoidance of the more emotive term 'bodyline' is worth noting), replied, 'We intend to play exactly as we played in Australia,' he made haste to add that Larwood had gone home and that New Zealand wickets were probably unsuitable for leg theory anyway. And, indeed, although Voce played in two of the games and Bowes wrought havoc with the New Zealand batting in the second Test, nothing remotely resembling 'bodyline' seems to have been seen. England's superiority was manifest without it, and Jardine was probably fully conscious of the diplomatic advantages of retaining the New Zealand sympathy which he clearly possessed.

In any case, the master practitioner, as Jardine had said, was no longer with the side. Larwood was suffering so much with his feet that he played no more cricket after the Sydney Test, and obtained permission from Jardine and the managers to go straight home, rather than accompanying the party on the tour of New Zealand. Pataudi went with him. They travelled across to Perth by train – at one of the stops on the way, according to Larwood, their compartment was invaded by an aggressive group of larrikins, booing, hissing and throwing pomegranate seeds at them, one of the very few pieces of personal unpleasantness he encountered on the tour – and from Perth caught ship for India, Suez and England, and the reception that awaited Larwood there.

The rest of the MCC party made their way home from New Zealand by what at the time it was fashionable to call the 'all-red route': by the New Zealand Shipping Company's *Aorangi* across the Pacific to Vancouver, across the continent by the Canadian Pacific Railway, and then home by that company's *Duchess of Atholl* from Montreal to Greenock. One notes again how intimately the sentiment of Empire was involved in these MCC tours between the Wars. Cricket, of course, was exclusively an 'Empire' game (as no other major sport was). References to the function of the tour in promoting the unity of Empire crop up everywhere. Some of them I have noted already. They appear strongly again in the pride taken in the party's use of the 'all-red route',* and in the fact that throughout the eight-month world tour the only time the party set foot on non-British territory was when the *Aorangi* called at Hawaii. All across Canada cheering crowds and official receptions awaited them.† At Greenock, a pipe and drum band came out in the tender to welcome the conquering heroes home, and yet another mayor and yet another speech awaited them on the quayside before the team broke up and went their individual ways home. It was a moment of heady and glorious national triumph and rejoicing; but it was not to last long. The wounds of 'bodyline' were still open, and there was still trouble to come.

* The instinctive connotation of 'red' has altered strangely in the last fifty years.

† In Vancouver a Canadian journalist did his best to explain 'bodyline' to his readers, summarizing its results as 'the bruising up of several of the Australian players just when they were planning to sock the old pill for a loop'.

PART II

Retrospective

CHAPTER 5

The Origins of Bodyline
Fast Bowling before 1932

But before we follow the further development of the controversy, it is time to turn and take stock. We have seen the effect of the English bowling tactics, and the Australian reaction to them; but we have yet to answer two very important questions. What exactly *was* 'bodyline', and how did the decision to employ it against the Australians come to be made? In this chapter and the next I shall try to answer these questions – neither of which is nearly as simple as both may look at first sight. In this chapter I shall be looking at 'bodyline' as an episode in the history of cricket techniques.

Technology has a history of its own, in cricket as in all kinds of human craft – take warfare as an example: every new weapon, and every new form of tactics, confers a momentary advantage on its first practitioner, and each in turn calls forth another weapon, or another form of tactics, to counter it. Thus the use of poison gas, regarded cold-bloodedly, was a rational response to the advantages conferred on the defender in the early phases of the First World War by the enormous multiplication of modern fire-power. But equally the history of technology is inadequate by itself, because to any given technical dilemma there is usually a range of possible counters and possible responses, and the choice between them is determined less by technology itself than by social pressures and individual psychology: the use of poison gas by the Germans in 1915 was rational, but it was not inevitable, and to understand it you have to look at factors such as the minds and characters of the leading members of the German government and high command, their moral beliefs, their understanding of the situation in which they found themselves, and the pressures of public opinion under which they acted. It is that aspect – if you like, the psychological as distinct from the technical aspect of the 'bodyline' controversy – that I shall be examining in the next chapter.

It is possible to define 'bodyline' fairly accurately as fast, short-pitched bowling directed at the batsman's body and bowled to a packed and close-set leg-side field; but we shall make poor sense of it if we approach it in this fashion. To grasp the point and the significance of 'bodyline', we need to understand how it arose; and to do that, we need to go back into cricket history a long way before 1932. As a point of departure, let it be said at once that all fast bowling is inherently intimidatory, in the sense that it has always achieved some of its successes by its ability to frighten the batsman. As Maurice Leyland once said with robust Yorkshire good sense, 'Nobody likes fast bowling – but some don't show it.' If a hard ball moving fast hits you, it hurts: reduced to its barest elements the thing is as simple as that, and I do not suppose the fast bowler has ever yet been born who was not pleased to see a batsman flinch away to leg as he bowled. Anyone who has ever played the game at all, were it no more than an under-11 game in the remotest corner of the playing field, knows that much. Larwood himself said, in the book that he wrote (or, rather, that was ghosted for him) at the height of the controversy, 'Very fast bowling always has been intimidating. It has always resulted in the batsman being hit more or less' – and, taken at face value, it would be hard to refute this, though one may feel that the more or less makes a deal of difference. Certainly from the days of the early round-armers onward, many nineteenth-century fast bowlers

130

Larwood in his delivery stride: a classic picture. Note the height of the left foot, about to pound into the ground. It was trouble with this foot that caused Larwood's breakdown in the last Test and prevented him bowling during the 1933 season

Woodfull hit over the heart in the 'Australian XI' match at Melbourne. This is the picture that did much to form the Australian image of 'bodyline'. Bowes exhibits a typical Yorkshire degree of sympathy at forward short leg

The Perils of the Leg Trap:
W. M. Woodfull hit by Larwood.

This time the leg theory claimed a distinguished victim. W. M. Woodfull, batting for an Australian XI against the M.C.C. at Melbourne, was struck over the heart by a thunderbolt from Larwood. He was able to continue his innings after ten minutes. J. R. Jardine has called Australian attention to fast bowling on the leg stump, with its occasional painful consequences, being a feature of all cricket, from village greens to Test matches. This is probably true. In any case, Australia, who in the twenties begot those incomparable terrorists, Gregory and Macdonald, must not complain of Larwood and Voce in the thirties. But apart from any particular case, and granted such tactics being common, the awkward question remains to be answered : Is it cricket ?

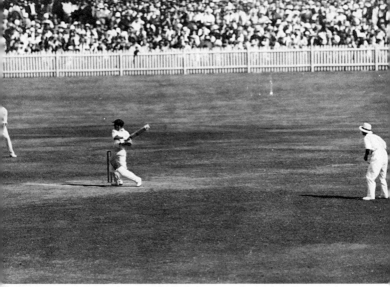

Bradman square-cutting from outside the leg stump in the Adelaide Test. The distance Bradman has moved wide of the leg stump is obvious. Only one short leg is visible: Bradman's tactics may already have forced Jardine to strengthen his off-side field

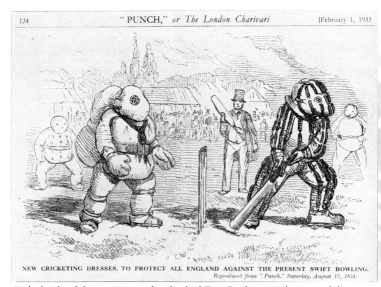

NEW CRICKETING DRESSES, TO PROTECT ALL ENGLAND AGAINST THE PRESENT SWIFT BOWLING.
Reproduced from "Punch," Saturday, August 12, 1854.

At the height of the controversy after the third Test, *Punch* very aptly reprinted this cartoon of 1854. Obviously the issues raised by 'bodyline' were not completely unfamiliar to the Victorians

The Adelaide Oval during the third Test

Oldfield hit on the head at Adelaide: the second of the incidents in the third Test that brought the 'bodyline' affair to the flashpoint. Note that Oldfield, a fraction of a second after the impact, is well outside the off stump. Note, too, the absence of a proper leg trap

This photograph, with its accompanying comment, published in an English periodical while the controversy was at its height, is of great interest, illustrating as it does the very different types of attack that could be covered by the terms 'leg theory' and 'leg trap', and the English tendency to confuse them. Quinn here would presumably have been bowling round the wicket and to a fairly full length, relying on swing rather than bounce to induce catches. The position of the short legs is quite different to that used by Larwood and Voce in Australia, who (see next illustration) normally had at least as many in front of the wicket as behind it. Note, too, that a field placing such as this would be impossible under the modern Law banning more than two fieldsmen behind the wicket on the leg side

Leg theory in full blast in the fourth Test: Woodfull ducks to a short ball from Larwood. Jardine – at square leg, in characteristic posture – calculates the effect of it. Note that point is apparently the only fieldsman in front of the wicket on the offside

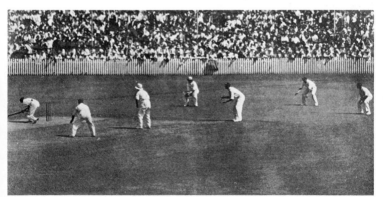

This picture, taken in conjunction with the one above, is a perfect illustration of the difficulties created for the Australian batsmen by the unpredictable bounce of the pitches. Here too Woodfull has ducked to a short ball, but the ball has failed to rise and has hit him in the ribs – in fact, as far as the height of it is concerned, it looks as though he might almost have been in danger of an LBW decision

The members of the special sub-committee set up by the MCC in May 1933 to handle the controversy

Lord Lewisham, President of the MCC 1932–33

Sir Stanley Jackson

Lord Hawke, Treasurer of the MCC at the time of the controversy

William Findlay, Secretary of the MCC

P. F. Warner

Hore-Ruthven, as Governor-General of
Australia after the War

J. H. Thomas, the Dominions Secretary in the National Government

Jardine leading the England side onto the field during the second Test at Melbourne. On this occasion he is wearing the silk choker but not the Harlequin cap. Sutcliffe and Wyatt, senior professional and vice-captain, are to the left and right of him respectively

Low's inimitable comment on the 'bodyline' affair

THE NEXT TEST.- AMAZING SCOOP!

WITH CHARACTERISTIC ENTERPRISE THIS NEWSPAPER HAS ARRANGED WITH THE SUPERNATURAL AUTHORITIES (OLD LOW, LOCAL AGENT) TO PRESENT THESE SNAPSHOTS OF THE NEXT TEST EVEN BEFORE IT HAPPENS.

Bradman getting sock on jaw from Larwood.

Bradman's bat hurled at Larwood.

Fieldsmen stumping Bradman with himself.

Jardine bites Woodfull.

Australian Government considers cable from M.C.C. to say that bthat biting is cricket and advising play-the-game sir.

STOP PRESS—Australia declares war.

must have been pretty frightening at times, especially given the unpredictable wickets of the period: most of us can probably call to mind the 'bumping pitch' of Newbolt's famous poem, and remember, from another cricket poem of the period, that Jackson's pace was 'very fearful'. When one bears in mind too the minimal protection that the batsmen of the time wore, it is obvious that batting against fast bowling in the nineteenth century must have required a stout nerve and considerable physical courage, and there is no doubt that batsmen took a lot of nasty knocks from time to time.

All this is true, but the difference between this and Larwood's and Voce's bowling in 1932–33 is still fundamental. By and large, it seems to be true that, though the fast bowlers of the time undoubtedly sometimes frightened batsmen, and may have been pleased when they did so, they did not deliberately try to intimidate them by threatening to hit them: they did not, in other words, bowl at their bodies. Perhaps some of them may have regarded the occasional short one as all in the day's work, but that was as far as it went. The nineteenth century was an age in which what the cricketers of the 1930s would have called 'off theory' was completely dominant, for fast bowlers above all. That is, they bowled at the stumps or just outside the off stump, and they aimed to take their wickets either by hitting the stumps or by catches at the wicket and in the slips. Swing, it must be remembered, was practically an unknown phenomenon (it was still possible to find experienced cricketers as late as the 1920s who denied that cricket balls ever swung) and the use of the seam still unknown. Fast bowlers aimed to beat the batsman by the straightforward weapons of sheer pace, of lift, and of the action breakback of which a bowler like Tom Richardson was such a master. Given also the element of uncertainty in the wickets of the day, they felt no need to resort to direct intimidation.

The narrow aristocratic elite who still controlled the game in most of its manifestations would have frowned on

131

such methods; and what is perhaps more important, the batting styles of the time were such as to give the bowler a fair chance without them. They were typically aggressive, front-foot, off-side styles, based on a firmly anchored right foot: their natural perfection was the cover-drive. We are naturally asymmetrical creatures, and there are few games into which this asymmetry has entered so deeply as into cricket, where the left hand-right hand distinction is crucial, and not merely incidental. Most – though not all – batsmen find off-side shots easier to play than on-side ones. Oddly enough, even aesthetics tend this way: the hook and the pull can be as effective as the drive and the cut, but it seems undeniable that they are less beautiful (perhaps the only truly beautiful leg-side shot is the leg glance, and only one great batsman, Ranjitsinhji, had ever cultivated that to the perfection of which it is capable); and maybe in a culture as aristocratic as that of nineteenth-century English cricket, even that consideration counted for something. Maybe it is possible to go further, and to suggest that nineteenth-century cricket was dominated by the batsman, and therefore tended to the off-side style of play that comes most naturally to most batsmen. We are entangled here in all the complexities of English social distinctions, but I think it could well be argued that typically at that time the gentleman batted, the player bowled (think of the school professional!), and that since the gentleman, economically and socially, called the tune, he determined the lines on which the game should be played.*

Perhaps this is fanciful, but the fact that cricket in the nineteenth century was fundamentally an off-side game is not; and the style of batting that went with this, though it

* It may be remarked that the traditional format of *Wisden*, the near-official almanac of cricket, was a perfect reflection of this upper-class dominance of the game, with its extensive coverage of cricket at Oxford, Cambridge, and the public schools – but no other universities, and no other schools – and its total neglect of the highly accomplished, but entirely non-genteel, league cricket of the North.

opened to the batsman a wide range of glorious and profitable strokes, also offered opportunity to the bowler, and to the fast bowler not least. This was true in two respects in particular. The anchored right foot, in the first place, meant that if the bowler pitched the ball on or outside the off stump, the batsman was necessarily playing across the line of the ball to some extent. This inevitably involved very fine timing, and meant that the chance of an edge, and a catch to the wicketkeeper or the slips, was never dishearteningly far away. Secondly, it also meant that the stumps were exposed: if the ball beat the bat, there was nothing to prevent it hitting the wicket.

With this last point in particular we touch on one of the major, but least recognized, sources of 'bodyline'; and it deserves a little fuller consideration accordingly. Prior to the end of the nineteenth century, the deliberate use of the pads was severely frowned upon: it was one of the things that gentlemen did not do (on the rare occasions when Ranjitsinhji was hit on the pads, he regarded it as proof that he had played a bad shot). Pads were meant to protect the batsman against accidental injury: the underlying assumption was that batsmen would no more deliberately use their legs to protect their stumps than bowlers would deliberately aim at those legs to injure or intimidate the batsman. And since a batsman who wants to protect his wicket with his pads will generally find his back leg – i.e., the right leg for a right-hander – the most convenient for the purpose (because it is closer to the stumps, and can therefore cover them more effectively), a style of batting based on the anchored right leg also militated against such methods. Obviously there were exceptions – a batsman playing back to a short ball pitched on the wicket or just outside the off stump always had to move his right foot across the wicket; but this was a different thing from deliberate use of the pads as a second line of defence, which was still frowned upon. That it was nevertheless sometimes done is shown by the appearance in the 1774 revision of the Laws of the earliest form of the LBW Law –

133

included specifically because one contemporary batsman 'was so shabby as to put his leg in the way and take advantage of the bowlers'.

Throughout the nineteenth century, this continued to be the approved attitude to pad-play – as late as the end of the century H. A. Vachell, in his once-famous schoolboy novel *The Hill*, took it for granted that at a quintessentially patrician occasion like the Eton and Harrow match, it would be an occasion for universal chaff if 'a batsman interposed a pad where a bat ought to have been'. An even better demonstration of the attitude is the illustration which appears in plate 7. This comes from the first edition of the well-known Badminton handbook on cricket, published in 1888, and was obviously meant as an illustration of a typical LBW dismissal. Here it is clearly not a case of the batsman being defeated by the bowler, but of a batsman infringing the ethical norms of the game. An unwritten distinction runs through the Laws of Cricket between ways of getting out based on the skill and dexterity of the bowler and the fieldsmen (like bowled and caught) and those which are seen as penalties for misbehaviour by the batsman (like obstructing the field and handling the ball). The point is that the LBW rule originated in this latter class, and that the feeling that deliberately guarding one's stumps with one's pads was unsporting persisted up to the end of the century.

As long as a particular form of behaviour continues to be widely regarded as unsporting, the form of dismissal associated with it remains rare – again, it is enough to refer to obstructing the field – because the moral sanction is enough to ensure that it will rarely be practised. By the late nineteenth century, deliberate pad-play was in a sort of moral no man's land. It was certainly practised to some extent – Arthur Shrewsbury was a great pioneer of it in the 1880s. Shrewsbury, though, was a professional: it is possible to read a lot of significance into the tale of the occasion when he was batting with the young F. S. Jackson against the Australians in the Lord's Test of 1893, and took

134

occasion to say to him, 'Back up with your pads, sir, or Charlie Turner will get you out.' The point is that it was not the way that gentlemen were expected to bat at the time. Accounts suggest, too, that even Shrewsbury rarely if ever padded up without offering a stroke. He merely ensured that, if the ball beat his bat, there would still be a second line of defence in his pads to protect his wicket. In any case, in that era of great amateur batsmen, pad-play was still very generally frowned upon, and little practised in consequence. One result of that was that if a bowler beat the bat, the way to the stumps was usually clear for him, and this encouraged bowling aimed at the wicket and pitched straight or on the off side (if a ball pitched outside the leg stump, a batsman could not *help* getting his legs in the way): another result, equally important, was that it was possible to get by with a minimal LBW law, which demanded two exacting conditions for a dismissal – that the ball should not merely have been going to have hit the stumps, but that it should have pitched on the line of them as well. LBW dismissals were in fact rare, though significantly they were increasing: it has been calculated that in Tests between England and Australia, they averaged 4.64 per match between 1877 and 1900, 7.55 between 1901 and 1914, and 11.21 between 1919 and 1933; and any glance at pre-1914 scoresheets will bear out the impression that these figures give.

The increase in pad-play was already giving concern before the War, and it was recognized at once that LBW Law in its existing form was quite inadequate to stop it, once it became ethically acceptable. As far back as 1888 – when Shrewsbury was at the peak of his career, in fact – the first-class counties asked the MCC to modify the Law by eliminating the requirement that the ball should pitch on the wicket. This was a clear reflection of the increasing popularity of pad-play: the MCC did not act on the suggestion, but made its position clear by issuing a strong condemnation of the practice of defending the wicket with the person rather than the bat, and hinting that stronger

135

measures might be necessary if the practice continued. The problem did not go away. Fourteen years later, in 1902, the counties' suggestion was revived, and at the annual general meeting of the MCC that year the proposal to eliminate from the LBW Law any reference to the point where the ball pitched was actually carried, but by an insufficient majority to come into force.

Fast bowlers still found that the styles of batting of the day earned them a reasonable return if they pitched the ball up on or about the line of the off stump. It was, indeed, a golden age of fast bowling, with names like Tom Richardson, Lockwood, Kortright, Walter Brearley, the South African Kotze and the Australians Cotter and Ernest Jones to conjure with. In terms of sheer pace, some of these were probably as intimidating as any fast bowlers have ever been – Kortright is often said to have been the fastest of all time, and two other lesser-known names, N. A. Knox of Surrey and W. B. Burns of Worcestershire, cannot have been far off his pace: *Wisden* bears tribute to the fear that Knox in 1906 often inspired in batsmen, and Pelham Warner claimed that Burns actually anticipated 'bodyline' in the Middlesex *v* Worcestershire match at Lord's in 1910, bowling fast and short on the leg stump to a packed leg-side field. Some of the others, too, were not above occasional deliberate use of the short-pitched ball. Ernest Jones and Cotter were both described by one who remembered them well as 'pretty rough': Gilbert Jessop, of all people, is said to have complained of Brearley's bowling on several occasions; and the amateur fast bowler S. M. J. Woods openly recommended the use of the short-pitched ball as 'an excellent method of attacking a nervous batsman' and is even said to have made deliberate use of 'beamers' – fast full pitches at the batsman's head, the most dangerous balls in a fast bowler's repertoire. Clearly it would be expecting too much of human nature to suppose that there was ever a time when the occasional deliberate use of the bouncer was unheard of; but the general impression that emerges from the records, nevertheless, is that none of the fast bowlers of the period made intimidation their main aim, and above all none of them made systematic use of the bouncer.

When cricket was resumed after the First World War, a great deal had changed – more than was at first realized. We are a long step nearer 'bodyline', and not only in terms of the passage of time. It is significant that the first two Test series after the War, the Australian series of 1920–21 and the English series of 1921 which immediately followed it, were dominated, as no such series had ever been before, by the figures of two great Australian fast bowlers, Gregory and McDonald, and memories of them and of their bowling still ran fiercely through English memories, and through much English comment, at the time of the 'bodyline' controversy a dozen years later. Gregory had first made his name with the Australian Imperial Forces team that made a great impact in England in 1919, when regular county and Test cricket had not yet been resumed, but it was only back in Australia in 1920–21 that English batsmen were first exposed to the joint onslaught of him and McDonald, and only in England in 1921 that they felt the full blast of it; and it was they, together with the leg-spinner Arthur Mailey, who more than anything determined the result of those two series. With Gregory and McDonald, fast bowling grew up a stage. They were, for one thing, the first great *pair* of fast bowlers, so closely associated on the field and in the imagination that the mention of one invariably conjures up the name of the other – like Lindwall and Miller, Hall and Griffith, or Lillee and Thomson. There is more to this than the mere accident of their being contemporaries: Richardson and Lockwood were also contemporaries in both the Surrey and England sides, but they never operated as a pair in the sense that Gregory and McDonald did. Because swing was little exploited, fast bowlers of the pre-War generation were not particularly linked with the new ball: it was common for slow bowlers to open the attack, and fast bowlers were often expected to operate in effect as stock bowlers, bowling long spells in the middle of the innings. There was therefore no particular necessity for them to operate together, and the modern idea of the fast bowler as essentially a shock bowler, bowling his eight or ten overs while the ball is new and then put out to grass till the next new ball comes along, was unheard of.

Gregory and McDonald changed all that. Under Armstrong's captaincy, they habitually opened the Australian attack together, and in two at least of the five Tests in 1921 the issue was virtually settled on the first morning, the English upper order batting torn to tatters by the pace and fury of their attack. Like all the great pairs of fast bowlers that were to follow them, they operated on the nerves of the batsmen as much as on their reflexes: with the two of them working in harness there was no respite, no breathing-space, but a ceaseless, battering onslaught that threatened in the end to crack even the toughest concentration. That they often frightened their opponents there is no question, nor that they bowled a lot of bumpers in the process. When the series was over, the editor of *Wisden* remarked that:

... some of our batsmen, knowing that they would have to face Gregory, were out before they went in. Since Knox bowled his fastest in 1906 I have never seen batsmen so obviously intimidated. McDonald struck one as being really the finer bowler of the two, but Gregory was by far the more alarming. Gregory was apt when he pitched at all short to get up dangerously high, but old cricketers were apt to be sarcastic when they saw batsmen frightened by long hops. They perhaps remembered Mr R. D. Walker's dictum years ago that the batsman who could not take care of himself ought not to play cricket. Finding the effect of the rising ball so great Gregory would have been almost more than human if he had not now and then dropped one short with intention.

The comment splendidly illuminates, not only the qualities of Gregory's bowling, but the attitudes of the time. This is an Englishman writing about Australian fast bowlers who have been wreaking havoc on English batsmen, but the dominant tone is admiration, linked with disdain for batsmen who allow themselves to be intimidated. This was an age when the fearsome bumper was not yet distinguished from the contemptible long hop, and when it was taken for granted that a fast bowler would rarely, if ever, deliberately bowl short, and when, if he did, it was felt that part of the blame properly belonged to the batsmen for showing themselves vulnerable to such bowling. There can be no doubt too that they and McDonald owed something, perhaps a lot, of their success to the lack of any bowler of comparable pace on the English side. The same effect has been seen repeatedly in Test series since the Second World War: the side that has true fast bowlers when the opposition has none is at such an enormous advantge that, in every Anglo-Australian series in which this disproportion has existed, it has always won. Miller and Lindwall, Frank Tyson, John Snow, Lillee and Thomson, have all successively won series for their sides. In the particular case of 1921, part of the English disadvantage probably arose from sheer lack of practice against bowlers of comparable pace; but there is not much doubt about another effect of such one-sided situations that has been noticed since, that fast bowlers who know their opponents lack the means of retaliation are more inclined to bowl bumpers than those who know that their own batsmen, and perhaps they themselves, will have to face a similar barrage when their turn comes. Their own batsmen can be relied upon to drive that point home, if they fail to see it for themselves. Nobody with an elementary knowledge of human nature will be surprised at this. Gregory and McDonald felt no such restraint: they reigned unchallenged over the English cricket scene in 1921, and (as the editor of *Wisden* noted in the passage quoted above) they would have been more than human if they had not taken advantage of it. But their example did mean that from then on the deliberate use of the bumper was a weapon that lay very close to the hands of other fast bowlers in similar circumstances.

Their thoughts were all the more likely to turn in this direction as a result of the way in which batting techniques were developing in the 1920s. Batting before the War had been first and foremost an art of aggression: batsmen were expected not merely to score runs, but to score them stylishly and to score them fast. There were of course exceptions, men like W. H. Scotton and R. G. Barlow, who made a virtue of sheer survival, but they stood out by their rarity. Indeed, the whole pace of the game was fast – far faster than nowadays. Deliberate time-wasting was virtually unheard-of: twenty overs an hour a normal rate of play, even with fast bowlers on: first-class matches, including Test Matches, were regularly completed in three days, though the run aggregates were no lower than they are now. In the 1920s all this changed. More and more batsmen concentrated on perfecting defensive techniques, and on run-getting based on accumulation rather than aggression. In the pre-1914 'Golden Age', bowlers had expected batsmen to 'go for them', and had placed their fields and plotted their length and line of attack accordingly: increasingly now they found these traditional strategies unrewarding, as batsmen more and more refused their baits, shouldered arms to anything of a fair length pitched outside the off stump, and were content to wait their time for the manifest long hop or half volley.

The reasons for the change, as for all such fundamental changes of style and attitude, go deep and are a field for speculation. One of the most important of them was that in the 1920s amateurism was beginning to lose its hold on the game. Although the traditional rigid taboos remained – the separate changing-rooms, the prefix 'Mr' and the initials printed on the score cards, the convention that a side must have an amateur captain* – they were being emptied of content. Amateurism, for one thing, was becoming 'shamateurism'. In the changed economic circumstances of the post-War world, a declining number of people could afford to spend four months of every year doing nothing but play cricket. Increasingly amateurs were having to work for their livings, which, except for the lucky few who could find exceptionally tolerant employers, meant either playing only occasionally (which inevitably weakened amateur control of the game – Jardine himself is a good example of this option), or finding a way of making a living out of cricket itself – by writing for the press, by becoming secretary of a county club, or whatever – which inevitably meant that the player's attitude to the game itself underwent a change. As amateur control weakened, so professional attitudes became more dominant; and for professionals the game was their living, and the first rule is that you do not do anything which may endanger your living. Time was when that meant playing the game in a way which appealed to its erstwhile aristocratic patrons; but in the 1920s, it increasingly meant your position in the averages – sheer runs scored or wickets taken, without regard to the elegance of the methods employed.

This typically professional attitude was reinforced by cricket's increasing financial dependence on its gate takings, and hence on the crowds who brought them – crowds whose vicarious involvement in the game was not primarily aesthetic or dilettante, but (especially at international level) fiercely combative: a demand for sheer results, a demand for victory, or at least avoidance of defeat. As Warner once said sadly to an Australian interviewer, 'Cricket has changed. It is Big Cricket now. The barracker, and those who stand shoulder to shoulder

---

* During the 1932–33 tour, Findlay, the MCC Secretary, expressed genteel distaste at the news that the amateur and professional members of the MCC party in Australia were on Christian name terms.

to him, pay the score. And consequently the barracker likes to call the tune.'

It seems to be a general law that professionalism in any game always takes the form of elimination of risk, of safety first – see (they tell me) modern soccer. Certainly this was the way that batting was going in the 1920s (and when at the end of the decade the onset of the Depression implanted in every professional's mind the knowledge that the alternative to scoring his thousand runs or taking his hundred wickets was the dole queue, the tendency naturally became all the stronger). The supremely gifted – Hammond, say – could afford to defy the trend, and bat as his predecessors had batted before 1914; but most could not afford it. This tendency in cricket was noted and deplored time and time again in the 1920s by those who had known the game before the War: Warner is one representative figure, but an even better one is Neville Cardus, whose cricket writings are shot through to such an extent with nostalgia for the golden age of pre-1914 cricket and laments over the decadence of the contemporary game that it is fair to call these their dominant motifs.

The cult of safety-first had a lot to do with the growing preference for back over forward play, which was one of the main features of first-class cricket in the 1920s. The increasing vogue of swing bowling had something to do with it too: with the ball moving more in the air, batsmen more and more wanted to commit themselves as late as possible and watch the ball right on to the bat, which pointed inevitably in the direction of playing off the back foot rather than the front. It also meant that to balls outside the off stump, they were less inclined to play a shot at all and more inclined to shoulder arms and let them go (the acknowledged master of this style of cricket was Phil Mead of Hampshire, one of the leading run-accumulators of the period, whose skill in judging whether a ball would miss the stumps by a couple of inches and hence could safely be left alone by all accounts approached the supernatural). Hence, the movement back across the stumps with the right foot as the ball left the bowler's hand had become instinctive with many batsmen – carried to extremes, this produced the 'two-eyed stance', the bane of the traditionally minded purists of the period, in which the batsman's chest was opened to the bowler so that he faced directly down the wicket, instead of facing cover-point and regrding the bowler over the left shoulder as tradition dictated. It was argued that the two-eyed stance robbed the game of its greatest beauties, by inhibiting all the classic off-side strokes, except perhaps the square cut, and indeed by making driving of any sort all but impossible. Fast bowlers were not normally aesthetes, but they regarded the matter from a more practical angle. This style of batting was making it increasingly difficult to hit the stumps, and, with all the traditional inhibitions against pad-play gone by the board, the LBW Law was no help, because it still bore the form it had taken in the days when the deliberate use of the pads was regarded as a form of sharp practice which no gentleman would countenance anyway. It still required, for a batsman to be given out, that the ball should have pitched on the wicket, should hit the batsman in front of the stumps ('between wicket and wicket' was the technical phrase), and of course would have hit the wicket if not so obstructed. These conditions are exorbitantly difficult to satisfy.

To this, of course, the obvious answer might seem to be a reform of the LBW Law, which had twice been attempted before the War, and there were not wanting in the 1920s those who said as much – within the MCC, R. H. Lyttelton in particular was indefatigable in urging the case for it. But throughout the 1920s the MCC resolutely set their face against the idea of such a change, perhaps because it might seem in some way to recognize and legitimize the change in batting style which traditionalists so much deplored. In the absence of such a change, however, bowlers – especially pace bowlers, the chief sufferers – were driven to seek a solution for themselves. If batsmen could stretch the conventions of the game in one direction, why should not bowlers stretch them in another? That solution took two forms – leg theory, and the increasing use of the bouncer. If batsmen were increasingly resorting to safety-first, negative tactics, concentrating less on scoring runs than on eliminating risks of getting out, very well, two could play at that game: let bowlers concentrate less on taking wickets than on making it as difficult as possible to score runs. If batsmen refused to incur risks by playing strokes outside the off stump, very well, take the risks to them by bowling bumpers to try to unsettle them (and the distance between 'unsettle' and 'intimidate' is not great). Maybe not many bowlers sat down at their drawing-boards and worked it out as directly as that; but it was the natural logic of the situation, and as the decade went on an increasing number of bowlers followed it.

Of the two strategies, leg theory at least had a coherent history going back before the War. Leg theory is a tiresomely elusive subject to discuss, because it covered a range of what were really very different methods of bowling. Its accepted meaning was any form of bowling which eschewed the traditional off-stump line and concentrated instead on the leg stump, or even outside it.* But this might apply to several very different strategies. In the nineteenth century, leg spinners seem commonly to have bowled on the leg stump or outside it, relying on catches in the deep and the reluctance of batsmen to make deliberate use of their pads to protect the stumps, and this was probably the earliest form of 'leg theory'; and it is also true that the idea of keeping attacking batsmen quiet by bowling on or outside the leg stump was exploited on occasions at least as early as the turn of the century. But

* The term 'leg theory' is in itself a tacit recognition of how it had come to be taken for granted that bowlers would naturally concentrate on an off-side attack. There is indeed something unnatural in any form of leg theory, in that the commonest form of bowling, right arm over the wicket, tends to slant to the leg side anyway, and a ball pitched on the leg stump, still more one pitched outside it, will therefore normally miss the wicket in any case.

the term seems first to have come into general use in the period between 1900 and the outbreak of the War, when it was used to describe the very different tactics of George Hirst and Frank Foster. Hirst and Foster were the first of the great fast left-handers. Both were inswingers: Hirst, indeed, is often reckoned to have been the first true swing bowler, if by that is meant the first man to rely primarily on the movement of the ball in the air to obtain his wickets (facing him with the new ball was said to be like trying to play a series of fast returns from cover). Both seem normally to have bowled round the wicket. With a left-arm inswinger bowling round the wicket, the normal legward slant of the ball is drastically accentuated: such bowling is bound to induce edges on the leg side rather than the off side, and the field has to be set accordingly. Frank Foster, when he went to Australia with Warner's team in 1911-12, bowled to a full-blown leg trap, three or four short legs clustered round the batsman in an arc from silly mid-on to leg slip, with another one or two men back on the fence behind them for the skied hook in case he dropped one short.

England won the rubber in 1911-12 by four matches to one, and the combination of Foster and the great and glowering Sidney Barnes is often quoted as the most formidable pair of bowlers England ever sent to Australia. But from our point of view it is Foster's methods rather than his success which concerns us, for in all the voluminous controversy that sprang out of Jardine's tour of 1932-33, no two precedents were as commonly invoked, especially on the English side, as Gregory's and McDonald's bowling in 1920-21 and Foster's in 1911-12. It is a parallel that Foster himself, as we have seen, indignantly denied. But there is no question that Foster gave leg theory a new meaning, nor that his field settings were almost identical with Jardine's placings for Larwood and Voce twenty years later. The very important differences lay in his line and his length. Foster insisted, and the evidence bears him out in the main, that he invariably bowled at the wicket, not at the batsman, and that he consistently bowled a full length. Even so, the record suggests that the element of physical menace was not entirely lacking from his bowling: bowling round the wicket, it is not surprising that he often swung into the pads, and, given the relatively flimsy nature of pre-War pads, being hit repeatedly even on the pads by Foster was evidently no joke. If not an 'express' bowler, as Larwood was, he nevertheless came off the wicket very fast indeed, and there is good contemporary evidence to suggest that the Australian batsmen found batting against him a painful experience and that his bowling aroused some critical comment on these grounds – a fact that explains his obvious sensitivity on the point as expressed both in his memoirs, published before the 1932–33 tour, and in the press during the tour when it was suggested that 'bodyline' owed a good deal to his own example and advice.

This, then, was a second form of 'leg theory', based on fast rather than slow bowling, and involving the use of a leg trap instead of the fast bowler's traditional cluster of slips. In the mid-1920s leg-theory was given a new twist by the appearance of Fred Root of Worcestershire. Root was remotely in the tradition of Hirst and Foster, but with two major differences: he was right-handed, and his pace was little if at all above medium. He was, of course, an inswinger, varying this with a ball that went the other way off the seam. He moved the ball a lot, and he was the first of a succession of fast-medium bowlers who flourished greatly up to the Second World War and after it, inswingers bowling a full length, pitching about off stump, hitting about middle and leg or passing just outside the leg stump, but aiming to get most of their wickets by catches in the two- or three-man leg trap. The idea was to force batsmen to play, but to move the ball far enough legward, i.e. outside the line of their bodies as they moved across the stumps, to make it difficult for them to get sufficiently over the ball in playing it to keep it safely on the ground. Root had sensational success when he first employed these tactics in the mid-1920s, and considerable success against the Australians with them in 1926: the trouble with them was that, with the LBW Law as it then was, it was almost impossible for a bowler of Root's type to get an LBW decision, and batsmen increasingly found that they could pad up to this kind of bowling and refuse to play a stroke at all with near-total impunity – another step in the direction of safety-first batting.

Leg theory could therefore mean a number of different things and different bowling strategies: it could refer to fast, medium-paced, or slow bowling (it could even be applied to off breaks bowled, Laker fashion, round the wicket to a leg trap), to inswingers tending from off to leg and to leg breaks tending from leg to off, to fundamentally aggressive and to fundamentally defensive styles of bowling, and to field settings based on a tight leg trap as much as to settings with no short legs at all. A term as vague as this was inevitably a fruitful source of confusion. What all these modes had in common was their eschewing of the traditional off-stump line, and that was about all that they had: though one might add that, anyway up to 1930, none of them was in any way intimidatory (this on the assumption that Foster's bowling of 1911–12 could not be classed as such).

But if one resort of bowlers frustrated by the batting styles of the 1920s was to leg theory, another, by the end of the decade, was to increasing use of the fast bumper. We have seen something of the prehistory of this, up to Gregory's and McDonald's bowling in England in 1921. Gregory and McDonald were probably at their fastest in that series, although both still had years of cricket ahead of them: Gregory played in both the 1924–25 and the 1926 series,* while McDonald left Australia to play as a professional for Lancashire with great success for the rest of the decade. But they had no immediate successors in either Australia or England of anything like their pace.

* Wyatt still remembers Gregory's first five balls going over his head in the Australians' match against 'An England XI' at Scarborough in 1926.

There were fast bowlers of course, but Gregory and McDonald had been more than fast bowlers: they both belonged to the much narrower and more elusive category of the *very* fast, the category which newspaper columnists of the 1920s dubbed 'express'. Australia, as the decade went on, came increasingly to depend upon the dynasty of great leg-spinners, Mailey, Grimmett and O'Reilly, who formed the mainspring of their attack until the second War. In England, the first true 'express' bowler of the inter-War period did not emerge until the appearance of the young Larwood in 1926; and from 1930 on, the England sides of the period came to depend as much upon pace, in the persons of Larwood himself, Voce, Allen, Bowes, Clark and Farnes, as the Australians did upon spin.

At the beginning of the period, though, fast bowling, for reasons already outlined, was a thankless task. The bowler of quite exceptional pace, like Larwood, might still be able to take wickets by the traditional methods; but most found that the combination of perfectly prepared batting wickets, increasingly defensive styles of batting involving the use of the pads as a second line of defence, and an LBW Law that was no help, made these methods increasingly unrewarding. Even Larwood found the going pretty hard in Australia in 1928–29, and in 1930 he was mercilessly put to the sword by the genius of the young Bradman. In these circumstances, it was no great wonder if some fast bowlers decided that the batsmen were having things too much their own way and looked to the bumper as a possible solution, a possible way to shock the batsman out of his composure: not so much as a means of getting him out directly maybe, but as a means of breaking his concentration, of inducing a careless or nervous shot at another ball; and there is no question that the use of the bumper was on the increase in the later 1920s.

At this point leg theory and the deliberate use of bumpers began to blur. The batsman's classic reply to the bumper is, of course, the hook – it will be recalled that as late as 1921,

Wisden drew no distinction between the intimidating bumper and the inept long hop, and when the 'bodyline' controversy was at its height in 1932–33, one stock gambit among the defenders of 'bodyline' was the assertion that the batsmen of the golden age would simply have hooked it out of sight.* But the hook is usually a lofted shot, and for a fast bowler deliberately basing his attack on the use of bumpers, the first and most obvious move was to put a man, or two men, back on the long leg boundary: once this was done, and given that the exact placing of a hook against a very fast bowler is almost impossible, hooking could be made prohibitively risky (although a batsman with fast footwork, a first-class eye, and the gods on his side, might still get away with it on occasion, as McCabe did spectacularly at Sydney in the first Test in 1932). This, nevertheless, was still fundamentally a defensive field setting: if a batsman did not choose to hook, he did not have to. The situation was different if a bowler shifted his line legward, to bowl at the batsman's body rather than his stumps, and if he simultaneously set a ring of close short legs, as well as two or three men back on the boundary behind them: if he then bowled three or four bumpers an over with the object of forcing the batsman to play a shot to protect himself and thus inducing catches in the leg-trap, this was 'bodyline'.

Whether this stage was actually reached before the English tour of Australia in 1932–33 is a matter of considerable controversy: what is not in doubt is that this was the way that fast bowling was tending around 1930. There have been various claims for the anticipation of 'bodyline' tactics before 1932 – most of them emanating from the pro-'bodyline' camp, since part of their case was the claim that they were doing nothing new. Much here though depends on the exact definition of 'bodyline'. If it

* According to the Australian fast bowler Ernest Jones, this was Grace's reaction to Jones' experiments with bumpers: 'I sends the first through his ruddy whiskers, and after that he keeps on hitting me for four off his blinkin' ear 'ole.'

means no more than fast short-pitched bowling purpose-fully directed on or about the line of the batsman's body, Larwood himself later* claimed to have bowled it as early as the Adelaide Test of 1928. It has also been claimed that Constantine bowled it for the West Indies during their tour of England in 1928, and during the English tour of the islands in 1929–30. The difficulty, fairly clearly, is one of definition: how many bumpers have to be bowled before the use of them can be described as 'systematic', and how far legward do they have to be directed before they can fairly be described as aimed at the body?

If it means fast short-pitched bowling bowled to a leg trap, the field is much more restricted: prior to the English season of 1932, the only notable experiment of this sort seems to have been in Australia, by Jack Scott of New South Wales against Victoria at Sydney in 1925, and the main lesson of this seems to have been one frequently reiterated by later experience, that bowling of this kind was liable to be both ineffective and very expensive unless it was very fast, directed with pinpoint accuracy, and bowled to a precisely set field.

But in spite of these references to the West Indies and to Australia, it was in England that the tendency to increasingly frequent and deliberate use of the fast bumper was most in evidence around 1930. This may have been simply because there were a lot of fast bowlers in England at the time: it probably owed more to the fact that in England alone was cricket a fully professional, six-days-a-week game, and consequently it was there that the pressures of professionalism and mass spectator interest were felt most intensely. In particular, the aggressive use of the bouncer came to be associated especially with three bowlers: Larwood, Voce and Bowes. It is no accident that all three were selected for the 1932–33 touring party to Australia, nor that two of them, Larwood and Voce, played

* In *The Larwood Story*, written in collaboration with Kevin Perkins and published in 1965.

for the same county, Nottinghamshire, under the captaincy of Arthur Carr.

The county ground at Nottingham was, of course, Trent Bridge, famed between the Wars for the superb quality of its wickets, and it is not very surprising if fast bowlers who had to spend half their seasons there were driven to try unorthodox tactics; but even more important than the quality of the Trent Bridge wicket was the quality of the county captain. Carr was rough and tough, and it is hard to avoid the impression that he enjoyed the reputation of being so. From 1930 on he had in Larwood and Voce far and away the most lethal pair of fast bowlers of any county in England. He was well aware of the fact, and of the advantage that it gave him, and he was not the man to forgo an inch of that advantage.

In view of later events, it is ironic that, of the three bowlers I have mentioned, Larwood was probably the one who had made least deliberate use of the bouncer before 1932. Being by some way the fastest of the three, and gifted with the ability to move the ball away from the bat in the air and bring it back sharply off the pitch, he was no doubt the one who had least need to. He was also the senior of them: born in 1904, he was five years older then Voce and four years older than Bowes, and his first-class career had begun as early as 1924, whereas Voce did not play his first county game until 1927, and Bowes not until 1929. Larwood had already played in three Test series against Australia by 1932. He was generally recognized as the finest fast bowler in England, as well as the fastest. But, although he certainly made the conventional occasional use of the bumper, and although any bumper bowled at his pace was bound to be a nasty proposition, he had never before 1932 been accused of going beyond the mark in his use of them, or of deliberate intimidation (this in spite of his own claim, already mentioned, to have resorted to fast short-pitched bowling on the leg side as early as the Adelaide Test of 1928).

His Nottinghamshire colleague, Voce, on the other

hand, had been associated with the use of the bouncer almost from the start of his career as a fast bowler. Voce did not start his professional career as a fast bowler at all. He was a left-hander, and it was as an orthodox slow left-hander that he first joined the county staff in 1927. *Fast* left-handers have always been rather rare birds: in England in particular, most of them get firmly pushed by their coaches in their youth into the strait tradition of the classic slow left-hander, the finger-spinner bowling round the wicket to an off-side field – the tradition of Rhodes, of Verity and of Lock. Voce started his career as a bowler of this type; but in 1928 he changed his style, and it soon became apparent that as a fast bowler he was going to be a formidable proposition, particularly in combination with Larwood – it was another example, like Gregory and McDonald, of a fast bowler's effectiveness being immensely enhanced by the companionship of another bowler of similar pace at the opposite end.

The Larwood-Voce combination was particularly effective because their methods, as distinct from their pace, were in strong contrast. Larwood, of course, was an extremely fast right-hander, bowling over the wicket and generally moving the ball away from the bat in the air (though no bowler as fast as he was moves it much – or needs to). Voce, a bigger, burlier man than Larwood, was not as fast as Larwood, but a genuine fast bowler rather than fast-medium, though perhaps not quite in the 'express' category. He was an inswinger – in the tradition, therefore, of Hirst and Foster, but unlike them bowling over the wicket as much as round it.* His line, therefore, was very different from Larwood's, and straighter than Hirst's and Foster's. This may have made it more difficult for him to get an inside edge, but it gave him a better chance of LBW decisions and also made it harder for the

* It is surprisingly difficult to get precise information on this point, since commonly neither scorebooks nor press accounts throw any light on it; but it does appear that during the 1932–33 tour at least the bulk of his bowling was done over it.

batsman to keep out of trouble by moving inside the line. Naturally enough for a bowler of his type, he bowled to a close-set leg trap – in other words, he was a practitioner of 'leg theory' in the same sense as Foster. From the first, too, he seems to have made a good deal of use of the bouncer – for instance, in Nottinghamshire's match against the 1930 Australians.

Voce had gone to the West Indies with the England touring team the previous winter, and had done well enough there to be a candidate for a place in the England team for the 1930 Tests against Australia. Omitted from the team for the first two Tests, he had his chance to show what he could do when the Australians came to play Notts before the third Test. He gave Jackson, Kippax and McCabe a very rough time indeed, hitting them on the body repeatedly, and though he faded later in the match and did not in fact play for England that summer, he left the Australians with an abiding impression of how nasty a proposition he could be.

Voce's line was such that he was in any case bound to be bowling very close to the batsman's body. To that extent, it might be argued that the increasing use of bumpers was an especially strong temptation for him. Certainly the sort of method he adopted against the Australians at Nottingham in 1930 brought him to the very brink, by the strictest definition, of what was later to be called 'bodyline': if it still fell short of it, it was only because, apart from the leg trap, he was still bowling to a field divided in orthodox fashion between the two sides of the wicket.

Bowes, the third of the trio, was a different proposition again. Bowes was a gangling, six-foot-three-inch Yorkshireman: his bowling in 1932 did much to help Yorkshire win the county championship that year, and made a profound impression on English cricketing opinion in doing so. But he had been brought up in the hard school of north of England cricket, where the ethical niceties of the amateur-dominated cricket of the South had never been given much shrift, and in view of the way things were going in English cricket in the 1930s it is not surprising that he soon decided that the bumper was the weapon to cultivate. Although he lacked extreme pace, his great height made an adequate substitute, enabling him to make the ball lift from short of a length on any but the most placid of wickets in very ugly fashion indeed. In the seasons of 1931 and 1932 he made a name for himself by the freedom with which he used the bumper: he hit a lot of batsmen and took a lot of wickets, attracting a good deal of unfavourable comment in the process.

In Bowes' bowling, the distinction between the regular use of the bumper and leg theory in any of its forms was still clear: he relied largely on the outswinger, he did not reckon to bowl down the leg side, and he did not employ a leg trap. But not only did he threaten life and limb of the batsmen opposed to him, he also trod on a lot of prestigious toes in the process. There was a famous confrontation at the Oval in the Surrey v Yorkshire match of August 1932. Bowling to Hobbs, the grand old man of English cricket, then in his fiftieth year and at the end of his career, he repeatedly bumped the ball head-high to him. Hobbs had been brought up in the school of pre-1914 cricket, when fast bowlers did not do these things. He did not like it, and he protested gently in the batsman's traditional way, coming down the pitch pointedly to pat a spot about two-thirds of the way to the bowler's wicket. 'Not there,' said Bowes, 'here' – pointing to a spot behind the bowler's wicket – and equally typical of the unflinching Yorkshire approach to the game was the comment of George Macaulay, Yorkshire's notoriously tigerish fast-medium bowler: 'Give him another.' (In view of what was to come, the significance of the incident was greatly increased by the fact that the Surrey captain was Jardine, and that Warner was watching the game as correspondent for the *Morning Post*.) Nor did the incident end there. Bowes went on bowling his bumpers, amid noisy protests from the Surrey crowd, who shouted for him to be taken off; and how high feelings had mounted was shown when Macaulay, bowling to Jardine in the course of an obdurate innings of 35 which lasted three hours, delivered two fast full tosses straight at his head. As a demonstration in miniature of how quickly and dangerously intimidatory fast bowling could change the whole temper of a game, it could hardly be bettered.

Warner, that epitome of the cricketing ethics of the golden age before 1914, had not liked what he had seen; and he said so outspokenly in his report for the *Morning Post* in an article which was repeatedly and embarrassingly to be quoted against him in Australia in the course of the next twelve months. The gist of it was taken up and elaborated further in an article that appeared the following week in the *Cricketer*, the leading (indeed, practically the only) cricket periodical of the inter-War period. Warner was the editor of the *Cricketer*,* but the article in question was not by him, but by the *Cricketer*'s leader-writer, 'Second Slip', who was in fact a former captain of Cambridge, Frank Mitchell. Mitchell's views and values nevertheless closely echoed Warner's, on most occasions as on this one. Of Bowes' performance at the Oval he said:

> That *is not bowling*: indeed, it is *not cricket*, and if all the fast bowlers were to adopt his methods there would be trouble and plenty of it. Bowes is a fine natural bowler ... but he would be a far better bowler if he concentrated on length and cut out all the short stuff.
>
> He is not doing justice to himself, to his ability, or to the game of cricket by such methods ... I am a great admirer of Yorkshire cricket. We all love their keenness and the zest with which they play, but they will find themselves a very unpopular side – if there is a repetition of last Saturday's methods.

There was a veiled threat in the last sentence whose point was to be keenly felt by Nottinghamshire, if not by

---

* A post whose compatibility with his membership of the MCC's Selection Committee at this time was sometimes questioned.

Yorkshire, in two years' time. This, unmistakably, was the voice of the traditional pedigreed cricketing Establishment of the South: there is even the appeal to the final unanswerable, because indefinable, criterion of the traditionally acceptable – Bowes' type of bowling was 'not cricket'. Bowes might reasonably have answered that, if it was *not* cricket, it was rapidly becoming so. Yet it would be a great mistake to dismiss the article as nothing more than a blimpish appeal to the supposed standards of a vanished past. If he re-read his article a year later, 'Second Slip' might have taken legitimate pride in the accuracy of his foresight, for in it he put his finger on at least one of the central objections to 'bodyline', the bad feeling that the use of it undeniably bred, whether in players or in spectators. There was indeed trouble and plenty of it, and in Australia England did indeed find themselves a very unpopular side.

Bowes' bowling in that match at the Oval brought controversy momentarily to a head, but it is clear that he was doing little, if anything, more than other fast bowlers were increasingly doing in 1932. Indeed, 'Second Slip's' article evoked a letter which appeared in the *Cricketer* a fortnight later which said as much: the writer, while not defending Bowes' methods, pointed out that he was far from being the only offender, referring to McDonald's bowling *against* Yorkshire themselves in the recent 'Roses' match, when Oldroyd was seriously injured by one of his bumpers, and also, significantly, to Larwood's and Voce's recent bowling against Worcestershire, when several Worcestershire batsmen had to retire to have their injuries attended to. However, in his suggested remedy, where Warner and Mitchell had appealed to the traditional ethics of the game, this correspondent was more robustly old-fashioned: he claimed that the remedy lay with the batsmen, who should hook this sort of bowling out of sight – as, according to him, their pre-War predecessors would have done. We have already come across this view, that the intensive use of bumpers was not so much ethically wrong as technically inept, and that if it succeeded, that fact was an indictment of the standards of contemporary batsmanship; and we shall come to it again.

However, I have said enough to show the point that the technical development of cricket, and specifically of the styles of batting and fast bowling, had reached by 1932. We have seen how the changing styles of batsmanship, taken together with the limitations of the existing LBW Law, were forcing bowlers in general, and fast bowlers in particular, to change their tactics, and how this change was accelerated by the weakening hold of the game's traditional amateur upper class patrons, and the increasing dominance in the game of the influence of money, of professionalism and of the mass gate-paying public. We have seen what this meant in practice – an increasing resort to 'leg theory' in its various forms, and an increasing resort to the deliberate and systematic use of the bouncer; and by 1932 the two tendencies were converging, most conspicuously perhaps in the bowling of Voce. What all this amounts to – I think – is that by 1932 first-class cricket had reached a stage where 'bodyline' was a natural next step. It was not an *inevitable* next step – in particular it was not inevitable that it should be adopted in the exact time and circumstances in which it was in fact first seen – but it would have been unthinkable (neither Jardine nor anybody else would have dreamed it up) if fast bowling had *not* been developing in the way it had. However, the changes in the methods of fast bowling had come about so far almost entirely as a matter of instinctive adaptation by bowlers themselves. For intimidation to be adopted as a deliberate strategy directed to a precisely placed field, and consistently adhered to, by a decision on the part of a captain, was something new: something for which the pressures of international cricket were a necessary condition. We have seen how the technology, if one can call it that, essential to 'bodyline' was evolved: it is time now to turn to the evolution of its theory and its psychology, and to the very remarkable man through whom that evolution was brought to its climax.

CHAPTER 6

The Origins of Bodyline

Jardine

Douglas Jardine was born in 1900 in Bombay, where his father, himself a distinguished cricketer who had scored a century in the Varsity Match, was a barrister at the Bombay Bar. It does not seem to me too fanciful to trace the origin of some of the younger Jardine's most marked characteristics in later life to that background: the sharply legalistic turn of mind, the unquestioning sense of the membership of a ruling elite coupled, unavoidably, with a hint of patronage and contempt when dealing with the other peoples of the Empire. Nor was an education at the Winchester and Oxford of that epoch likely to do much to eradicate such characteristics. Jardine's angularity of character was early apparent: it was probably the main explanation for his failure to cap a distinguished cricket career at both school and university by being elected to captain Oxford.

There is no question of Jardine's cricketing ability. At Oxford he averaged 33.64 for his four years in the side; in 1921 he scored 96 not out in the University's match against Armstrong's all-conquering Australians, his first encounter with them.* After coming down from Oxford, limited

---

*It has indeed been said that this match was the origin of his unrelenting conviction that no gloves were to be worn in contests with the Australians. Armstrong had insisted that the fixtures immediately preceding the Test Matches in 1921 should be curtailed to give his side a

financial means prevented him playing regularly for his county, Surrey (one more sign of the growing financial pressures on amateurism in the 1920s). But in 1927 and 1928 he headed the English batting averages with figures of 91.09 and 87.15 and in 1928 he made 193 for the Gentlemen against the Players and was selected for two of the Tests against the West Indies. It is not surprising that that year he achieved the coveted distinction of being selected by *Wisden* as one of its five 'Cricketers of the Year'. 'As with all really sound batsmen,' the accompanying commentary read, 'fast bowling possesses no terrors for him' – a remark full of significance in view of later events, and one which probably echoes the increasingly intimidatory nature of fast bowling at the time. It went on to describe him as 'the most reliable of amateur batsmen', and added that 'provided he can spare the time, nothing appears more likely than that he will be in the next team that visits Australia'.

Jardine, a tall man, was a fine upright batsman in the classic mould, playing very straight in defence. In his early years he scored his runs at a fair pace as well, though there was always a streak of obduracy and of concentration bordering on grimness in him: he was never the happy warrior type so glorified in amateur tradition. Predominantly a firm right-foot man, he was in particular, as *Wisden* noted, a magnificent player of fast bowling. Against the spinners he was never as happy, the limitations of his footwork finding him out – a weakness that explains his

proper rest before the Tests, and with his accustomed obduracy carried his point, not without a good deal of resentment on the part of the MCC. The result of this was that the game against Oxford was reduced to two days, and at the close of the second day the Australians refused to bowl the extra over or two that would have given Jardine the chance of achieving the rare feat of an undergraduate scoring a century against them. The incident was minor enough (and there is much to be said for the Australian attitude that once you have fixed a time for drawing stumps, you should stick to it); but it is not hard to see that in a tenacious memory it might rankle.

relatively poor batting performance in Australia in 1932–33.

As *Wisden* had predicted, he went to Australia in 1928–29 with Chapman's side, and did very well there: he scored three successive centuries in state matches and played in all five Tests, making 98 in the fourth Test at Adelaide, where he and Hammond set up a new record for England's third wicket against Australia. But if the tour was a success for him in cricketing terms, socially it was somewhat less happy. Jardine and Australian cricketing public seemed to have been designed by nature to fall foul of each other. Jardine was every inch the pedigreed upper-class Englishman, a type that has been mocked, satirized, and resented in about equal measure in Australia ever since the demotic strain in Australian culture came to the fore late in the nineteenth century. His batting looked like that, and he made a point of wearing the badges of his class: the famous Harlequin cap and the white silk choker. It was not that these things were necessarily damning in themselves: as always, a great deal depended on the style. Chapman sometimes wore a club cap on the field, and his popularity in Australia was totally unaffected by it; but Chapman was a genial, hail-fellow-well-met extrovert, confident and easygoing, a personality at the opposite end of the spectrum from Jardine's. There is a story, which is at least *ben trovato*, of an Australian battalion arriving in Egypt in 1915, prior to going to Gallipoli, and being placed under an English commanding officer who appeared before them on the parade ground wearing a monocle (surely the precise equivalent of Jardine's choker?). Next morning the entire battalion appeared on parade with a penny in one eye. The Englishman surveyed the scene without comment, took out his monocle, threw it up in the air, and caught it perfectly in his eye. 'How many of you chaps can do that?' he enquired, and from then on, all his problems were over.

Jardine was not like that. He could not unbend (the rigidity was even physical: you can sense it in the photographs of him), and it is evident that he returned from the Australian tour in 1929 with an abiding resentment of the Australian cricketing public, and above all of the 'barracker', whose wit and abuse, exercised at his expense in the outfield, he had taken in the back without a muscle twitching in his face – as he took that blow on the hip from Alexander in the last Test in 1933 – but which had entered deep, and festered, and for which Australia would have to pay in due course. If he had acquired an abiding resentment of the spirit in which Australian cricketers approached the game from his encounter with them in 1921, he added to this a perhaps even deeper resentment of the spirit in which Australian spectators watched it in 1928–29: a dangerous combination.

Jardine played comparatively little first-class cricket in the next two years, due to his professional commitments, and played in none of the 1930 Tests against Australia. But an unexpected turn of events in 1931 brought him sharply back into the limelight. As has been mentioned earlier, England's Test Match record since 1930 had been undistinguished, to the discontent of the public and the growing disturbance of the MCC, especially with the prospect of sending a team to Australia in 1932–33 to confront Bradman on his own wickets looming ahead. For the 1931 season, the MCC appointed a new Selection Committee of Warner, P. A. Perrin of Essex and T. A. Higson of Lancashire, and to reconstruct the England side that committee turned to Jardine as captain. It was in many ways a surprising choice, for Jardine's previous experience of captaincy had been slight – as we have seen, he had not captained Oxford, and he did not captain Surrey until 1932 (and then, effectively, only for one season) – and, in view of later events, it is highly ironical that his chief advocate on the committee seems to have been Warner. But if what the Selection Committee were looking for was an acute cricketing brain, combined with a natural authority and a total concentration on the task in hand, they had chosen the right man, for Jardine had all these characteristics, and, moreover, was a highly credible candidate for a place in the

England side on his merits as both a batsman and a close-to-the-wicket fieldsman. Although he had not yet captained Surrey, he had had the advantage of playing in the Surrey side for several years under P. G. H. Fender, a personal friend and, in the opinion of many contemporary observers, the possessor of the sharpest cricketing mind in the country – a man whom many thought should himself have been selected to captain England in the 1920s. Jardine proceeded to justify his appointment by leading England successfully to victory against both New Zealand in 1931 and India in 1932 – not that the opposition was of the highest quality in either case.

There was a revealing glimpse of his characteristics as a captain in the Lord's Test against India. Lord's, notoriously, had, until a few years ago, no sightscreen at the pavilion end because it would obstruct the view from the pavilion. During the England innings, Jardine had noticed the difficulty of picking up full tosses against the background (since full tosses are faster on to a batsman than good-length balls, and, unlike them, cannot be sighted against the grass), and, when England took the field, he astonished his fast bowlers, Voce and Bowes, by instructing them to bowl full tosses. Both, according to Bowes, jibbed at it. There is no reason to think that Jardine meant them to bowl *high* full tosses – beamers – deliberately aimed at the batsmen, like the two Macaulay was to bowl at Jardine himself at The Oval later in the season – but both Bowes and Voce apparently felt that to bowl full tosses deliberately was stretching the ethics of the game a bit far (or was it just that a full toss offended their professional pride in the same way as a string out of tune might offend the professional pride of a violinist?). The incident anyway is doubly characteristic of Jardine – characteristic, that is, both of the acuteness of his observation of the game, and of his belief that cricket, or at any rate Test cricket, was meant to be played hard.

In any case, Jardine's performances in these two series left the selectors in no doubt that he was the man to take the MCC team to Australia in the winter of 1932–33. Though the appointment was in general well received, their confidence was not universally shared. Rockley Wilson, Jardine's old cricket master at Winchester, who had himself toured Australia with the 1920–21 side, is reputed to have said that Jardine might win the Ashes, but lose the Empire; and Ernest Crutchley, the British Representative in Australia, whose later role in the controversy we have seen, made an exceptionally perceptive comment in his diary one night on board the *Orontes* on the voyage out after a dinner at which the MCC party had been present: 'There was much good speechifying but nothing said of any note. The usual stuff about the Test Team being ambassadors of Empire. I wonder! If the crowd are as hostile to Jardine as they have been in the past I can see anything but good coming of the visit.'

But these doubts were confined to a very small minority: Warner himself demonstrated his faith in Jardine by agreeing to go with the team as joint manager. In view of what was to follow, one must assume that the Selection Committee had less than perfect understanding of the man they were sending. They had a correct appreciation of Jardine's talents – they clearly wanted a hard captain, and they had got one – but not of his limitations.

What the state of fast bowling was in England in 1932 we have already seen: the time has come now to assess Jardine's thinking. It was, after all, in a way paradoxical that it should be Jardine who masterminded the adoption of 'bodyline'. That 'bodyline', as it was bowled in Australia by Larwood and Voce in 1932–33, was at odds with the ethics and aesthetics of the game, at least in their more traditional, conservative and high-minded forms, seems to me to be not worth disputing now (whether it was as much at odds with the way that ethic had been developing since 1918 may be another question). But if there was one country in the world where the game was dominated by a cricketing Establishment in whose mind the traditional ethic was still dominant, that country was England: so one would think, and so most contemporaries undoubtedly thought at the time. Most people – certainly most Englishmen – if asked before 1932 whether England or Australia were more likely to adopt a method of attack based on intimidatory fast bowling would doubtless have plumped for Australia, remembering Gregory and McDonald and reflecting that this sort of thing was to be expected of a crew of colonial roughnecks, but certainly not of a country where cricket was still under the control of the aristocratic and tradition-dominated MCC. And surely it was least of all to be looked for from a team captained by so seemingly typical a figure of the English Establishment as Douglas Jardine.

That this analysis would have been wrong is now obvious: why was it wrong? Perhaps it is in any case mistaken to suppose that cricket's traditional ethos was more deeply rooted in England than in Australia: nobody could have subscribed to it more wholeheartedly than Woodfull, and a short course in the novels of Henry James might be in order to remind us that simple high-mindedness may be a more typical product of young (dare I add colonial?) cultures than of metropolitan ones. It is also true, and should be sufficiently obvious after what was said in the last chapter, that the fact that cricket in England was a six-day-a-week professional sport, rather than a week-end, mainly amateur one as it was in Australia, had already made it in some ways a harder and more ruthless game than its Australian equivalent. But to a very great extent the explanation of how England came to use 'bodyline' must be looked for in Jardine's mind and temperament.

Jardine's character is readily recognizable as that of a very sensitive, intensely inward man who hid his sensitivity behind a hard and brittle surface. An upbringing in Anglo-India, and still more at Winchester in the second decade of the twentieth century, could be guaranteed to teach him not to wear his heart upon his sleeve. This was equally true of all his contemporaries, but Jardine was unusual in being very sensitive and very proud, easily hurt, but ready to do anything rather than admit it. A trait that comes out in many of the stories about Jardine is the seemingly impassive and impenetrable surface that made the more bewildering his sudden changes of attitude: what was passing in his mind and his mood was his own secret, to be revealed only at the moment when he felt like it and (so many of the stories suggest) with a timing which guaranteed its maximum effect (his refusal to announce his team selections until the last minute is typical).

This armour which both protected and concealed the natural self within was no doubt a necessity to him, but the trouble with it was that it did not prevent the shafts entering – it merely denied the archer the satisfaction of knowing that he had hit. Hence the sort of mutually escalating exasperation that set in between Jardine and the Australian crowds: the crowds more and more enraged by Jardine's seeming indifference, Jardine bitterly resenting their barracking, but all the more determined not to show it. It comes out well in a story that Larwood tells about him in the climactic third Test at Adelaide: the England team came off the field at the end of the Australian first innings (in which Woodfull and Oldfield had both been hurt) to a very hostile reception by the crowd, and Jardine's response, according to Larwood, was, 'Listen to the bastards yelling. I think I'll go in myself and give the bastards something to yell at' – and he then deliberately chose his brightest Harlequin cap to go out in, knowing that it would anger the crowd still more.*

That Jardine felt bitterness is clear enough: unfortunately, the price that he paid for his pride, for his determination never to show his critics that they hurt him, was that he was never able to come to terms with the bitterness, to confront it and control it – instead, it controlled him. Jardine was fatally disqualified as the captain of a touring team in Australia because he went out

---

*It is a pity to spoil a good story, but it is only fair to point out that Jardine had already opened with Sutcliffe in the first innings. Still, the words may well have been spoken as Larwood reports them.

there in 1932 with a deeply implanted resentment of the Australians already rankling within him. It is easy to criticize fifty years after the event, but it is nevertheless true that if the MCC Selection Committee knew as much, they should never have appointed him; and perhaps they should have known. It is also true that Jardine, feeling as he did, should not have accepted the invitation. He did in fact at first show no enthusiasm for it – whether for this reason or another there is no evidence – and had to be persuaded into it by his father; but in any case, I have just said that Jardine was never able to look his bitterness in the face and recognize it, and if that was the case, he could not be expected to realize how fatally it unfitted him for the job. On the way out to Australia, he took most of the team aside individually to tell them that the only way to beat the Australians was to hate them. Even if this was deliberate exaggeration, such an attitude was hardly a recommendation for a job which was supposed to include that of an ambassador of Empire.

Jardine therefore came to the task of selecting the team and considering his tactics for Australia with a resentment simmering within him which from the outset made it unlikely that the softer amenities of the game would weigh very much with him; but there were other aspects of his character which pointed the same way as well. He was never one of the moral idealists of the game, as Warner and Woodfull were, men for whom those softer amenities I have just mentioned were the very essence of the game itself. Nor was he one of the aesthetes, like Cardus. His recent experience had been under Fender, a captain for whom the game was, above all, a contest, to be fought hard and with unbuttoned foils. This approach was a natural one for Jardine too; and to it he added a lawyer's mind, inherited perhaps from his father and reinforced by his own legal training. In Fender, the sharpness of his mind was only one aspect of a free, balanced and warmly human personality; in Jardine, the mind was acute, detached and cold, as a lawyer's mind needs to be, facing the tactical

166

decisions of the cricket field with the rigid self-sufficient logic of the solicitor interpreting a statute, and with as little regard for extraneous considerations.

Jardine was not inhuman. He was a fond husband and father, and, if not a man of many friends, he was very close to the friends he had. But there is always something a little inhuman about the workings of a legal mind, its ability to abstract and isolate, to consider problems in detachment from their human setting, to draw sharp black-and-white distinctions. It was that kind of mind that Jardine had and that he brought to the consideration of cricket. Insofar as cricket is a contest fought according to a set of artificial rules, it made him a superb captain; insofar as it is a form of human social activity, a very inadequate one. It is not that Jardine was given to sharp practice, and he was punctilious on the traditional courtesies of the game: in the first match against New South Wales in 1932, when Oldfield was injured (nothing to do with 'bodyline' on this occasion) he earned much favourable comment by allowing the New South Wales reserve wicketkeeper, Love, to replace him behind the stumps, although he was not even the official twelfth man.

But 'bodyline' was not like that – the whole issue of intimidatory fast bowling had always been fluid and undefined: different men had had very different notions here of what was cricket and what was not, and moreoever, as we have seen, the notions themselves had changed considerably with time. It was in areas like this, where there was wide room for honest difference of opinions, that Jardine felt free to give the ruthless lgoic of his mind free scope; and he expected his opponents to do as much in return.

There is no doubt that, in laying his plans for the MCC tour of Australia in 1932, Jardine was faced by an exceptionally difficult problem – perhaps indeed he has never been given due intellectual credit for solving it, as solve it he undeniably did. The Australian batting triumphs of the 1930 series, the threat above all of Bradman, loomed most ominously over the coming series, and, as we saw in the first chapter, it was anything but clear where England might look to find the answer to it. After his successes in the 1928 series, several influential English commentators – Fender notable among them – had claimed that there were flaws in Bradman's technique which would find him out on English wickets and which would prevent him succeeding there. Criticism of this sort Bradman invariably took as a personal challenge, and his reply to it in 1930 could not have been more crushing – 974 runs in seven Test innings, at an average of 139.14: overall, 2,960 runs at an average of 98.66. If he could do that on alien wickets, what would he do in 1932–33 on his own?

It was above all this problem that Jardine had to solve: what to do about Bradman, to stop him winning the series for Australia off his own bat (and Australia had an imposing batting side even apart from him – Woodfull, Ponsford, Kippax, McCabe, and so on). The most minute observation had detected at most two tiny cracks in Bradman's mastery in the summer of 1930. On wearing wickets, he had shown some fallibility against the leg-spinners, R. W. V. Robins getting him out cheaply in the second innings at Lord's, and Ian Peebles causing him some embarrassment in the fourth Test at Old Trafford. But Robins, although invited, could not come on the 1932 tour, and Peebles had lost a lot of his form and was not invited. In any case, to judge by the experience of the 1928 tour, Australian wickets were practically everlasting. England did take two leg-spinners to Australia in 1932, Tom Mitchell of Derbyshire and the young Freddy Brown; but from the way he handled them out there, it is clear that Jardine cannot have put much faith in their potentialities (and indeed no English leg-spinner has ever achieved very much in Australia to this day, except when Bosanquet first baffled them with his newly invented googly in 1903–04).

The other hint of a possible weakness in Bradman was an even slimmer one: for a short time in Australia's second innings at the Oval in the final Test Bradman and the other young batting discovery of the tour, Archie Jackson, had had to face Larwood and Tate on a wicket lively after rain. Several observers, Larwood among them, thought that it was apparent that Bradman did not like it, and often backed away to leg, whereas Jackson* played it with no sign of fear. Not by any means all observers thought so, and the facts are still disputed; but, rightly or wrongly, some *had* drawn the conclusion that Bradman might have a weakness against top-class fast bowling that was lifting at all sharply. The rub of it was, of course, that rain-affected wickets were even rarer in Australia than they were in England.† It should be understood too that there had been no suggestion at all that Larwood's and Tate's bowling at the Oval that day had made anything but perfectly fair use of the conditions: they had not crowded the batsmen with short legs, and they had not bowled bumpers (and indeed they had not got either batsman out). They had certainly not anticipated 'bodyline'.

I have been told by Jardine's daughter that it was the experience of watching a film of that episode that planted the seed of the idea of 'bodyline' in his mind – 'I've got it,' he is supposed to have said, 'he's yellow.' The story is characteristic of Jardine, and whether it is true or not it is clear in retrospect that Jardine decided early to build his attack in Australia round his fast bowlers, and decided too that he wanted the Nottinghamshire pair, Larwood and Voce, as its spearhead. Both were natural decisions: fast bowling was a field in which England unquestionably had the edge over Australia in the early 1930s. Larwood was acknowledged as the finest fast bowler in England, and Voce had amply shown in numerous county matches how dangerous he was in combination with Larwood and had himself played successfully for England in three Test series (though never against the Australians, and never yet in

* Who, incidentally, was to send Larwood a telegram of congratulation on his bowling in the Adelaide Test from his deathbed.
† It is important to bear in mind that between the Wars the wicket was not covered once the match had begun.

joint harness with Larwood). But fast bowling in itself was no answer to Bradman: everything depended on how it was used. Jardine was the last man not to give full consideration to this in advance. He was an acute and precise tactical thinker and it is clear that during August and September 1932, as he, together with the MCC Selection Committee, was working out the composition of the touring party, he took enormous pains to work out the tactics he would use in Australia. To guide him in that choice of bowling tactics, there were several things which pointed in similar, if not the same, directions: the growing tendency of batsman to concentrate on back play in order to get in line with the ball; the increasingly aggressive use of bumpers by bowlers like Voce and Bowes; and the brief period of Bradman's apparent discomfort at the Oval. There were also reports which reached him from Australia via Fender that the Australian batsmen were increasingly favouring the technique of playing fast bowling off the back foot and of moving across their wickets as they did so, with the object of directing most of their shots to the relatively lightly guarded leg side. The question is exactly what conclusions Jardine drew from these data, and exactly how far, before leaving England, he had pursued them.

In most accounts of the 'bodyline' affair, a central place in the evolution of 'bodyline' is given to a famous dinner at the Piccadilly Hotel grill-room in early August 1932 at the end of the traditional Surrey *v* Notts Bank Holiday fixture at the Oval. The party consisted of Jardine, the Notts captain Carr, and his two fast bowlers, Larwood and Voce, and it has often been supposed that it was there that what came to be called 'bodyline' was first discussed. Carr himself, as we have seen, realizing the uniquely formidable weapon he possessed in Larwood and Voce, had already appreciated and to some extent developed the aggressive use of deliberate short-pitched bowling – especially by Voce – but Carr never approached Jardine as a clear analytic thinker about the game. The classic account of what transpired at the dinner is Larwood's, as related to Kevin Perkins in 1965:

> Jardine asked me if I thought I could bowl on the leg stump, making the ball come up into the body all the time so that Bradman had to play his shots to leg ... We thought Don was frightened of sharp-rising balls and we reasoned that if he got a lot of them over the leg stump he would be put off his game *and intimidated* [my italics], and eventually, having to direct his shots to leg all the time, would give a catch to one of the onside fieldsmen.

Larwood's account of the conversation is of interest in several ways: he also says that he did not at the time think of the tactics that Jardine was suggesting as being anything very new, having in mind Root's bowling and also Voce's habitual methods. Larwood's account of the whole 'bodyline' affair in *The Larwood Story*, the book that he wrote with Perkins, is admirably frank and fair-minded (which is more than can be said of the literary contributions to the controversy of some of the other participants in it). For instance, he makes no bones about the fact that 'bodyline' was conceived of originally as a means of curbing Bradman (though he adds that Jardine did suggest at the dinner that, if it worked against Bradman, it might be worth trying it against the other Australian batsmen as well). There seems to me no reason at all to doubt that his account of the meeting and the conversation is frank and substantially correct. Yet we have to remember that it was written thirty-three years after the event: there must at least be a possibility that Larwood's recollections were affected by his memories of what actually happened on the tour. And, even apart from that, there are points in his description of what Jardine said that bear finer examination.

It is worth noting first of all that Larwood was to be the principal executor of the strategy. This, of course, tends to be a feature of first-person accounts; but here it accords exactly with the facts. Larwood was much the more experienced fast bowler than Voce: he knew Australian conditions at first hand, and throughout the series it was Larwood who was to be viewed by the Australians as the incarnation of 'bodyline' bowling, and its real cutting edge – a judgement amply born out by the English bowling analyses. Voce was an invaluable second, but he was a second. But what exactly was it that Jardine was asking of Larwood?

The most interesting point here is that it certainly does not sound like a barrage of bumpers. Bowling 'on the leg stump, making the ball come up into the body all the time'; 'sharp-rising balls'; 'if he got a lot of them over the leg stump he would be put off his game and intimidated, and eventually, having to direct his shots to leg all the time, would give a catch to one of the onside fieldsmen'. There is no mention of length, no direct mention even of a leg trap: the emphasis is on line and lift. The ball is to rise higher than the leg stump, certainly, but on an Australian wicket a bowler of Larwood's pace would need to bowl very little short of a length to achieve that; it is to be directed at the body; it is designed to intimidate, and to confine Bradman to leg-side shots; the eventual objective is to get him caught on the leg side. It sounds as though what Jardine had in mind was bowling just short of a length coming up hip- or chest-high, but certainly not head-high: not short enough to hook, and, by its direction at the body, confining the batsman to cramped defensive pushes on the leg side, with the accompanying risk of giving catches to close-set fieldsmen. It is very probable that Jardine's intention in the first place was largely defensive – to deprive Bradman of the brilliant range of attacking shots which he had displayed to such devastating effect in England in 1930 – as much as to get him out.

It does not emerge from Larwood's account whether there was much talk about field placings on this occasion, although it is obvious that the type of bowling discussed would require a predominantly leg-side field. The heavy concentration of fieldsmen on the leg – often seven of them

– was to become one of the chief defining characteristics of the 'bodyline' attack; and this is very typical of the clarity of Jardine's thinking, his insistence on following a chain of reasoning through to its logical conclusion. Both he and Fender insisted on the importance of a fielding side *concentrating* its attack – in Australia especially, where conditons generally were weighted so heavily in favour of the batsman. This meant bowling to a particular length and line with such accuracy that a batsman's shots were necessarily restricted to one limited area of the field – and Larwood's extreme accuracy was one of the characteristics that made him particularly suitable for Jardine's purposes – and then setting a field to block these shots with equal accuracy. Bowes still remembers Jardine's insistence on the absolute necessity of concentrating *either* on off or on leg theory in Australia for this reason; any attempt to combine the two involved a fatal dispersion of the field. It must be one thing or the other, and this was dramatically represented by the way Larwood would open his attack. While the ball was still new he could use his natural outswing, bowling an off-stump line to packed slips and a conventional off-side field; then the moment would come when Jardine would clap his hands over his head and beckon, and immediately there was leg theory in full array, clustering short legs, long leg behind them, and Larwood pounding the ball down remorselessly on the leg stump or just outside it. Or again there was that incident in the first South Australian game at Adelaide, when Bowes asked Jardine repeatedly for an extra man on the leg side, to be told that he could not have one, but he could have five – an incident which perfectly encapsulates Jardine's evident love of taking the wind out of people with his sudden and startling changes of direction, but even more perfectly his insistence on concentration of the field. To anyone with a taste for the academic turn of mind, the clarity at least of Jardine's thinking is attractive.

The origin of Jardine's leg theory field settings certainly owed something to a number of visits that he paid after the dinner in the Piccadilly grill-room to Frank Foster, whose leg theory (as we saw) had been so successful in Australia in 1911–12. These visits came into prominence later, when at the height of the controversy Foster came out in strenuous denunciation of 'bodyline' and denials that he had had any notion of the type of bowling tactics that were in Jardine's mind at the time of these discussions. According to Foster, Jardine had sought his advice purely about field placings for an attack directed, as Foster's had been, at the leg stump: it is to be presumed that Foster supposed that Jardine had the left-handed Voce chiefly in mind.

These points about the origin of 'bodyline' are important, partly because they throw light on exactly what Jardine had in mind, but more because of a curious query that hangs over them. It has come to be the accepted belief that 'bodyline' was hatched in England before the tour began; that if a precise moment of birth has to be defined, it was the dinner in the Piccadilly grill-room; that Jardine went out to Australia with the blueprint for 'bodyline' clearly worked out in his mind – and even, according to one version, common knowledge among the rest of the MCC party; that it was deliberately held back until the 'Australian XI' game at Melbourne, and then unleashed with full force with the aim of intimidating the Australians, and especially Bradman, before the first Test. This has always been the prevailing view in Australia – that it was a cold-blooded, premeditated conspiracy – a view reinforced by and perhaps originating in the Australian image of Jardine as secretive, ruthless and inhuman.

Larwood's account in *The Larwood Story* broadly supports this version, with its account of the dinner in the Piccadilly grill-room and its outright statement that the form of attack to be adopted was common knowledge among the team on the way out to Australia (his earlier book, *Body-Line?*, published immediately after the tour, says nothing about the origin of the idea). Carr and Voce have confirmed the story of the dinner, although without giving any details of what took place at it. Yet of the English survivors of the

174

tour, Allen, Wyatt, Ames and Bowes all agree that they had heard nothing to suggest the use of 'bodyline' – and I am referring to the tactics, not the name, which admittedly was not in use until after the first Test – until the tour was well advanced. Allen and Wyatt do not believe that 'bodyline' in any precise sense was premeditated at all. Wyatt – who was Jardine's vice-captain, and (one would think) ought to have known if anyone did – still thinks that the tactics were evolved in the course of the tour, and that he himself was largely responsible for the evolution, when, captaining the side in the match against the 'Australian XI' in Melbourne, he found the Australian batsmen so consistently moving across their stumps to play the ball that he was forced willy-nilly to concentrate his attack on the leg side. He remembers explaining this to Jardine afterwards (and this was the match which is generally regarded as having witnessed the first use of 'bodyline' tactics by the MCC in Australia).

Fender's recollections, of having discussed with Jardine before the tour began the possibility that the Australian batsmen would do just this, and the implications that this would have for the direction of the English attack and the field placings if so, support Wyatt's view, at least insofar as they too suggest that 'bodyline' started life as a reaction to an Australian initiative rather than as a gratuitous and unscrupulous stroke of tactics on England's part.

Fender was a close friend of Jardine as well as his county captain until 1932, and has himself been suggested as the source of the idea of 'bodyline': certainly, if 'bodyline' had been deliberately plotted before the tour began, one might have expected Fender to know about it. Yet he denies any such knowledge, and told Richard Streeton, his biographer, that he received letters from Jardine in Australia saying that his predictions as to the Australians moving back across their stumps had been proved true, and that he was already having to place five or six fieldsmen on the leg side, and, as things were going, would soon have to put 'the whole bloody lot' there.

Unfortunately, these letters were destroyed in the War: they would, of course, exactly match Wyatt's account. Moreover, a fragment of a letter of Jardine's, written to Findlay, the MCC Secretary, in early December, certainly does survive* which, unless Jardine is to be suspected of complete disingenuousness, goes some way to support Fender's version and reveals something of the way Jardine saw his own tactics at the time:

> So far our bowling has in general been a shock and an unpleasant surprise to the old hands of Australia. The papers have put up a squeal rising to a whine about bowling at the man. Nothing of the sort, but we have by dint of hard and, I hope, clear thinking got a field suitable for attacking the leg stump instead of the old off side theory.

In the book that he wrote after the tour Jardine also claimed that it was because the Australian batsmen made such a practice of moving across their wickets to play the fast bowlers that they were so often hit; and this must be set beside his letters to Fender and Findlay, and Wyatt's recollections. Were the Australians in fact moving back across their stumps and concentrating all their shots on the leg side to an unprecedented extent? Certainly they were doing it a lot: the decisive proof of that is the number of them who were out LBW or, still more significantly, bowled behind their legs by the fast bowlers during the tour, since, generally speaking, bowling a batsman round his legs is an uncommon form of dismissal, and for a fast bowler very rare indeed. Ponsford in particular was repeatedly out in this way. But, aside from the fact that some of these dismissals, especially late in the series, should be ranked as effect rather than cause – i.e., that they resulted from batsmen trying to get out of the way of

---

*It is quoted in a letter of Findlay's – one of the few relevant documents to survive among the MCC records.

176

short-pitched balls by moving inside the line, only to find the ball bouncing less high than they expected and failing to clear the stumps – the difficulty is that all batting had been developing this way since the War, and whether the Australians were actually doing it more systematically than it had been done in England in recent years is hard to estimate. There is little doubt, as we have seen, that the method had originated with Shrewsbury and other English professionals in the late nineteenth century, and it was often regarded as a typical bit of professional batting technique; and it was only in England that cricket had been professionalized. Still, so many good English authorities agreed in 1932–33 that the Australians were taking the practice further than ever before that I am inclined to accept it, and to see in this one important explanation of the English resort to leg theory in Australia.

But although the leg-side field may indeed have been *strengthened* in response to Australian batting methods, there can be no doubt that both the general notion of an attack directed on the leg stump or outside it, and therefore to a predominantly leg-side field, and the use of a close-set leg trap, preceded this: there were precedents for both in England before the tour began.

It is fair too to note that the leg-side field was used for Bradman, even when he was making a practice of moving further to leg and trying to force the ball on the *off* side: clearly there was no question here of the field setting being a response to the batting methods. The Australians too vehemently maintained that Larwood and Voce bowled on the line of their bodies wherever they were standing – Victor Richardson in particular claimed to have tried the experiment of standing wider and wider of his leg stump, only to find the ball following him whatever he did – and on this point at least a definite conclusion seems possible, since both Larwood and Voce have since admitted that this was true. The admission was made with particularly disarming frankness by Larwood in *The Larwood Story*. But this was at Adelaide, and whether it had been true from the outset is another matter: it may be that 'bodyline' started more innocently, and that it was only at and after the second Test that it became as frankly intimidatory as this.

It seems to me that far the easiest solution lies in some reconciliation of the apparently conflicting accounts, and a good point of departure for this is Jardine's own account. In his book *In Quest of the Ashes*, published in 1933 after his return from Australia, although not mentioning the dinner at the Piccadilly Hotel, Jardine does imply that the use of leg theory for his fast bowlers had been discussed before the tour. However, he plays down its novelty, pointing out that it had been anticipated on various occasions, and says that he originally conceived of it as nothing more than a tactic which might occasionally prove useful when batsmen were well set, but that by the time of the 'Australian XI' match at Melbourne 'an almost totally unsuspected weakness on the leg stump' had been observed by the MCC in several of the leading Australian batsmen, and that thereafter they consequently resorted to leg theory increasingly against the batsmen in question (who included Bradman and Ponsford, but not, according to Jardine, McCabe, Richardson or Fingleton – though his inclusion of Fingleton, one of the chief victims of leg theory, with McCabe and Richardson is inexplicable).

It must be said that *In Quest of the Ashes*, written at the height of the public controversy, does not read throughout like a completely frank book; but the account of the origins of 'bodyline' here fits in reasonably well with Wyatt's recollections, and also with Larwood's later memories of the Piccadilly Hotel meeting, though not with his other statements implying that 'bodyline' was planned in detail there and introduced in the 'Australian XI' match as a result of a premeditated strategy.

It seems easier to suppose that in retrospect too much significance has been attached to the Piccadilly Hotel dinner, which was no more than one of a series of consultations that Jardine held (with Fender, with Foster, and very possibly with others too) in the summer of 1932, in the course of working out the tactics to be employed in Australia during the forthcoming tour; that in the course of these consultations, Jardine did decide to adopt some form of leg theory for his fast bowlers, but that this was in some degree tentative, and in any case fell well short of full-blown 'bodyline'; that when tried on the field in Australia, it proved unexpectedly rewarding, and thereafter rapidly developed to an extent and in a direction which Jardine had not anticipated, but which he supported when it occurred.

This suggestion seems also to provide the most plausible solution to another problem. I am told by Jardine's daughter that her father always maintained that the selection committee were aware that he intended to use leg theory against the Australians, and that the bitterness he undoubtedly felt later when the MCC renounced the use of 'bodyline' was due to this fact: he felt that they had let him down. There are obvious difficulties in the way of accepting this at face value. It seems to make the recorded actions and statements of the MCC during the controversy and after it inexplicable – and the reactions of Warner in particular, who had been the chairman of the selection committee, even more so – and it equally leaves it unexplained how so many of the touring party, including the vice-captain, remained in ignorance of Jardine's intentions and thought that 'bodyline' was something that was evolved in the course of the tour. However, it is possible to make some sense of it if what Jardine had discussed with the members of the selection committee was 'leg theory' of the sort already familiar in England – that is, with no emphasis on direct intimidation – and that this developed into full-blown 'bodyline' in the course of the tour – this would, incidentally, help to explain Foster's violent revulsion against the later English tactics, if 'bodyline' as it evolved during the series was something substantially different from what had been in Jardine's own mind at the time of his conversations with Foster. The confusion would then have arisen from Jardine's failure to admit, and perhaps failure to recognize, that it had developed far beyond his own original intentions and in the process had changed its nature.

However, any theory will leave some loose ends untied about the exact point at which 'bodyline', in the form in which it finally came to be known and hated in Australia, first took clear-cut shape in Jardine's mind. A study of when it was first actually used on the field might be expected to throw a lot of light on the issue, but in fact it helps surprisingly little – largely because 'bodyline' is not all that easy to define, and in retrospect various observers made various different claims for its first appearance, which, in the nature of things, it is very difficult to verify afterwards. It is a point in favour of what may be called the 'conspiracy' theory that Larwood appears to have experimented with 'bodyline', or something very like it, to a full-fledged 'bodyline' field, in two county matches, against Essex and Glamorgan, late in August 1932 – the Essex match, indeed, came immediately after the meeting at the Piccadilly Hotel. The record of the early matches in Australia is unhelpful. It is usually reckoned that 'bodyline' first saw the light of day at the 'Australian XI' match in Melbourne in mid-November. On the 'conspiracy' theory, the usual explanation is that it was deliberately held in reserve until the last two matches before the first Test, when it was unveiled with the set purpose of intimidating Bradman, who played in both of them (for the 'Australian XI', and for New South Wales in Sydney). That Larwood himself was deliberately held back, there can be little doubt: prior to the 'Australian XI' match, he had bowled only eleven overs on the tour. But if there was such a plan, it seems quite incredible that Jardine should choose the match at which his secret weapon was to be unveiled to go off fishing, leaving the attack to be handled in his absence by his vice-captain, Wyatt, without even telling him of the plan's existence; and in the New South Wales match Larwood was again omitted from the side, though Voce certainly seems to have bowled at his roughest, hitting Fingleton (who made a century) repeatedly.

The facts fit the 'evolution' hypothesis at least as well as they do the 'conspiracy' one, and the record of the first two Tests appears to bear this out, for in the first Test Larwood bowled mostly 'off theory', whereas by the beginning of the second Test in Melbourne there is no doubt that 'let theory' had come to occupy a central place in Jardine's thinking, as is clear from his highly significant conversation, already recounted, with Allen in the English dressing-room before the game began, in which he tried to persuade him too to adopt 'leg theory' tactics, which, as we have seen, were exploited by the three professional fast bowlers throughout the game. This certainly looks like 'evolution'; but the 'conspiracy' theorists come back with the rejoinder that if the full 'bodyline' attack was not unleashed at Sydney in the first Test, that was only because Bradman was unfit and was not playing: as soon as he was back in the side for the second Test, England returned to 'bodyline' without qualification.

And so the argument goes on. As I have made clear, I think myself that the truth lies somewhere between the two extreme hypotheses – that 'bodyline' was fully worked out before the tour began, or that there was no planning at all, and 'bodyline' was a mere improvisation on the spot.

This is not of course a new suggestion: Alan Kippax, I believe, got it almost exactly right in his very sensible book *Anti-Bodyline*, when he said: 'It is possible that what was meant to be "leg theory" passed imperceptibly into "bodyline".' We have to remember that given the stern attitude to the series that Jardine himself possessed and that he did his best to instil into the rest of the team, given their memories of the 1930 series, and given, above all, the state of English fast bowling at the time and the selection of the side, it was hardly to be expected that the English pace attack would be anything but full-blooded. Voce and Bowes were already well-known for their free use of the bumper, and Voce for the regular use of a leg trap. It is worth noting that when, back in England following the tour, both Jardine and Larwood published books about it at the height of the controversy, this is essentially the line they took: that 'bodyline', so-called, was at most a modest extension of tactics that were already in use, and had been for years.

The 'Australian XI' match at Melbourne certainly demonstrated beyond doubt that the Australian batting was vulnerable to Larwood and Voce bowling at top pace, on a leg-side line and short enough to make the ball lift nastily at the batsman, and, as I see it, 'fast leg theory' hardened into 'bodyline' between this match, starting on 18 November, and the third Test, starting on 13 January. The three intervening first-class fixtures, the first match against New South Wales and the first two Tests, saw intermediate stages in its development, and they also saw the idea assuming increasing clarity in Jardine's own mind, as he realized that in this technique he had the means of winning the Test series – the manifest discomfort of all the leading Australian batsmen in the face of it was evidence enough of that. The leg-side direction of the attack, planned before the tour began and reinforced by the experience of Australian batting methods in the earlier matches of the tour, remained: its effect was now reinforced by the increasingly frequent and systematic use of the short lifting ball and the crowded leg trap.*

It was also during this same period that the public recognition of 'bodyline' as a radically new and controversial method of attack took place. The Australian press were feeling their way towards it from the time of the 'Australian XI' match onwards, and the term itself

---

*At the time when he hit Woodfull in the 'Australian XI' match, Larwood was bowling to three short legs and one man back – a pale shadow of what was to come. By the time of the following match against New South Wales, Voce was bowling to a four- or five-man leg trap. Warner, writing to Findlay after the first Test, was already very critical of 'leg theory', but – significantly – of its line rather than its length: he says that during a 35 minute spell, Larwood bowled only three balls on the wicket, but adds that he 'kept more or less a length'.

originated during the first Test, by tradition as a journalist's piece of telegraphic shorthand, and soon proved its superior staying power over several other experimental names for the new phenomenon. It is beyond question that the influence of the press, especially the popular press, in both countries worked to heighten and exacerbate, if not actually to create, the 'bodyline' controversy; and no single development did more towards this end than the appearance of the word, which immediately became itself a cause of conflict. The term so perfectly reflected Australian perceptions of English methods that it came into universal use in Australia almost immediately;* and once coined, it made a clear-cut entity of the English tactics and impressed an image on them that, in Australian eyes at least, they never thereafter lost. Once 'bodyline' was given a name, it became a thing: a thing to raise the tempers of newspaper readers in both countries, a thing that crowds flocking to the grounds where the MCC were playing expected to see and looked forward to hating.

It may even be suspected that the name did something to make the thing clearer in the minds of Jardine and the English players themselves, and to give it a sharper edge: certainly, Jardine being Jardine, the adoption of the word by the Australian press and public and its implication of unfairness were unlikely to do anything but cause him to grit his teeth and resolve more defiantly than ever to stick remorselessly to his tactics and to use to the uttermost the advantage that they gave him – and 'give the bastards something to shout about'. Clearly by the time of the second Test Jardine had a clear conception of the hostility those tactics aroused: when he was trying to persuade Allen to adopt leg-theory methods at the beginning of that match, he tried to needle him by telling him that the other England players were passing the word around that Allen

* Though one must not exaggerate: the staider Australian papers largely avoided it in their descriptions of the games throughout the tour.

183

was too frightened of endangering his popularity with the crowds to do it.

This is one of the reasons why it seems to me that it was the Adelaide Test which completed the crystallization – so to speak – of 'bodyline': it was here that the collision with Australian public opinion became open and unbridgeable. There were other reasons too: most importantly, it was the Adelaide Test which finally put it beyond all doubt that 'bodyline', if persisted in, was a winner. The Melbourne Test had left many, perhaps most, Australians with the impression that 'bodyline' had been conquered: Adelaide showed that this was an illusion, and therefore made its continuance certain. In particular, it showed that Bradman's century at Melbourne was, if not a flash in the pan, at least misleading as an indication that even Bradman had any convincing counter to 'bodyline'. But more than that, it was the events at Adelaide that finally gave 'bodyline' its inescapable identification with violence and direct intimidation. I believe leg theory, in Jardine's original intention, had been primarily a matter of the *line* his bowlers should bowl. Certainly from the first there was a good deal of short stuff mixed in with it: this was true particularly of Voce, who throughout the series seems to have bowled more bumpers than Larwood. By the time of the Adelaide Test, though, it had become clear that it was the element of intimidation that was the true cutting edge of 'fast leg theory'; and it was Larwood's bowling on a relatively lively wicket in that Test that made that element more naked and more lethal than ever before. Once he had discovered what he could achieve with the short-pitched, steeply rising ball, it was inevitable that Larwood would go on using it; and from then onwards it was this aspect of 'bodyline', even more than its line, that dominated all discussion.

At the same time, the image of 'bodyline' as a form of brutal intimidation was fixed in the public mind by the accidents to Woodfull and Oldfield – even though both might have happened if 'bodyline' had never been heard of, and if Larwood throughout the tour had bowled as conventional fast bowlers had always bowled.

And, finally, the violence of the crowd reaction, and the outbreak of the war of the cables, fixed 'bodyline' in another way: it made it certain that Jardine would persist in it, and persist in it in its most aggressive form. It is just possible that another captain might have found a way to conciliation after Adelaide, without abandoning all the advantages that 'fast leg theory' had given him; but to the hostility of the Australian crowds and public, Jardine would not yield an inch.

This refusal to lift a finger to meet the demands of the press or the clamour of the crowds had marked Jardine's conduct of the tour from the outset. His attitude to cricket was patrician in a way that by 1932 was old-fashioned: in effect, he simply denied the right of press and public to exert an influence on the game. In his eyes, they were there on sufferance: if they enjoyed themselves, so much the better, but their first obligation was to keep quiet and behave themselves. The game was an affair between the players, and on it neither press nor public had a right to be heard. As he was to put it himself in his own book on the series, 'the arena, hitherto sacred to eleven players on either side, has been invaded by newspapers, broadcasters, and spectators'. At bottom this was the pre-1914, patrician view of cricket as an aristocratic recreation. It took no account of the realities, above all the economic realities, of the post-War game, and by 1932, when the concentration of press and public interest on the Anglo-Australian Tests was greater than ever before, it was anachronistic.

This contempt for the public, whose support was essential for the continuing existence of the first-class game, is closely related to a remarkable feature of the 'bodyline' affair that has not, so far as I am aware, been commented on before: the fact that 'bodyline' was employed by England not at home, where the crowds might have been expected to be at least relatively sympathetic (at any rate if the result was to win the series for England), but in Australia, where the crowds were bound to be hostile. The fact in itself is no doubt accidental: if Jardine had been asked to captain England at home against Australia in similar circumstances, there is every reason to think that he would have used exactly the same tactics as he in fact used in Australia: or if he did not (since it is arguable that 'bodyline' was more effective on hard Australian wickets than it would have been likely to be on softer English ones), the reasons would have been purely technical. Jardine simply, and very typically, left crowd reactions out of the equation entirely. Yet in doing so he was running formidable risks. The situation during the 'bodyline' Tests in Australia was like that of a city surrounded by a besieging army, itself encircled by another and much greater army of the citizens' compatriots. There were the two Australian batsmen, facing Larwood's and Voce's bombardment, surrounded by a grim ring of grasping English fieldsmen: the image, it might seem, of desperate resistance in the face of brutal aggression. And there, outside the pickets, was the crowd: forty to sixty thousand Australians, hungrily anxious for an Australian victory, seething with anger at English tactics, yet forbidden by the conventions and the very concept of the game to leap the fence and come to the rescue of their beleaguered and assaulted fellow-countrymen. It was as artificial and explosive a situation as one could conceive, one that pointed with acute precision to the fundamental paradox of the theatre and of spectator sport, in which the spectator experiences intense identification with the actors but is excluded from the action.

In creating such a situation, Jardine ran a fearsome risk of shattering the artificial convention on which it all rested. More than one of the English fieldsmen at Adelaide thought that the crowd were on the point of coming over the fence at them. Hele, one of the umpires, saw a spectator put a foot on the fence, and claims that he heard afterwards that one of the police inspectors on duty called out to another spectator, 'Why don't you jump the fence? I won't stop you'; and if one man had taken the leap, it would probably have been enough to have loosed the torrent. It is not at all impossible to imagine a scene in which serious injury might have been done to Jardine at least: even, perhaps, a death. Jardine gambled on the assumption that the fishbowl convention – the convention that the action on the field is totally insulated from the spectators and their emotions, as though by a sheet of unbreakable glass – would hold; and it is a tribute to the toughness of the social conventions in the 1930s that hold it did, just; but the risk was extravagant.

CHAPTER 7

The Meaning of Bodyline

We have now reached the point at which the natural evolution of fast bowling techniques, and the personality of Douglas Jardine, converged to produce the result known as 'bodyline': for, whatever view is taken of its origins, and the exact point of the tour at which it was first consciously adopted, nobody doubts that, at latest from the second Test onwards, it was deliberately and consistently adopted by Jardine as the foundation of the English attack. Both factors were essential to its genesis: if fast bowling had not been evolving in this direction anyway, it is most unlikely that the conception of 'bodyline' would ever have occurred to Jardine or to anyone else; and in all probability no other captain whom the MCC might have appointed would have had the hardihood to use it.*

I use the word 'hardihood' advisedly, and without prejudice. I have said already that I think the use of 'bodyline' in Australia, against Australia, implied an irresponsible degree of contempt for or indifference to public opinion and probable crowd reactions. But I also think that it took a captain of exceptional strength of character and independence of mind to think through the logic of fast leg theory to this point and to shoulder the

*Fender or Carr might perhaps have done so, but by 1932 neither was a credible candidate for the England captaincy. Apart from Jardine, the only obvious candidate was Wyatt, who would never have countenanced 'bodyline'.

burden of obloquy involved in the use of it. It was his courage, and his unflinching readiness to accept the responsibility and to take the worst of the unpopularity that was going, that best explains the remarkable loyalty that Jardine commanded from his side;* and there has always been an English school of thought that sees in Jardine the English counterpart of a captain like Warwick Armstrong, and in the eventual repudiation of 'bodyline' a craven capitulation to an explosion of Australian indignation that at bottom was no more than an expression of wounded *amour propre*: it was not for nothing that Fender called his account of the 1934 series, after 'bodyline' had been disowned and Jardine, Larwood and Voce had been eased out of the England side, *Kissing the Rod*. But the central issue remains to be faced: what, exactly, *was* 'bodyline' as bowled in Australia in 1932–33, and was it or was it not an intolerable breach of cricketing ethics?

I have fallen into the use of the word 'bodyline', and in doing so I am already to some extent prejudging the issue. 'Bodyline' was the term coined by the Australian press to describe the English tactics. It singled out vividly what in Australian eyes was the most obvious characteristic of the new style of bowling – that it was directed at the batsman's body, and not at the stumps. As such, the term was no doubt intended as a pejorative, and certainly taken as such in England. During the tour, the English press rarely used the word, and if they did, put it in inverted commas to distance themselves from its implications: the MCC, in their reply to the Australian Board of Control's first cable from Adelaide, expressed ignorance of its meaning, and Jardine consistently denied that his bowlers were bowling at the batsmen's bodies: he said they were attacking the leg stump, and if Australian batsmen were getting hit, that was because of their habit of moving across the wicket to play the ball. The English term for their tactics was 'leg theory', or, more specifically, 'fast leg theory', and if

* Hedley Verity named his son after him.

189

'bodyline' was a pejorative, this equally was a meliorative, since it carried with it the claim, which Jardine repeatedly made, that the tactics were nothing new, but at most a modest extension of the various versions of leg theory which, as we have seen, had been becoming increasingly fashionable in the 1920s. It is a fine example of the well-known phenomenon by which rival names for the same thing become weapons in a war of words – 'Falklands' and 'Malvinas' is a highly current example at the moment of writing – and the fact that 'bodyline' has become the accepted term accurately indicates who won the war.

None of the English survivors of the tour today denies that Larwood's and Voce's bowling (and Bowes', in the solitary Test Match in which he played) was deliberately intimidatory. Even Jardine himself, though he never said so in so many words, might have admitted as much. In the book that he wrote after his return to England, *In Quest of the Ashes*, he claims that the main aim of 'fast leg theory' is to force the batsman to play at more balls: to counter, in other words, the increasing tendency to pad up to anything outside the off stump and play no stroke, leaving the fast bowler to tire himself out. Fast leg theory achieved this aim, according to Jardine, because it is harder to judge if a ball is missing the leg stump than if it is missing the off stump, and also because of the danger of being bowled off the pads if you play no stroke. This is one of the points in *The Quest for the Ashes* at which it becomes very hard to maintain faith in the book's complete frankness. Jardine here discusses 'fast leg theory' as though its distinguishing characteristic was purely its direction. I said in the last chapter that, though this may have been the case originally, it had clearly ceased to be so by the time of the third Test at Adelaide at the latest.

In Australian eyes certainly, what distinguished 'bodyline' was as much its shortness of length as its leg-side direction – if nothing more than the batsmen's pads had been hit, there would have been very few complaints of intimidation – and if 'fast leg theory' did indeed force the

Australian batsmen to play more balls, there seems little doubt that one of the main reasons for this was to protect themselves against being hit. It is much to Sir Stanley Jackson's credit that he fixed on this point acutely at an early stage of the controversy and long before he had had a chance to see the new bowling for himself. In an article in the *Daily Telegraph* in mid-March, he drew the distinction between legitimate 'leg theory' and 'bodyline', arguing that 'leg theory' depended on swing for its effect and hence required a full length, whereas if a fast bowler bowled *short of a length* on or outside the leg stump, he was necessarily relying on intimidation. But most English discussion of the controversy ignored the distinction. Jardine does indeed concede that batsmen must expect to be hit occasionally when facing this type of bowling; but the implication is clearly that this is an accidental by-product, not the object of the bowling, and that the better the batsman, the less he will be hit, emphasizing the significance of the fact that Bradman himself was hit only once, and then not seriously. Bradman's method of playing 'bodyline' from well wide of the leg stump did indeed minimize the risk of being hit, and it was just as well: considering the almost demigod status of Bradman in the eyes of Australian cricket followers in 1932–33, it is hard indeed to say what might have happened if Larwood had hit Bradman as he hit Woodfull and Oldfield at Adelaide.

But there is, of course, truth in what Jardine said: in general, the better the batsman, the less likely he was to be hit, though how far this goes as a legitimate defence of 'bodyline' may be questioned. None of the Australian tail-enders were hit in the 1932–33 series, but that was because 'bodyline' was not used against them. The convention that fast bowlers did not bowl short at batsmen who could not be expected to defend themselves was already well established, and was fully observed in 1932–33; and in any case, there were easier methods of getting them out, all the more since the Australian tail was unusually and notoriously long and vulnerable in that series. But of the

191

regular batsmen in the Australian order, it was certainly true, as one would expect, that it was those whose footwork was most limited who suffered most, notably Woodfull, Fingleton and Ponsford. Bradman's footwork was always one of the most remarkable qualities of his batting. He decided early that, whatever the answer to 'bodyline' might be, there was nothing to be said for being hit by it, and said as much; and his record in the series demonstrates amply that his footwork could be put to this use as effectively as he commonly used it for more aggressive purposes. It is of course also true that Jardine may well have considered that by thus forcing his most dangerous opponent to put one of his greatest attacking assets to a fundamentally defensive use he was anyway gaining major advantage.

Let us clear the ground a little. I have said that 'bodyline' in its full sense was evolved between mid-November 1932 and mid-January 1933, in the course of five matches – those against the 'Australian XI' and New South Wales, and the first three Tests. Prior to these matches, and in the minor games in Tasmania and against country sides which took place between them, no accusations of anything resembling 'bodyline' were made. After the third Test, the MCC played six more first-class matches in Australia: the two remaining Tests, one against Queensland, and the return games against New South Wales, Victoria and South Australia. In none of the four State games does 'bodyline' seem to have been used – certainly not to an extent to arouse serious comment or controversy. Jardine was no doubt anxious to rest his fast bowlers between the Tests as much as he could, and in fact in only one of these four games, that against Queensland, did Larwood play. By this stage of the tour at any rate, 'bodyline' proper was reserved for the Tests; and it is worth nothing that, on any strict definition, it was utilized only on seven matches in the entire tour.*

* Arguably only on six, for the first match against New South Wales

It will not do, therefore, to think of the English attack on the tour, nor even of the pace attack, as consisting entirely of 'bodyline'. Of the five pace bowlers in the side, Allen and Tate – if he is to be reckoned as a pace bowler – never bowled it; and the others, Larwood, Voce and Bowes, did not bowl it all the time, even in the Tests.* In all the Tests, Larwood and Voce – Larwood especially – alternated between 'leg theory' (for our purposes now, let us say 'bodyline') and conventional 'off theory'. In particular, 'bodyline' was never used against tail-enders – the lowest it seems to have reached down the order was Oldfield, batting No. 7 at Adelaide – and Larwood regularly opened his attack at the beginning of an innings bowling 'off theory' in order to exploit his outswinger while the ball was new. 'Bodyline' was essentially a tactic for the ball with the shine gone off it, since it meant bowling short of a length, and if a bowler wants to make use of the shine of a ball to swing it, he must bowl a full length to give it space to swing – as Jackson had pointed out in the *Daily Telegraph*. For the true 'express' bowler like Larwood, swing, it is true, is always a secondary weapon – at a pace around 90 m.p.h., no ball will swing very much – but it was nevertheless worth his while to make what use he could of it while the ball was new: Fingleton never forgot the ball with which Larwood bowled him at the start of the Australian second innings at Adelaide, which started on the line of the leg stump, swung

* Bowes played in only one Test, plus the 'Australian XI' match, and he too therefore bowled very little 'bodyline' on the tour, perhaps because he was not really fast or accurate enough for it. Indeed, it is striking how his bowling, which had aroused so much criticism in England in 1932, passed almost entirely without comment in Australia.

must be regarded as a marginal case. Larwood, with whom 'bodyline' was usually identified, did not play in it, and although Voce bumped the ball a lot and bowled to a leg trap, both were characteristic of his normal methods, and might have passed without comment but for Larwood's bowling in the 'Australian XI' match immediately previously. There is a case, therefore, for saying that 'bodyline' was reserved entirely for representative games.

at Larwood's top pace, and hit the top of the off. But on the hard Australian pitches and very rough outfields of the period, on which the ball lost its shine very quickly and before long could be as rough as the sole of a boot, Larwood after three or four overs was usually ready to switch to the 'leg theory' attack – we have seen that, when Woodfull was hit at Adelaide, Jardine switched to 'leg theory' after only two overs (though Larwood thought the ball *was* still swinging then).

Throughout the Tests Jardine used his fast bowlers in fairly short spells, varying 'leg theory' with more conventional tactics as psychological and tactical consider-ations dictated. The two modes of attack were completely distinct: at any given moment there was no doubt whether a bowler was bowling leg theory or not. Voce bowled it most of the time, since his normal method was so akin to it anyway; but the clarity of Jardine's tactical thinking, and particularly the necessities of field setting, ruled out any possibility of combining the two forms of attack. We have seen that one of the principal origins of Jardine's tactics lay in the idea of tactical concentration, of directing the attack, and therefore the field placing, exclusively to one side of the wicket or the other. It is obvious that, if you are bowling to seven men on the leg side, anything pitched offward of the middle stump gives an opportunity to the batsman. Remorseless accuracy was the first quality that Jardine demanded of his bowlers.

The use of 'bodyline', therefore, was not continuous; but this is not in any way to deny that it came to form the real core of the English attack in the Tests, as it certainly did. 'Bodyline', or the threat of 'bodyline', dominated all the Tests, at least from Melbourne onwards: the qualification is important, for it is clear that 'bodyline' achieved much of its success by its ability to demoralize batsmen, to destroy their concentration, and sometimes to take prohibitive risks against other bowlers in their anxiety to make some runs before having to face the next spell of 'bodyline' – we have seen how Verity in particular profited from this reaction in the later Tests. 'Bodyline' might not be bowled for more than a quite small proportion of an innings, but with Larwood and Voce on the field the threat of it was present all the time, and a batsman could never know whether, at the end of the over in progress, Jardine would not throw the ball to one or the other of them and, with a clap of his hands over his head, summon up his shoal of short legs.

With this field set, not only was the bowler committed to bowling on or outside the leg stump: he was also committed to bowling short of a length.* It was the logic of concentration carried to its natural conclusion. The typical 'bodyline' field included a single mid-wicket, or wide mid-on, and nobody else in front of the wicket on the leg side more than half a dozen yards from the bat: to bowl a full length to such a field must necessarily have been to invite forcing shots into the wide arc between square leg and the bowler. Larwood and Voce therefore bowled short; but there are degrees of shortness, and, above all, there are the problems raised by the variation in bounce that was an outstanding quality of Australian wickets on this tour. When bowling 'bodyline', both Larwood and Voce used the bumper freely – Voce, by most accounts, more freely than Larwood, sometimes three or four of them in succession. The bumper is unpleasant, and is meant to be. It can on occasion be bowled with the hope of inducing the batsman to hook, and hole out at long leg, but this is not usually its main aim, which is to intimidate the batsman, to unsettle him, to break his concentration: it is designed less to get the batsman out directly than to make him more liable to error later in the over, or in the next over. But if the bounce is predictable, it can be ducked or avoided: the batsman does not need to play it, and in fact usually does not try. It is when the bounce is not predictable, as was so markedly the case in Australia on that tour, that life for the batsman

*Larwood indeed later argued that 'bodyline' was actually less dangerous than the occasional use of random bouncers, because the field setting gave the man fair notice of what to expect.

becomes very much harder. When Larwood and Voce dropped short of a length, the ball might rise sometimes waist-high, sometimes chest-high, sometimes head-high. There has always been variable bounce, and it is a matter of conjecture why it was so pronounced in 1932–33; but that it was so is borne out not only by the accounts of players and observers, but also by the number of Australian batsmen who were dismissed in the series either bowled or leg-before playing no stroke, when balls which they judged would rise above the level of the stumps failed to do so, and also by the number who were hit while ducking. Nothing undermines a batsman's confidence more than uncertainty about the height at which the ball is going to bounce, and with a bowler of Larwood's pace the effect is multiplied, because the time for adjustment is so short as to be almost non-existent: the batsman had only a fraction of a second to judge whether to hook, to play a defensive stroke, to duck or try to move out of the line, or simply to take the ball on the body. If he opted for the hook, there were one or two men in the deep behind square leg for the catch; if he chose the defensive stroke, he had all the problems of trying to keep down a chest-high and steeply rising ball with four or five short legs clustered round within half a dozen yards of him. To avoid the ball was often simply not possible, except for a batsman like Bradman of exceptionally quick reactions. There remained the stoic reaction of taking it on the body, as several of the Australian batsmen repeatedly did. But this kind of physical battering, repeated over after over, innings after innings after innings, match after match, inevitably took its toll of any man in the end, sapping concentration and weakening resolution. It has been remarked that, although several of the Australian batsmen produced one or two outstanding innings against 'bodyline', Bradman alone performed against it with any degree of consistency.

This is a reasonably objective account of 'bodyline', which (I hope) any observer on either side would accept as broadly accurate. As we have seen, the serious differences begin when one tries to define the line on which Larwood and Voce bowled, and whether or not they deliberately bowled at the body – as Jardine always denied. Larwood himself, in his descriptions of his own bowling as given to Kevin Perkins thirty years after the event, is inconsistent on the point. He says more than once that he bowled on the line of the leg stump, but he also says that the Australian batsman (Richardson), who claimed that when he took guard further and further outside the leg stump he still found Larwood's bowling coming straight at him, was perfectly right, and that if he saw the batsman moving as he came up to bowl he deliberately altered his line of delivery to follow him. Part of the answer probably does lie in the habit of several of the Australian batsmen of moving back across their stumps to play the ball, as we have seen – obviously, if they did this, a ball on the line of the leg stump could also be a ball on the line of the batsman's body.

But it is not a complete explanation, as Richardson's story shows. That they bowled to intimidate neither Larwood nor Voce ever denied: indeed, both have agreed that they did. It is not, perhaps, quite the same thing as trying to hit the batsman, though it certainly comes perilously close to it: if a batsman is intimidated, it is presumably the prospect of being hit that frightens him. In his earlier book, *Bodyline?*, written just after the tour, Larwood said frankly that he thought he could hit most batsmen on a fast wicket if he wanted to, and there seems little reason to doubt this; but he denied outright that he had ever deliberately tried to do so.

It is clear at least that the object of 'bodyline' was not actually to injure the batsmen, to knock them out: even the most hostile critics rarely suggested this (though some did). Its object was rather – to put it simply – to drive the batsman into fatal error by fear of pain. It might achieve this directly, by catches in the leg trap from batsmen trying to fend the ball off their bodies, or indirectly, by driving them into misjudgements of balls that were not short of a length, or into indiscretions against other bowlers; but the root motive in either case would be the same, and the method was such that it was inevitable that batsmen *would* sometimes get hit.

The point has already been made that a pair of top class fast bowlers is worth more than twice either of them singly, and that it was the combination of Larwood and Voce that made 'bodyline' the formidable thing it was – especially when we bear in mind that both were supported by the presence of Allen, the third fast bowler, who never bowled 'bodyline', but who lacked none of the pace and aggression to keep Australian nerves and reactions at full stretch.* But that Larwood deserved the title 'the spearhead of the English attack' was doubted by nobody. It will never be possible for those who were not there to recapture the intensely ephemeral reality – few things are more irrecoverable than the great sporting performances of the past in the days before television – but the sense of greatness, of something stretching into another whole dimension than the common run of even world-class fast bowling, still hangs about the accounts of his bowling on that tour. He was not merely tremendously fast, though that he certainly was. Almost all the Australians agreed that he was by some margin the fastest they had ever played against: certainly significantly faster than Voce or Allen though Allen especially was also very quick on that tour. But that was only part of his menance. Bradman thinks that Tyson, in 1954–55, was faster through the air than Larwood, but not the more formidable bowler. Larwood, for one thing, had pinpoint accuracy, to a degree quite exceptional for a fast bowler; but, in the views of many of those who played him, it was his bounce that was

---

* Allen was faster than Voce and took considerably more wickets in the Tests (21 to 15) at practically the same average cost. Voce missed the fourth Test and was unable to bowl much in the second innings of the third; on the other hand, Allen's figures suffered in the fifth Test, when he bowled a lot in spite of not being properly fit. Larwood took 33 wickets. Between them, the three English fast bowlers thus took 69 of the 93 Australian wickets to fall to the ball during the series.

his most difficult quality of all. Larwood had the knack of making the ball fly unpredictably, from very little short of a length – especially on the hard Australian wickets. His run up to the wicket was all springy, flowing rhythm, the accumulated energy of it concentrated totally in the final catapulting pivot over the rigid left leg. When he pitched the ball short of a length, it would often rocket explosively up at the batsman's chest or head at a speed that defied controlled reaction. Bill Bowes remembers it very clearly: when he or Voce bowled a short one, he says, it would bounce like a tennis ball; when Larwood did it, it was like a stone skimming on water. The illustration is vivid: we all know the way a flat stone, bounced on smooth water, will rise with no apparent loss of speed at all.

The technicalities of all this are worth a moment's thought. In normal circumstances, a ball will bounce off a flat surface – such as a cricket pitch – at the same angle at which it went on: hence the greater the height from which the ball is delivered from a given distance, the more steeply it will lift. But this is not the whole story. Larwood was a small man, though a well-built one – considerably shorter than Voce, let alone the six-foot-four-inch Bowes, who should therefore have been able to make the ball lift more steeply than he could. But he was considerably faster than them; and although the speed of the ball does not affect the angle at which it leaves the pitch, it is the critical factor in determining how long it will hold its vertical line – how long it will go on rising – after it does so. In fact, Larwood's lack of height may have been a positive asset, for the shorter the bowler, the finer the angle at which the ball will hit the pitch, and the finer the angle, the less speed it will lose in bouncing. Pace off the pitch, and angle off the pitch, in fact, are in inverse relationship. Larwood's deliveries did not lift exceptionally steeply, but they went on rising much longer than most fast bowler's deliveries;* and, as we have

*I am very much obliged to a colleague, Bob Parker, for his guidance of an ignorant arts graduate through the simpler mysteries of trajectory and bounce.

seen, the batsman's problems were further compounded by the unpredictability of the bounce.

The venom of 'bodyline' of course varied with the wicket. As a technique, it was especially well adapted to a country like Australia, of hard wickets, where the ball lost its shine quickly, but came off the pitch faster and bounced higher than at home. But even Australian wickets varied: a number of observers, in fact, remarked that in 1932–33 they were much less consistently hard and fast than in 1928–29, which had been an enormously high-scoring series. 'Bodyline' was least effective in the Melbourne and Brisbane Tests, though at Melbourne, on a slow wicket which took spin from the start to an extent to give rise to dark suspicions in the English camp about its preparation, its ineffectiveness was only relative. The English battery of fast bowlers bowled Australia out for 228 and 191, but the English batsmen fared even worse against the Australian spinners, Ironmonger, O'Reilly and Grimmett. At Brisbane the wicket had so little bounce in it that even Larwood had difficulty in getting the ball up head-high, and the English attack was further limited by the absence of Voce and the intense heat; but even so Larwood took seven wickets in the two innings and was mainly responsible for taking the heart out of the Australian batting.

At Sydney and Adelaide the wickets were faster, and the fast bowlers profited accordingly. By all accounts, the wicket at Adelaide in the third Test was the liveliest of the whole series: it is not a coincidence that it was here that the two most serious injuries of the series, and the most violent crowd scenes, occurred. In fact the wicket was at its most volatile on the first morning, when England, batting first for the only time in the series, lost their first four wickets for 30 runs: what would have happened if Larwood, Voce and Allen had had first use of it is an interesting subject for speculation.

As it was, Wall, at well below their pace and bowling no more than an orthodox fast bowler's normal ration of short ones, was a quite sufficiently nasty proposition, and

Hammond at least, who was not a hooker and was never very happy when the ball was flying about his ears, made no pretence of liking it. When he was out, caught at the wicket off Wall – George Hele, the umpire, thought that he actually glanced the ball deliberately to Oldfield – on the way back to the pavilion, he said to O'Reilly, 'If that's what the game's coming to, it's time for me to get out.' It is a revealing incident – assuming that Hele's memory is to be trusted – for Wall at his fastest was an infinitely less formidable proposition than Larwood, and it tends to support the view strongly held in Australia that if it had been the English batsmen who had been exposed to the 'bodyline' attack, they would have been no more successful, and no less resentful, than their Australian counterparts.

In coping with the 'bodyline' attack, the Australian batsmen had no worthwhile previous experience to go by, and we have already seen that in practice their reactions varied. The most aggressive response to a fast bowler pitching short is to hook; but the hook is a dangerous, though spectacular, shot. Batsmen, even first-class batsmen, tend to divide fairly sharply into the hookers and the non-hookers: we have just seen that Hammond, for instance, belonged to the latter category, and of the regular Australian batsmen only Bradman, Richardson and McCabe were habitual hookers. McCabe's famous 187 at Sydney in the first Test was largely based on the shot, which he used with particular profit against Voce,* and Richardson used it effectively in the first innings at Brisbane. But the hook was a dubious counter to 'bodyline'. If a batsman counter-attacked in this way, Jardine would post three men on the boundary between fine-leg and square, which made hooking a perilously chancy enterprise. Against bowlers of Larwood's pace, the margin for error was very small indeed (it will be remembered that it was in trying to hook that Oldfield was hit on the head at

* According to Fingleton, he scored only 16 runs in front of the wicket on the off side in the course of this innings.

Adelaide); and we have seen that Larwood's most dangerous delivery in particular was not so much the bumper as the ball of slightly fuller length which rose waist- or chest- rather than head-high, and which could rarely be sighed off the pitch accurately enough to permit of hooking.

It is significant that of the two innings just mentioned, McCabe's was played in the first innings of the first Test, when Larwood had not yet gone over to full 'bodyline' methods, and Richardson's at Brisbane, where Larwood did not have the support of Voce and was handicapped by an exceptionally unresponsive wicket. It is very significant that neither of them ever played a comparable innings again later in the series,* and perhaps even more so that Bradman, the most technically well-equipped of all the Australian batsmen and in ordinary circumstances a magnificent hooker, virtually excluded the shot from his repertoire altogether in the 'bodyline' series because he thought it too risky. It may have been his experience in the first innings of the Melbourne Test, where he played on to Bowes when attempting the stroke, which brought him to this conclusion: certainly he seems to have made little use of it in the course of his match-winning century in the second innings, and thereafter he increasingly evolved his own quite different and unique technique of playing 'bodyline', which, as we have seen, was based on moving away wide of the leg stump and forcing the bowling to the off side with a cross bat.

I have made the point earlier that there is a sense in which this, intellectually, was the most satisfactory response to 'bodyline', since 'bodyline' was based on the attempt to confine the batsman's strokes to a single narrow arc of the field, and Bradman was countering this directly by forcing the ball into the wide open spaces on the off side: it was also a very respectably successful attempt when one looks at Bradman's scores in the last three Tests – 8 and 66

*Hele records that after his great innings McCabe himself said, 'I was lucky – I could never do it again.'

at Adelaide, 76 and 24 at Brisbane, and 48 and 71 at Sydney – and especially when one contrasts them with the comparative figures for the other Australian batsmen. But both Australian and British observers had reservations about it. It was a fearsomely risky technique, since it meant leaving the stumps completely exposed, and given the variable bounce of Australian pitches on this tour, this was almost bound to be fatal in the end (as in the first innings at Brisbane, where Bradman was bowled leg stump by Larwood while trying to force him through the covers); and it was the mood of reckless aggression that it reflected that twice gave Verity Bradman's wicket – in the second innings at both Adelaide and Sydney.

Although Bradman in this mood played brilliant and hectic innings, he played no really long one. It was a desperate remedy, and one that probably no batsman in the world but Bradman had the speed of eye and footwork to attempt with any prospect of success; and – so some thought anyway – at a time when what was needed to steady the nerves and revive the flagging morale of the other Australian batsmen was a demonstration that 'bodyline' could be worn down and mastered by methods within the compass of ordinary mortals, Bradman's adoption of it drove them instead to the conclusion that, if this was the only counter to 'bodyline', for them there was no hope at all. According to George Hele, the umpire, Woodfull actually wanted to drop Bradman from the side after his 66 in the second innings at Adelaide – he had instructed his batsmen to stand in line to the bowling, and Bradman had defied him.

Bradman has always been an extremely private person: he has had to be, to resist the intense pressures of publicity that have beaten upon him for most of his life. I can imagine an argument that he saw 'bodyline' primarily as a private challenge and forged a private answer to it, whereas in fact it was not that. The error, if there was one, was pardonable, for there is no doubt that 'bodyline' had originated and evolved very largely as an anti-Bradman weapon, and to Larwood at least it may well have been a private thing, for Larwood had a considerable score to settle with Bradman for the treatment he had received at his hands in 1930. 'If that little bugger can get him out, wait till I get at him,' he said, as he watched Bradman in some discomfort when facing Allen bowling very fast down a strong wind in the 'Combined XI' match at Perth at the beginning of the tour. But although for Jardine too the main problem was how to get Bradman out, and though Jardine too had a private score to settle in Australia, his score was not against Bradman, but against Australia, and 'bodyline' to him was not a means to humiliate any one man, even Bradman, but to win the Tests; and it was no counter for Bradman to find a method of playing 'bodyline', if he was the only one who could use it. So the argument might run, but what it is worth I do not pretend to be able to say.

Larwood himself was interesting on this, in his conversations with Kevin Perkins on which *The Larwood Story* was based. It is common ground that 'bodyline', bowled badly, could be extremely expensive: Larwood's own early experiments with it in the Notts matches against Essex and Glamorgan late in the 1932 season both ended in run feasts for the opposition, as did Jack Scott's experiment with something similar against Victoria in Sydney in 1925. To be successful, 'bodyline' demanded both very great pace and supreme accuracy: even then, so Larwood thought, it *could* have been successfully counter-attacked by skilful and determined use of the hook, and Richardson and McCabe came close to achieving this. Larwood too felt that Bradman and Woodfull led the Australian batsmen into a blind alley, by forswearing the hook (though Woodfull in any case was never a hooker) and adopting methods which were either unsound (in Bradman's case) or merely passive (in Woodfull's), and that this both undermined Australian morale and convinced the English side that it was worth persisting with 'bodyline'.

All this is very controversial. Larwood never had to face

his own bowling (and told Kevin Perkins that he himself might possibly have thought it unfair if he had ever seen it from the spectator's angle – let alone the batsman's); Bradman has never swerved from his opinion that 'bodyline' as bowled by Larwood and Voce, was unplayable by any orthodox means; and nobody is in a worse position to pass judgement on such an issue than a bespectacled academic behind a typewriter. Still, is is worth noting that opinions did, and do, differ on the issue, as did the Australian techniques at the time. Apart from McCabe, Richardson, and Bradman, the other front-rank Australian batsmen all adopted mainly passive techniques against 'bodyline': either ducking, as Woodfull repeatedly did, or taking the ball on the body when it seemed to be lifting too dangerously for a dead-bat defensive stroke – the method usually favoured by Ponsford and Fingleton. Ponsford batted with a towel wrapped round his chest, and actually turned his back on the ball at times. For batsmen not distinguished by unusual speed of footwork – as on the whole was true of Woodfull, Ponsford and Fingleton – it was almost impossible to avoid being hit with some frequency in any case. This may have served to emphasize the ugly face of 'bodyline' – Fingleton remarked how, in the first New South Wales match, when Voce hit him and the other NSW batsmen repeatedly about the body, the close fieldsmen who at first came up and gathered round after each incident to see how the batsman was and give him a sympathetic word, gradually ceased doing so and stood off in either embarrassment or assumed indifference. But this kind of moral pressure was not going to cut much ice with Jardine, and it was small compensation for the steady undermining of concentration and resolution that was the inevitable effect of such repeated battering. The effect of 'bodyline' was psychologically *cumulative*; and it is worth remembering too that most of the leading Australian batsmen were married men. Their wives knew what had happened to Woodfull and Oldfield, and they had to watch their husbands go out to bat in the knowledge that the same or worse might be about to happen to them. 'Bodyline' worked on the batsmen through *their* anxieties, as well as through the batsmen's own fears.

How often batsmen were hit is obviously a point of some importance in reaching a judgement on 'bodyline'. Both Jardine and Larwood took the line that fast bowlers had always hit batsmen from time to time, and that the better the batsman, the less he would be hit. This is true, but there is no question that the Australian batsmen were hit far more often on the 1932–33 tour than in any past series. How far they were themselves to blame for this by moving back across the stumps has already been discussed: suffice it to say here that it does not seem that this can be anything more than a very partial explanation. That some were hit far more than others, and that Bradman was never badly hit at all, is true, as we have seen; and we have also seen that the difference mostly reflects their choice of tactics when facing the 'bodyline' attack. In fairness, it must also be said that, though several took a painful battering, no Australian batsman was seriously injured by 'bodyline'. The two worst incidents, those at Adelaide involving Woodfull and Oldfield, both occurred, by common consent, at times when the 'bodyline' field was not set, and the balls concerned were recognized by all those qualified to express an opinion as legitimate fast bowlers' deliveries. There is, though, great force in the contention that what ultimately made 'bodyline' unacceptable was the prospect of what injuries might be inflicted when inaccurate bowlers started bowling it to indifferent batsmen. This possibility was a source of great anxiety in Australia, where already before the end of the tour the appearance of experiments in 'bodyline' in grade and schools cricket, and of injuries resulting from them, was being reported. Most, if not all, the state cricket associations in fact acted swiftly to ban 'bodyline' in all games played under their jurisdiction.

The whole issue of injuries to the batsman needs to be seen against the background of the kinds of protective clothing available to batsmen in 1933. Pads and gloves were of course universal. as were boxes: pads in particular had come a long way since the flimsy affairs of pre-War days – an indication of the much more intensive use that batsmen were now making of them. But that was the limit – even thigh-pads seem not to have been in use, and body-padding and helmets were unknown. Necessity drove the Australian batsmen to improvise: Woodfull said that in the Adelaide Test most of them were wearing some form of body protection, and we have already seen in passing such novelties as Ponsford's towel and the use of cork padding for the chest at Brisbane. It is, though, very striking that the only form of head-protection that appeared seems to have been a curious three-peaked cap designed by Hendren to protect his temples against the West-Indies fast bowlers in England in 1933. Probably one of the factors here was the difficulty of finding any suitable materials for helmets in days before the evolution of the modern plastics industry; another, no doubt, was the repugnance of the cricketing Establishment to countenance the use of these ugly concessions to violence, a repugnance still widely felt today and no doubt much more effective in the 1930s, when the cricketing Establishment was much narrower and much more powerful. E. T. Crutchley, the British Representative in Canberra, whose role in the affair we have seen, wrote a most revealing letter to Warner when the controversy was at its height in February, in which he used this repugnance as a powerful argument against 'bodyline' itself:

What do batsmen wear pads and gloves for? Well, the same reason to my mind would not justify the wearing of helmets and chest protectors. Do we want that? No, too hot! Well then either stop deliberate short pitching by consent or have a no-ball line say 10 yards up the wicket!

For my part, I can only applaud, and it may well be that if 'bodyline' had lasted longer, helmets would have become conventional accoutrements forty years earlier than they in fact did.

There is a final point connected with the technical aspects of 'bodyline' which requires some attention here. It may well seem very surprising indeed that in a series in which the English tactics were so intensely controversial, the Laws were never invoked and the umpires never involved. It *is* very surprising. That it was so is, in large part, a high tribute to the two umpires, George Hele and George Borwick, who stood in all five Tests and whose conduct of them was never the subject of any serious criticism by either side. Obviously, though, the question of the relationship of 'bodyline' to the Laws of the game must have arisen in some people's minds. The difficulty wat that 'bodyline' was a new technique, and the Laws had been framed by men who had never conceived of such a method of attack: it had been excluded, if it had even been consciously considered, by the mysterious and impalpable conventions of the game rather than by its Laws. I have it on Bradman's authority that, to the best of his knowledge, the possibility of appealing to the umpires to intervene was never considered by the Australian team. It did occur to some. *The Times*, in one of the leaders that it devoted to the affair, used the failure of the umpires to intervene as an argument in favour of the fairness of 'leg theory'. More to the point, George Hele, in one of his conversations with R. S. Whitington on which the latter based his book *Bodyline Umpire*, relates that he and Borwick discussed the legality of 'bodyline' (more precisely, apparently, of the field setting on which it was based) before the first Test, and that on the Sunday of the Adelaide Test, after Woodfull had been hit, they went through the Laws again to consider their application to 'bodyline', but came to the conclusion that they could do nothing without an appeal – which never came. It is not in fact at all easy to see what they could have done under the Laws as they then were even if there *had* been an appeal, though Hele seems to imply that he and Borwick thought they could have done something. There was indeed Law 43, which lays it down that 'the Umpires are the sole judges of fair and unfair play': this has sometimes been interpreted as a sort of ultimate deterrent, giving umpires unlimited powers of intervention in cases not covered by the Laws. But it can hardly have been this that Hele had in mind, since it makes no mention of an appeal; and although it may have been on this that *The Times* leader-writer based his argument, he was probably wrong if he did, since there is not much doubt that the real intention of Law 43 is merely to make the umpires the sole interpreters of the Laws, rather than legislators in their own right. When discussion turned seriously, as it very soon did, to the possibility of banning 'bodyline' by legislation, it was invariably assumed that an addition to the Laws would be required for the purpose.

If the laws in their existing form provided no protection against bodyline, there remained in theory one other immediate response the Australians might have tried – retaliation. A good many Australians, I suspect, agreed with this in their heart of hearts, and felt that there was something demeaning and humiliating in the Board's attitude. Certainly the jeers of the English popular press, their taunts that the Australians, who had been ready enough to hand it out when Gregory and Macdonald were on the rampage in 1920–21, were showing that they could not take it now that they were on the receiving end, must have been very hard for Australians to stomach – and the press of each country was quick to reprint the more inflammatory utterances of their contemporaries in the other. The veteran versifier (and enthusiastic cricketer) J. C. Squire was even moved to verse on these lines, concluding with the not especially happy couplet:

> We won't believe the paradox,
> A whining Digger funking knocks.

It was, in fact, repeatedly rumoured in the later stages of the tour that 'bodyline' was to be turned against the MCC side. It was said that it was going to be tried by the Victorian fast bowler Alexander in the country match at Ballarat after the third Test, and again by the aboriginal Gilbert in Queensland's match against the MCC; but on both occasions authority, in the persons of the Victorian Cricket Association in the first instance and Gough, the Queensland captain, in the second, stepped in and forbade its use. We have seen with what delight the Sydney crowd reacted when Alexander did in fact hit Jardine during the last Test; and in the very last match of the tour, at Adelaide, the South Australian captain and Test Match batsman, Victor Richardson, who had been in the forefront of the 'bodyline' encounters in the Tests, a man of very different temperament to Woodfull and whose own inclination was clearly toward retaliation, used something resembling the English tactics, getting his opening bowler Williams to concentrate his attack on the leg side and setting a species of leg trap for him. It was, however, a very pale imitation: Williams was not a bowler of any real pace, and the 'leg trap', instead of crouching menacingly round the batsman, were fifteen or twenty yards back.

But none of these proposals for retaliation came to anything serious. Most evaporated entirely. In the case of the South Australia match, feeble though the imitation was, the Board of Control was disturbed enough to require an explanation from the Secretary of the South Australian Cricket Association; and in this can be seen the main reason why the idea of retaliation never came to anything. The fact is that Woodfull had set his face firmly against any such notion from the start, and that the Board gave him solid support in this attitude. It is true that Australia in 1932–33 in any case lacked the means for effective retaliation; but this was not the main reason for Woodfull's position, which was basically moral. Woodfull, a school-master – and later a headmaster – and the son of a Methodist minister, was a wholehearted believer in the idea of cricket as a school of morality. The whole idea of systematic intimidation as an element in it was fundamentally unacceptable to him, and he was consistent enough to see that this position would be undermined if Australia showed the slightest inclination to turn the Englishmen's tactics against them; and he carried the Board with him in this. He was not necessarily right: it is possible to feel that retaliation, or the prospect of it, might have been a relatively painless and effective way of making England think twice about 'bodyline'. Certainly the use of bouncers has sometimes been restrained by the reflection that two can play at that game, and that the other side may have bowlers who can bounce them as fast and as high as yours can; and we shall see that the Board of Control, or its representative, was itself not above deriving useful leverage from the threat of retaliation at a later stage. Woodfull's position, it is true, would have been stronger if it had not been public knowledge that Australia in any case lacked the means for effective retaliation in 1932–33, even if they had had the will; but it is impossible not at least to respect his position. Australia preserved its moral position intact. The 'bodyline' issue remained unresolved; but with the next Australian touring side due in England in a bare twelve months' time, it could not remain so for long. With the return of the MCC side to England, the 'bodyline' debate resumed with full intensity.

PART III

The Sequel

CHAPTER 8

The Controversy Resumed
(May–December 1933)

The MCC side landed at Greenock from the liner *Duchess of Atholl* on 6 May on the crest of a wave of national triumph and euphoria; and almost from that moment the wave began to ebb.

Even before their team's return, the MCC had good reason to be aware that the 'bodyline' issue was anything but dead and buried. A curtain-raiser was provided by the return of Larwood at the end of March. It will be remembered that he, together with Pataudi, had left the touring party in Adelaide at the conclusion of the Australian part of the tour, travelled by train to Perth, and from there caught a boat home. Pataudi went home to India; Larwood travelled on alone. It is an indication of the excitement the tour had aroused in England that the press dispatched a swarm of journalists to meet him at Toulon, and the *Sketch* went so far as to commission Arthur Carr, his county captain, to go out and interview him at Suez. Larwood had little experience of dealing with the press, and none at all of handling an issue as red-hot as this one, for it was clear that the representatives of the popular press, in search of sensational headlines and circulation figures, would be on to him at once about the most dramatic and controversial aspects of the tour – leg theory, the failures of the Australian batsmen against it, and the Australian barracking – and that Larwood might well let slip comments which could be blown up by the press into something very explosive indeed, especially when reprinted in Australia. The news of Carr's going was particularly disquieting, for discretion was the least of his virtues, and it is no wonder that both the Nottinghamshire CCC and the MCC took alarm, the former holding an emergency meeting to deprecate his trip, the latter despatching a hasty telegram to Larwood at sea, urging him not to give any information to Carr or anyone else. The danger was averted – in fact, by the time he reached Suez it seems to have dawned on Carr himself that he was acting less than wisely and he apparently lent his support to the MCC's telegram, urging Larwood to say nothing to the journalists awaiting him. But it was evident enough that Jardine and Larwood in particular would be under enormous pressure and inducements from the press to tell their side of the story when once they were back in England; and although the entire touring party were bound by the terms of their contract to write nothing for the press during the tour, once the party was home there would be no way to prevent them selling their stories.*

This might be considered a storm in a teacup: much more serious was the arrival, on 28 April, of a new cable from the Board of Control. The last official communication from them had been the cable of 8 February. The interval had been occupied, as far as the Australians were concerned, by the deliberations of the committee of whose appointment they had informed the MCC in their second cable, set up 'to report on the action necessary to eliminate such bowling [i.e., 'bodyline'] from Australian cricket as from the beginning of the 1933–34 season'. The committee consisted of R. J. Hartigan, one of the Queensland representatives on

---

* Ferguson, the team's baggage manager, has told the story of how he was received on the quay, at the team's arrival at Greenock, by a journalist brandishing a handful of pound notes, who accosted him with, 'Just talk to my paper and this lot is yours, and there's plenty more where that came from.' Larwood himself was later offered £1 a word for anything he cared to write.

216

the Board of Control and one of the only two of the Board's members with extensive experience of first-class cricket; Woodfull, the Australian captain; Victor Richardson, the vice-captain; and M. A. Noble, an ex-captain of Australia and one of the most respected figures in the Australian cricketing community. The committee, by its brief, was appointed, not to discuss 'bodyline', but to legislate it out of existence, and its composition reflected the fact: all four were known opponents of 'bodyline' (for that matter, it would have been hard to find prominent figures in the Australian cricketing world who were not), and significantly none of them were fast bowlers.

The committee's deliberations took time – as always in Australia, it was not easy for busy men who came from cities as far apart as Brisbane and Adelaide to arrange meetings – and the Board itself, whose meetings were equally difficult to arrange and equally rare for the same reasons, did not meet to consider its report until 28 April. The committee recommended an addition to the Laws, to be numbered 48(b), which would read:

> Any ball delivered which, in the opinion of the umpire at the bowler's end, is bowled at the batsman with the intent to intimidate or injure him shall be considered unfair and 'No-ball' shall be called. The bowler shall be notified of the reason. If the offence be repeated by the same bowler in the same innings he shall be immediately instructed by the umpire to cease bowling and the over shall be regarded as completed. Such bowler shall not again be permitted to bowl during the course of the innings then in progress.

The proposal was radical and far-reaching – particularly in its unprecedented suggestion that an offending bowler should be banned for the rest of the innings. If it had been in force during the 1932–33 tour, there can be no doubt that it would have been invoked, and that it would have made 'bodyline' impossible. In Australia, which had seen 'bodyline' and overwhelmingly repudiated it, it might be expected that the proposed new Law would meet with little opposition. But the Board had to consider another issue – how would such a radical addition to the Laws be received by the rest of the world cricketing community, and by the lordly MCC in particular?

It was the MCC itself, in its reply to the ABC's original cable, which had suggested that the Australian body should, if it felt it necessary, submit an amendment to the Laws for consideration by the parent body. It is quite clear that the MCC were not expecting the ABC to introduce a local Law, necessarily confined to the game within Australia, without consultation with London; but, such was the strength of feeling on the issue in Australia, that was what they proceeded to do. The original terms of reference of the committee appointed in January implied as much; and at their meeting of 28 April, the Board did not merely agree to report the committee's recommendation to Lord's and postpone the question of its actual adoption until their next meeting in September – which would have allowed time for consultation with London and discussion of the proposed amendment at the meeting of the Imperial Cricket Conference due in England during the summer, and would still have been in ample time for the beginning of the next Australian season. This would have been the conciliatory line: significantly, it was the line recommended by the Board's own representative on the drafting committee, Hartigan, and his Queensland colleague, Hutcheon (both of whom had consistently favoured conciliation, rather than confrontation, as the best line to follow in negotiations with Lord's). But the Board preferred a more militant line: they adopted the proposed Law on the spot, and submitted it to the MCC by cable only 'for your consideration and it is hoped co-operation by application to all cricket'.

The Board's right to legislate unilaterally in this fashion was highly dubious. There was no doubt that the MCC was the supreme legislative body for the game: the Laws were issued on its authority and were intended to apply to the game throughout the world, though it was normal for them to be ratified at meetings of the Imperial Cricket Conference, representing the governing authorities of all the cricketing countries of the Empire. There were three local provisions in the Laws, applying to Australia (or Australia and New Zealand) only; but they were confined to marginal matters – the sweeping and rolling of the pitch, the number of balls in the over, and the margin required to enforce the follow-on – and, though they had been introduced at the instance of the Australian authorities, they had been passed *by* the MCC. The ABC were now introducing a major amendment, which would make a very substantial difference to the way the game was being played, without reference to the MCC. It might be difficult to challenge their *power* to do this, but their *right* was certainly questionable: it was a precedent which opened the way for cricket to develop into several radically different games in different countries, and presumably for the death of the game at international level.

Even in Australia the Board's action did not in fact go unchallenged. The New South Wales Cricket Association, which, like the Queensland Association, had been critical of the Board's handling of the controversy from the start, although condemning 'bodyline' as heartily as anyone, now refused outright to adopt the new Law, denied the Board's competence to legislate for the game, and went so far as to back its challenge by forwarding to the Board counsel's opinion to the same effect.

So it might well seem that the ABC were taking a dangerously strong line in adopting so intransigent a position; and all the more so since a meeting of the Imperial Cricket Conference was due to take place in London during the summer. At this the 'bodyline' issue was almost certain to be raised, and on the face of it Australia – the only country which had so far witnessed 'bodyline' – might, by so pre-empting the issue rather than merely presenting its amendment as a proposal for discussion, risk ostracism at

219

it. There were, nevertheless, good reasons for the Board's attitude – the strength of feeling in Australia, which demanded resolute and uncompromising action, and the necessity which the Board clearly felt to take action to prevent the proliferation of 'bodyline' at all levels of the game in Australia in the forthcoming 1933–34 season. The Board had decided to be tough; and on this general point, if not on the particular issue of the line on which they had chosen to fight, they were soon to receive the strong support of their representative in London, Dr. R. Macdonald.

The arrival of the Board's cable multiplied the problems facing the MCC Committee. The Annual General Meeting of the Club was due on 3 May. The touring party was due back on the 6th, and once they were home, they would be free to release their stories to the press, who, for their part, were clamouring to get at them. Meanwhile, the new English season was just about to begin. The conjunction of events conveniently symbolizes the three main fronts on which, so to speak, the controversy was to be fought out during the summer of 1933; and given the confused and complex nature of events, it may help to try to keep the distinction in mind. All three fronts were English: in Australia, once the English touring side had departed, there was no longer any conflict to speak of, except perhaps as to the best means of eliminating 'bodyline'; to the proposition that, by one means or another, eliminated it should be, there was no serious opposition. But in England it is possible to distinguish the continuing retrospective argument about the series in Australia just completed: the events that took place on the field during the English season of 1933, and the public reaction to them; and the continuing negotiations between the MCC and the Australian Board of Control, which turned increasingly on the issue of whether there was indeed to be an Australian tour of England in 1934. It is also approximately true that the three 'fronts' involved different groups of combatants. The first was largely an affair of the press, especially the popular sporting press and its readers; the second an affair of the English cricket-going public, and especially of its more influential echelons; the third an affair of the inmost circles of the cricketing worlds of the two countries – in Australia, the Board of Control, in England, the Main Committee of the MCC, and the still more restricted sub-committee it had appointed for the purpose. There were certainly overlaps between these groups of combatants, and between the 'fronts' themselves: events on one front sometimes affected those on another, and the conflicts on all three fronts proceeded simultaneously. But, as I say, as a device to help clarify a very complicated story it may serve. The public controversy had died away for the time being with the departure of the MCC party from Australia in mid-March: it resumed with their triumphant arrival in England, and the opening of the new season in May, and it resumed on all three fronts almost simultaneously.

Now that the team were back, the debate on the rights and wrongs of what had happened in Australia could not conceivably be confined behind closed doors. The pace on this first front was set by an article by Larwood which appeared in the *Sunday Express* on 7 May – the day after the MCC team returned home, and the first moment at which Larwood was released from the ban on writing for the press written into his tour contract. In this he said, among other things, 'You ask me why Woodfull and Bradman couldn't stand up to my fast bowling. These are the true reasons: Woodfull was too slow. Bradman was too frightened. Yes, "frightened" is the word. Bradman just wouldn't have it.' This was precisely the sort of thing that the great British cricketing public did, and the MCC did not, want to read, and it was all too typical of the style that was to characterize events on this 'front' for the next eighteen months or more – crude, inflammatory and violently partisan. From the first they concentrated heavily round the two controversial figures of Jardine and Larwood, who by the spring of 1933 had become, in the eyes of most of the general public, the incarnations of 'bodyline', and, without any volition of their own, symbols for the instincts and passions of a large section of the public (in both countries) whose interest in and knowledge of the game was often not much more than skin-deep. Their very names became triggers to release pleasurable orgies of pommy-bashing in Australian hotels and denunciations of Australian larrikins and squealers in English clubs.

I suggested in the first chapter that the sense of nationalism, or pride in one's country, was in an unusually delicate and volatile condition in both Britain and Australia in 1932–33, roused to frenzied heights by the War, denied adequate expression after it, and deeply frustrated by the experience of the Depression. Certainly the depths of passion sounded by the 'bodyline' controversy would seem to support this, and what remains of the miscellaneous correspondence that poured in to both the MCC and the ABC on the issue bears this out.

This level of debate was not limited to readers of the *Star* and the *Sunday Dispatch*, but seems to have extended across most of the social spectrum, revealing surprising depths of snobbishness and bigotry in the process. Thus, on the one side, the attitude of Macdonald, the Australian Board of Control's representative in London, to Jardine can only be described as venomous. In one of his letters to the Board, written early in 1934 after the controversy had been settled, he remarked that:

Australia will have the satisfaction of knowing that she resented the introduction into Cricket of methods which (while quite natural to Mr Jardine) were wholly Teutonic in their character. To achieve victory at any cost, seems to be an attribute common to both Attila and Mr Jardine. If I do Attila an injustice by this simile I tender an apology to his belated memory.

The carry-over of attitudes bred in the First World War here is noteworthy. But it is not difficult to counter with equally savage judgements from England, not always

222

confined (as Macdonald's was) to the limits of private correspondence. Carr, the Nottinghamshire captain, in his highly polemical contribution to the controversy, *Cricket With The Lid Off*, remarked that 'Cricket is more or less purely and simply a matter of £ s d with the Australians ... I know plenty of professionals whom I would delight to have as guests in my own home, but I am afraid I cannot say the same thing about most of the Australians whom I have met.'*

To Australians, Jardine was the mastermind and Larwood the chief executive of a type of attack which grossly violated the ethical tradition of the game and which constantly threatened – and in Oldfield's case achieved – serious physical injury to the batsman. To Englishmen, Jardine was the courageous captain who had taken the Australians on at their own game and shown that Englishmen could be tough too (to counter the Australians, 'il faut cultiver notre Jardine,' remarked Nevile Cardus, in an execrable pun), Larwood was the super-bowler who had punctured the myth of Bradman the super-batsman.

Throughout the summer of 1933, the fires of the controversy were regularly stoked up by the appearance of new accounts of the tour, originating from one country or the other, and most of them highly polemical. By the early 1930s, the tradition of accounts of tours just concluded, usually written by sporting journalists who had accompanied them, and dropping red-hot from the press within a few weeks of the touring team's return home, was already well established; but no tour has ever bred as many books as that of 1932–33. The controversy was of course manna from heaven for the publishers (as well as for the press),

---

* One is reminded of the almost unbelievable quotation from one of C. B. Fry's press reports on the 1930 tour, reprinted by Fingleton in *Cricket Crisis*: 'In all this Australian team there are barely one or two who would be accepted as public school men ... and while I am writing this, curator X has just bowled another maiden over.' The element of pure snobbery, and reverse snobbery, present in all Anglo-Australian relations in the 1930s should not be overlooked as a factor in the 'bodyline' troubles.

and throughout the summer books succeeded each other from the presses of Australia and England at a rate the reviewers of the cricketing periodicals could scarcely keep up with. From Australia there came Arthur Mailey's *And Then Came Larwood*, R. W. E. Wilmot's *Defending the Ashes*, and Alan Kippax' *Anti-Bodyline*; from England, Hobbs' *Fight For The Ashes*, Bruce Harris' *Jardine Justified*, and – still more controversially – Larwood's *Body-Line?* and Jardine's *In Quest of the Ashes*. Of these, Mailey's and Hobbs' books can fairly be called measured and impartial, though both are critical of 'bodyline': all the rest are definitely partisan, often to the point of polemic.

Jardine and Larwood in England in 1933 were, of course, very much in the position that Bradman had been in in Australia after the 1930 tour: they were national heroes (the *Cricketer* commented significantly in May on the rapturous reception Jardine received from the Lord's crowd when he led the MCC in their match against the West Indies touring side), and in consequence very valuable literary properties; and it is not surprising that both received publishers' offers tempting enough to induce them to write books. It is some indication of the pressures of commercial money on first-class cricketers at this juncture that Fingleton records hearing that Larwood had quintupled his entire earnings for the tour in Australia by a week's demonstration of 'bodyline' at Gamage's after his return.*

The prominence of Jardine and Larwood in the controversy is obvious from the list of these titles and authors, and was still more heavily underlined in the sports columns of the popular (and especially the Sunday) papers, but one may very well doubt whether their public

* It would be interesting to have some details of how this demonstration was mounted, and especially of who was on the receiving end. Larwood apparently also produced a record on 'bodyline' for Columbia; I have slightly more information on this. It consisted not (as might be expected) of thuds, howls of anguish and shouts of 'How's that?', against a background of barracking, but of a conversation with Frank Foster.

prominence did either them or the case for 'bodyline' much good. An argument that could have been conducted usefully on the level of an impersonal examination of what 'bodyline' meant and what its consequences were for the game became distorted and perverted by the intensity of the focus on the two principals concerned. It was hardly surprising if the impression was given that these two men alone were the cause of the controversy, and that if they were removed from the scene, it would automatically be ended. It is also unsurprising if the pressure of intense publicity had effects on Jardine and Larwood themselves that were not always happy.

Certainly neither of the books that appeared in their name at this time seems, in retrospect, to have been likely to advance their cause in anything but the very short term. Both were concerned to play down 'bodyline', and to minimize the element of novelty in it: both indeed reject the term, with its implication of intimidation, and prefer to describe the English tactics as 'fast leg theory' instead. Larwood's is perceptibly the franker of the two – he does recognize, as his title implies, that 'bodyline' (or whatever term is preferred) *was* the central issue of the series – but even so it is a far less satisfactory book than *The Larwood Story* published thirty years later. Jardine devotes only one chapter to 'leg theory', and brushes aside the accusation that it depended for its effect on direct attack on the batsman as too absurd to require refutation. The main theme of the book, stated at the outset, is whether the continuance of Test Matches between the two countries is worth while, and this turns out to resolve itself entirely into the question of what, if anything, the Australian authorities are prepared to do to control the behaviour of their crowds! Conceivably, Jardine never realized that 'fast leg theory' had developed a dynamic of its own during the series, and had been transformed into something very different from his probable original intention – but it is impossible to think that it was anything but a misleading perspective from which to view the events of the tour.

In Quest of the Ashes is a bitter book; and it seems to me very much to be regretted that Jardine did not write instead a franker, more reasoned and more dispassionate account of his conduct of the tour – which could, I believe, have been done, and which would have done his reputation a much better service in the long run. One comes back again to the quite fundamental and total lack of sympathy – antipathy is hardly too strong a word – for his Australian opponents and for the Australian cricketing public that runs through incident after incident of the tour and through everything that he had to say about it afterwards. It can be discerned in the prefaces that he wrote for Larwood's and Bruce Harris' books as well as in his own: it seemed to make it impossible to write a defence of Jardine that was not simultaneously an attack upon Australia, and it damaged his own prospects in the sense that as time went on it made it increasingly unthinkable that he could ever lead England against Australia again.

If Jardine's book served to stoke the fires of the controversy (as it certainly did), Jardine at least refused to blow them up further by contributing to the rabid clamours of the popular press on the subject. Larwood, lacking Jardine's armour of patrician disdain for the press and all its works, and his comfortable income, was less immune to journalists' inducements: all the more when, as time went on, he began to feel that he was being let down by the policy-makers of the MCC and, wisely or unwisely, turned to the popular press as his only allies against them. We have already noted his first appearance in print, in the *Sunday Express* of 7 May; another outburst of his in October was to cause equal trouble, and there was more to come in 1934. What he wrote did him no good at all with the MCC, and did much to undermine his chances of ever playing for England again; and some of it makes sad reading today. But it is impossible not to have very great sympathy with him. He had no experience of dealings with the popular press, which exploited him ruthlessly for the purpose of nourishing the sensationalism on which it thrived; the financial inducements it offered were great; he received no responsible guidance where he might have looked for it from his county captain, Carr, whose public statements were as intemperate as his own; and he *was* badly treated by the cricketing Establishment, and it is no wonder if he did not always choose his allies against them wisely. It is no more than justice to him to point out that his last word on the 'bodyline' controversy, his book *The Larwood Story*, is still, to my mind, the frankest and fairest account of the affair ever written.

It must in any case be recognized that, if Jardine and Larwood in the course of 1933 did something to help their critics by failing to present their own cause in a very sympathetic light, their appeal to the court of public opinion – for that was what it amounted to – made it very difficult for the MCC to repudiate them (especially, of course, since it had already appeared to endorse Jardine's tactics while the tour was in progress). If Jardine and Larwood had said nothing to the press and published no word of their own, the MCC would have been greatly relieved – but probably still less likely to stick to its guns in defence of the legitimacy of 'bodyline'. Events on the other two 'fronts' of the controversy were already inclining the outcome the other way.

It was against this background that the MCC Committee had to consider their reply to the ABC's cable of 28 April and to carry on their negotiations with that body's representative, Dr R. Macdonald, and for this purpose they proceeded, at the beginning of May, to appoint a special sub-committee in strict secrecy. The MCC records do not reveal the membership of the sub-committee, but on the evidence of Macdonald's letters to the Board it probably consisted of Lord Lewisham (outgoing President of the MCC), Lord Hawke (past-President and current Treasurer of the Club, and also current President of Yorkshire CC), Sir Stanley Jackson (also a past-President, and a past captain of England in addition) and W. Findlay, the Secretary – a composition which is a sure sign of the importance of the issue in the MCC's eyes, for a quartet who carried greater weight in the English cricketing Establishment could scarcely have been found among its members.

Following this shrewd move, it is not surprising to hear that nothing was heard of the controversy at the Annual General Meeting which followed. Nothing was said of the Australian cable, and there was apparently no reference to the tour just concluded other than a routine and anodyne congratulation to Jardine and his side on their success in the President's address.

There was, though, one other event of high significance at the meeting – the election of the new President, who was none other than Lord Hailsham. Hailsham (the father of the present Lord Chancellor) was Secretary for War and a member of the National Government's Cabinet: his succession to Lewisham may have been arranged before the 'bodyline' crisis blew up, but his presence at the head of the MCC for the next twelve months meant the closest possible contact with government at the highest level, and, although no direct evidence has come to light, there seems every reason to suppose that his influence acted power-fully in favour of the government's desire to defuse the controversy.

It was with this body that Macdonald, in the course of the next five months, was to carry on the crucial negotiations on which the main issue turned – whether or not an Australian touring side was to come to England in 1934. Macdonald neither sought nor received any of the limelight during the twelve months of frequently heated and embittered controversy that followed the return home of the MCC touring side in the spring of 1933; but it is clear from the records of the Board that he played a crucial role in the difficult negotiations between them and the MCC, and had a great deal to do with shaping the final form of the settlement; and the record reflects great credit on the accuracy of his judgement of men and attitudes and on the strength and clarity of his mind. He seems regularly to have spent the winters in the United States, and it was with the detachment that that conferred that he had been able to follow the accounts of the developing crisis while the tour was in progress. He returned to London late in March, and the letter he wrote to the Board announcing his arrival vigorously outlines the attitude he maintained throughout the months that followed. He asked for instructions on the line the Board wished him to follow on the 'bodyline' issue, but he also stated his own opinion. He hoped that the Imperial Cricket Conference would take action to ban 'bodyline' from the game. If they did not, he recommended the cancellation of the 1934 tour of England. If the Board nevertheless decided to persist with it, the team must include three or four fast bowlers able and willing to retaliate. This was strong meat; and Macdonald's resolve was, if anything, strengthened by the widespread soundings he proceeded to take of opinion about 'bodyline' among the ruling circles of English cricket. These convinced him that there was widespread uneasiness about Jardine's tactics in Australia, and that if the Board took a sufficiently firm line, they would win their case. On 28 April, the very day of the meeting of the Board at which it was decided to adopt the proposed Law 48(b) immediately and unilaterally, he sent a cable putting the point in the clearest possible terms – 'Unmistakable evidence growing feeling England against adoption Bodyline Bowling. Respectfully submit we should maintain inflexible attitude making tour next year conditional on ban.' It is to be noted that Macdonald wished the Board to take their stand on the issue of the 1934 tour: he did not mention the possibility of unilateral anti-'bodyline' legislation by Australia (which in itself would have no effect on the tour), and in fact Law 48(b) was to prove something of an embarrassment to him. Nevertheless, with their agent in London taking this line, it is not so surprising that the Board decided that they could afford to be intransigent.

It is true that the 'bodyline' issue would have had to be thrashed out, with or without the impending arrival of an

Australian touring team. 'Bodyline' had been adopted as an expedient to deal with an immediate threat; but it could not be confined to that. As I have mentioned earlier it is my own view that it was, to some considerable extent, improvised on the field after the tour had begun; but whether this is true or not, it seems fairly certain that neither Jardine nor anybody else had given much thought to the long-term consequences of its introduction. It had, as we have seen, been used very selectively on the Australian tour, and not at all in New Zealand; but – like the atomic bomb – it could not be used once or twice to meet an immediate need, locked away in a drawer, and forgotten. Once it had been used and proved effective, other people were certain to try it sooner or later – unless they were stopped. But although it was not the fact that Australia were due to tour England in 1934 that kept the 'bodyline' issue alive after the return home of the MCC side in the spring of 1933, it was that that made it urgent; and it was the same fact that now, for the first time, shifted the balance of power when it came to negotiations between the cricketing authorities of the two countries in Australia's favour – that, and one other factor that we shall come to shortly.

Both the MCC and the Australian Board of Control shrank instinctively from the idea of cancelling a Test tour – in effect, of severing the cricketing relations between the two countries. So also did the country cricket clubs in England and the State Cricket Associations in Australia; so did the cricketing public of both countries; so, undoubtedly, did the two governments. In the minds of a large part of the public, cricket *was* the main and most intimate link between the two countries in the 1930s: a rupture here would be traumatic indeed. There would be intense public indignation against those responsible: there would be immense emotional, financial, and even diplomatic implications. Test cricket was big money, then as now: the proceeds of cricket tours were shared equally between the countries concerned, and in the depressed circumstances of the early

1930s the financial blow to the parent bodies and to the county clubs and state associations if a tour was cancelled would be very serious indeed.

The governments had other issues to consider. In February, Ernest Crutchley, who, as Britain's leading diplomatic representative in Australia, had to be especially sensitive on such matters, was appalled by the strength of anti-English feeling over the 'bodyline' issue in – of all staid places! – the Union Club at Canberra; Hore-Ruthven reported from Adelaide that feeling there was so strong that people were refusing to buy British goods. The arena of the controversy even extended to China. In March an Australian paper commented on the severe strain put upon relations between British and Australian residents in Hong Kong and Shanghai by the 'bodyline' affair, and on the aggressively pro-British attitude of the leading English journal in China, the *North China Daily News*. 'It is remarkable,' the Australian paper commented, 'how this "bodyline" business has militated against Australia in certain quarters in the Far East. It is impossible not to be struck by the heat it has engendered and by its bad effect upon our commercial interests in China. This may seem rather far-fetched, but it is nevertheless a fact that Australians engaged in business in Hong Kong and Shanghai have been embarrassed by it. I know of several deals lost to Australians because of it.'

This mutual exacerbation of feelings suits the book of neither government. The Depression had put strains on the relations between the two countries, as it put strains on the relations between almost all countries in the early 1930s; but all the instinct of both governments was to minimize these strains and to work towards reconciliation, and the last thing that either desired was to have its scope for manoeuvre limited by the eruption of a massive inflammation of anti-British or anti-Australian public opinion. This had already been apparent during the crisis following the Adelaide Test, when it is sufficiently evident that both governments brought quiet but considerable

231

influence to bear on the ABC and the MCC for a speedy and peaceful settlement. At that time, because it was England that was threatening to cancel the rest of the tour, the effect of the pressure was to induce a climb-down by Australia. When the issue of the 1934 Australian tour of England became the urgent one, the influence of the governments was still all for reconciliation; but now it was England who would have to make the concessions.

Both sides shrank from a breach; but they did not shrink equally, as, in these eyeball-to-eyeball situations, they very rarely do. In 1962, NATO backed down over the Berlin Wall; in 1963, the USSR backed down over Cuba. They did so in both cases because they thought that, at the point of crucial pressure, their opponent could exert more force than they could. The essential psychological position was not different in 1933; and the gist of it was that it was always the touring side that could exert the greater leverage, because it was they who could, with greater credibility, threaten the cancellation of the tour. For one thing, it was always morally far easier to refuse to send a team than to refuse to receive one. For another, the financial loss might be equal, but it would be the home crowds who would be deprived of the chance of watching Test Matches, and whose indignation would turn against their own cricketing authorities in consequence. We have seen how the determination of the Queensland crowds not to be deprived of their Test Match had weakened the Australian Board of Control's position in its controversy by cable with the MCC in February, two months later, the boot was on the other foot. It was in England that the next Test was due to be played, and in consequence it was the MCC who would bear the responsibility if it never took place. There were indeed voices in the press in both countries urging that a suspension of Test Matches might be no bad thing if they were to cause as much bad feeling as the series just concluded in Australia: if (in the eyes of Australian papers) the English were to persist in the use of blatant intimidation, or if (in the eyes of English ones) the

232

Australian public were to show themselves so incapable of accepting defeat in a sporting spirit. Nevertheless, there was never any serious doubt that England would go ahead with the series: the threat of cancellation came from Australia, where the Board of Control made it very clear in its continuing negotiations with the MCC that they would not go ahead with the tour without some adequate assurance that 'bodyline' would not again be used against them. It was a demand which it was very difficult for the MCC either to refuse or to meet.

It was difficult to refuse it because the threat of cancellation was serious and because the consequences of cancellation – in diplomatic and financial terms, as well as in terms of outraged public opinion – were unacceptable. But it was also difficult because an increasing number of people in England, including several whose opinions carried considerable weight at Lord's, were less than happy about 'bodyline'. Some, as we have seen – like Foster, Gilligan and Ranjitsinhji – had denounced 'bodyline' from the start. They were then a small minority; but, as the tour had proceeded, as press photographs, newsreels, and the descriptions of cricket correspondents multiplied, the contours of 'bodyline' gradually became clearer and disquieted some of those who saw them.

As we have seen, Macdonald reported to the ABC in this sense in his cable of 28 April. The confident tone of his cable may seem surprising, for the general impression of English opinion up to this point had been of overwhelming support for Jardine and his team, and events were to show that, though there were certainly some individual members of the MCC Committee hostile to 'bodyline', it was far into the summer before majority opinion on that body began to waver. However, the working of Macdonald's cable is probably significant. It was against the *adoption* of 'bodyline' bowling that he reported finding the weight of English opinion so impressive; and if that was the way he worded his enquiries, one can only further admire his shrewdness, for the course of events during the summer was to make it increasingly clear that support for Jardine and Larwood in Australia was one thing, since it involved deep-lying national allegiances; wanting to see the widespread adoption of their methods in England was quite another. In particular, 'bodyline' suffered from the major weakness that it was a technique that could benefit only the small minority of very fast bowlers, and of teams that possessed them. The rest, when they stopped to consider the issue coolly, might well think that they had everything to gain and nothing to lose by a ban on 'bodyline', and those who had suffered at the hands of Larwood, Voce and Bowes in previous seasons were likely to feel this with particular force.

Clearly, too, private correspondence, both with Australians and English observers in Australia, had an effect which, though limited in range, could, in the case of correspondents like Crutchley and Hore-Ruthven, be very influential. No documents are more eloquent of the way British verdicts on 'bodyline' shifted than Crutchley's diary and correspondence. On the way out to Australia on the *Orontes*, as we have seen, he already had his fears about the tour, but these were based on his doubts as to whether Jardine could expect fair treatment from the Australian crowds. This was still his reaction at the first news of the troubles at Adelaide; but by February he had swung right round, and was convinced that 'bodyline' was the real villain of the piece. Hore-Ruthven, whose role in London as an intermediary with the MCC and the Dominions Office when the controversy was at its hottest in January we have already seen, did not return to his post in Adelaide until the tour was over; but once there he made it his business to take very thorough soundings of local opinion on the issue, and reported to J. H. Thomas in London his conviction that there was justice in the Australian complaints. He also stressed the depth and intensity of the anti-British feeling bred by the affair. Faced with reports of this sort from its representatives in Australia, the natural reaction of the British government was to press for concessions and reconciliation (as has been its instinct in all its dealings with intransigent fragments of the former Empire for the last eighty years); and the links between the MCC and the circles of political power in Britain were amply close enough for such pressures to be swiftly felt.

There were then powerful influences at work inclining the MCC to give ground to the Australian position on the 'bodyline' issue; but the counteracting pressures were little, if at all, less strong. For one thing, the position they had taken up in the exchange of cables arising out of the Adelaide Test had gone far to commit them in defence of Jardine, in whom they had expressed the fullest confidence: it was not going to be easy to reverse that position, and admit, if only by implication, that the Board of Control had been right all along, and that the MCC team had won the series in Australia by methods they now admitted to be repugnant to the spirit of cricket. For another, if 'bodyline' had many critics in England by the spring of 1933, it – or at least Jardine and Larwood – had many outspoken supporters and admirers. In particular, to the mass of the English cricketing public, hallooed on and supported by the full voice of the popular press at its mot strident, Jardine was the captain and Larwood, seconded by Voce and Allen, the bowler who had brought back the Ashes in triumph – and if the Australians did not like their medicine, so much the worse for them. If the weight of opinion in the political Establishment was overwhelmingly in favour of concilia-tion by the spring of 1933, and the weight of opinion in the cricketing Establishment beginning to move the same way –·and both are probably true – there is no question whatever that the overwhelming weight of public opinion was vehemently on the other side. And this too was a consideration that could not be ignored: all the more since it was a weapon of which Jardine and Larwood would be able to make powerful use, if they were so minded.

The sub-committee set about its work in mid-May. Its first task was a post-mortem on the tour just concluded. For this, it had before it the reports submitted on their return by Jardine and by the managers, Warner and Palairet. It is a matter for great regret that these reports do not seem to survive, but it is clear that they must have been in violent conflict, for Warner, who had avoided public condemnation of Jardine's tactics during the tour, is known to have spoken his mind without reserve in the privacy of the MCC committee-room on his return – only to meet with incomprehension and incredulity. In this he was not alone. The sub-committee interviewed not only Jardine, Warner and Palairet, but also Larwood, Voce and Ames: they were apparently intending to interview Allen and Wyatt as well, but changed their minds after a confrontation between Allen and Findlay in the pavilion at Lord's. Allen had left the rest of the touring party in Vancouver, gone south to visit friends in the USA, and arrived back in London towards the end of May. He went straight to Lord's, to be greeted in the Long Room by Findlay with a group of other committee members. Findlay greeted him with commiserations for the terrible treatment the side had experienced in Australia, and the monstrous behaviour of the Australians. Allen, never a man to be afraid of speaking his mind, replied that he didn't know what Findlay was talking about, he had had a marvellous time: if he was ever asked to go to Australia again, he would jump at it. Findlay bristled up immediately – 'I refuse to believe,' he said, 'that any Englishmen ever bowled at a batsman.' 'If that's what you think,' replied Allen, 'the sooner you find out what really did happen the better.' The conversation ended then and there: Allen was not summoned to give evidence before the sub-committee, and nor was Wyatt, who was known to share his views. The incident reveals a lot about the state of opinion at Lord's at the end of May; and if the sub-committee's interviews were indeed restricted to the six mentioned above, of whom only Warner was a critic of 'bodyline', it is not surprising that they apparently rejected his views and accepted Jardine's version – the MCC's next cable, which must have been based on their report, strongly suggests this, although the sub-committee, alas, was seemingly too discreet a body to take any minutes of its proceedings: if it did, they do not seem to have survived.

There was yet another aspect of the matter that the MCC had to bear in mind – events on what I have called the second front, the beginning of the English season, and the very high probability that, given the successes of 'bodyline' in Australia, something would be seen of it in England during the summer. It is true that the inducement to use it was less strong in England, since on the one hand there was less pace and bounce to be got out of English wickets than Australian ones, and on the other, with the ball keeping its shine longer there was more to be gained by bowling a full length and going for movement through the air – but still it would be surprising if somebody did not try it. That somebody, though, would not be Larwood, for the damage to his toe proved to be so serious that he bowled only ten overs during the season, though playing a number of games for Notts as a middle-order batsman. Larwood's disability may have lightened the MCC's problems in one respect; but it cut both ways, because it also reduced the possibilities of English cricket followers forming a fair judgement of 'bodyline'. At the beginning of the season, the *Sunday Graphic* remarked: 'We must make the fullest use of bodyline [i.e., in the forthcoming season] in order that England may determine for itself whether there was any justification for the Australian protest.' That was very fairly said; but in the absence of its leading exponent the demonstration was necessarily going to be inconclusive as far as the bulk of the English cricket-going public was concerned.

Yet another factor in the situation was the forthcoming Test series against the West Indies, who were in England that summer. Was Jardine going to captain England in the Tests, and were – say – Voce – and Bowes going to open the attack, in the absence of Larwood; and how were they going to bowl if they did? What was more, if there was going to be any rough stuff, it might not be all on the side of

England: the West Indies already had a reputation for fast bowling, and in the last English tour of the islands, in 1928–29, several of the English batsmen had found Constantine, bowling very fast and frequently short of a length, a distinctly nasty proposition. Constantine, playing as a professional in the Lancashire League, was not a member of the 1933 West Indies party, but it was expected that he would be available for the Tests; and apart from him, the West Indies had another bowler of great pace in Martindale.

One way and another, it seemed certain that the MCC were going to have to pick their way over a lot of heavily mined territory before the season was over – and even more before the next Australian side were brought safe to shore in the spring of 1934.

In fact, although Larwood, practically speaking, did no bowling during the 1933 season, and Voce, probably also feeling the effect of his exertions in Australia, suffered a loss of form, most observers were in no doubt that fast bowlers up and down the country were bowling more at the batsman and less at the stumps, and were making more systematic use of the bumper, than ever before; and few of them liked it. To some degree the difference may have been in the sensitivity of the observers, alerted by events in Australia, rather than in the tactics of the bowlers; but it would be surprising if some fast bowlers were not attracted by the success of such methods in Australia, and the record leaves little room for doubt that there was more rough stuff being bowled in England in 1933 than in previous seasons. Again, it might be questioned how much of this was, in the strictest sense of the word, 'bodyline' as Larwood and Voice had bowled it in Australia – how much of it, for instance, was accompanied by a Jardine-style leg trap – rather than intimidation of a rougher and readier sort, especially since much of it seems to have originated spontaneously with the bowlers, rather than with a planned strategy on the part of the captain.

Jardine would have been the obvious man to look to for

this; but in fact Jardine, after a winter in Australia, was unable to take much time off for cricket in 1933. He led England in the three Test Matches against the West Indies, but captained Surrey only occasionally; and he seems never to have employed leg theory tactics for Surrey, probably because the county lacked fast bowlers suitable for the purpose. But English observers had never seen 'bodyline', and naturally assumed that what they saw was identical with the tactics that had caused such uproar in Australia; and what they saw disquieted them.

It was, not surprisingly, Bowes who made the running. Glamorgan, batting against Yorkshire at Cardiff at the end of May, were effectively intimidated by him; in the Whitsun Roses Match at Old Trafford a week later he hit Watson, the Lancashire opening bat, on the head and knocked him out; and in mid-June Macdonald reported, in one of his cables to the Board of Control, with what it is hard to regard as anything other than grim satisfaction, that he had already seriously injured five batsmen. A week later he also knocked out Keeton, the Nottinghamshire opener.

None of this was good propaganda for 'bodyline', seeing that the main line of defence offered for the English tactics in Australia had been a denial that they constituted a direct attack on the batsman, and an assertion that, if Australian batsmen were being hit, that was primarily the consequence of their own defective technique and their tendency to move right across the stumps in defence. Nevertheless – and we now turn back to the third 'front' of the controversy, the negotiations between the ABC and the MCC – when, on 12 June, the Main Committee of the MCC at last met to consider what answer it should send to the Australian Board of Control's cable of 28 April, with its announcement that the ABC was acting unilaterally in introducing its new Law 48(b) to ban 'bodyline' in Australia and its recommendation of the same Law to the MCC for general adoption, it was still in uncompromising mood. It had before it the report of the special sub-committee, and it is much to be regretted that we do not know what that report said; but the MCC's reply to the Australian cable, sent on the same day – 12 June – shows again the truth of what Allen and Warner had found on their return to England: that at the beginning of the season the bulk of English cricketing opinion, both informed and uninformed, was at one in its condemnation of the Australian position and in its lack of understanding of the issues involved. The MCC's lengthy reply read as follows:

> The MCC Committee have received and carefully considered the cable of the Australian Board of Control of April 28th last. They have also received and considered the reports of the Captain and Managers of the cricket team which visited Australia 1932–33.
>
> With regard to the cable of the Australian Board of Control of April 28th last, the Committee presume that the class of bowling to which the proposed new law would apply is that referred to as 'bodyline' bowling in the Australian Board of Control's cable of January 18th. The Committee consider that the term 'bodyline' bowling is misleading and improper. It has led to much inaccuracy of thought by confusing the short bumping ball, whether directed on the off, middle or leg stump, with what is known as 'leg-theory'.
>
> The term 'bodyline' would appear to imply a direct attack by the bowler on the batsman. The Committee consider that such an implication applied to any English bowling in Australia is improper and incorrect. Such action on the part of any bowler would be an offence against the spirit of the game and would be immediately condemned. The practice of bowling on the leg stump with a field placed on the leg side necessary for such bowling is legitimate, and has been in force for many years. It has generally been referred to as 'leg-theory'. The present habit of batsmen who move in front of their wickets with the object of gliding straight balls to leg tends to give the impression that the bowler is bowling

at the batsman, especially in the case of a fast bowler when the batsman mistimes the ball and is hit.

The new Law recommended by the Australian Board of Control does not appear to the Committee to be practicable. Firstly, it would place an impossible task on the umpire, and secondly, it would place in the hands of the umpire a power over the game which would be more than dangerous, and which any umpire might well fear to exercise.

The Committee have had no reason to give special attention to 'leg-theory' as practised by fast bowlers [my italics]. They will, however, watch carefully during the present season for anything which might be regarded as unfair or prejudicial to the best interests of the game. They propose to invite opinions and suggestions from County Clubs and Captains at the end of the season, with a view to enabling them to express an opinion on this matter at a Special Meeting of the Imperial Cricket Conference.

With regard to the reports of the Captain and Managers, the Committee, while deeply appreciative of the private and public hospitality shown to the English Team, are much concerned with regard to barracking, which is referred to in all the reports, and against which there is unamimous deprecation. Barracking has, unfortunately, always been indulged in by spectators in Australia to a degree quite unknown in this country. During the late tour, however, it would appear to have exceeded all previous experience, and on occasions to have become thoroughly objectionable. There appears to have been little or no effort on the part of those responsible for the administration of the game in Australia to interfere, or to control this exhibition. This was naturally regarded by members of the team as a serious lack of consideration for them. The Committee are of opinion that cricket played under such conditions is robbed of much of its value as a game, and that unless barracking is stopped, or is greatly moderated in Australia, it is difficult to see how the continuance of representative matches can service the best interest of the game.

The Committee regret that these matters have to be dealt with by correspondence and not by personal conference. If at any time duly accredited representatives of Australian Cricket could meet the Committee in conference, such conference would be welcomed by MCC.

This document was nothing if not unbending; and it does at least have the merit of restating clearly and concisely the basic elements of the English position on the controversy in uncompromising form. The disdainful references to the Australian use of the term 'bodyline' and the pedagogical tone of the disquisition on the differences between bumpers and leg theory in the second paragraph very fairly set the tone for what follows. It reads like a rebuke to a child in a tantrum, and it reveals the continuing failure of the MCC Committee to grasp (or its refusal to believe) the exact nature of Larwood's and Voce's bowling in Australia. The Committee goes on to reject flatly the suggestion that they had been guilty of 'direct attack', and to reassert the view that, if batsmen were hit, it was their own fault for getting in front of the stumps. They imply that Larwood's and Voce's attack was always directed *at* the leg stump, and not outside it; they refer only in the most general terms to their use of the 'leg trap', and, perhaps most significant of all, they make no mention whatever of the *length* of their bowling. It rejects the new Law proposed by Australia as impracticable (a view, incidentally, for which there was a good deal of support in both countries). It states flatly that it has had no cause for concern with the use of 'leg theory' tactics by fast bowlers. It then goes over to vigorous counter-attack in its denunciation of Australian barracking, and its implied demand that the Australian authorities should take strong action against it, under threat of (presumably) the cancellation of the next English tour of Australia, which was due in 1936–37.

In the whole lengthy cable, there are only two minor conciliatory notes: the concession that the MCC would keep its eyes open during the current season for the use of unfair tactics by fast bowlers, and would take the opinions of county clubs and captains on the issue at the season's end, and the suggestion that the controversy could most easily be resolved by the ABC sending representatives to England to discuss the issues in dispute over the table. It is perfectly true that one of the main obstacles to understanding lay in the fact that at no stage of the controversy did anything resembling a personal conference between the two governing bodies take place, such was the width of the communications gap – what Geoffrey Blainey has called 'the tyranny of distance' – between England and Australia in the 1930s, and that at the official level it had to be conducted almost entirely through the cramping medium of the submarine telegraph.*

The position that emerges from this cable is clear-cut. The Australians had no case: the tactics of the English fast bowlers in Australia had been orthodox, traditional 'leg-theory', based on an attack on the leg stump (presumably of full length), not on the batsmen. There was no need for legislation, and the proposed Australian Law was in any case impracticable and undesirable. There had indeed been cause for legitimate complaint during the MCC tour, but the Board of Control had got the boot on the wrong foot: it was the Australian crowds, not the English players, who had misbehaved, and if the Board wanted Anglo-Australian Test Matches to continue, they had better do something about it.

Unfortunately, the MCC Committee had mistaken the time of day. The effective threat of cancellation was no longer theirs to use, for it was Australia who were next scheduled to send a team to England, and not vice versa.

---

* In fact, of course, the ABC did have a representative in England during the summer of 1933, Macdonald. We can only assume that he was not regarded by the MCC as a sufficiently authoritative figure to conduct official negotiations on the Board's behalf.

And if it was indeed true when the cable was sent that 'the Committee had had no reason to give special attention to "leg theory" as practised by fast bowlers', 12 June must have been just about the last moment of the 1933 season when that position could be adopted with any plausibility at all. By the end of the month, the lengthening trail of injuries that Bowes in particular was leaving behind him must have been giving Lord's increasing cause for concern. But if any particular events can be singled out as marking the point at which what may be called official English cricketing opinion tilted decisively against 'bodyline' (and perhaps they cannot: it may be that the really decisive influence was being exercised behind the scenes by Hailsham and those other members of the MCC Committee, such as Lord Ullswater, Lord Bridgeman, Jackson and Sir Kynaston Studd, who had close connections with the world of politics and government), they were two matches that took place in July – the Varsity Match on the 10th, 11th and 12th of the month, and the second Test against the West Indies at Manchester between 22 and 25 July.

The Cambridge attack at Lord's was led by Kenneth Farnes – probably the fastest bowler produced between the Wars by either university – and in this match he bowled what was apparently as good an approximation to what Larwood had been bowling in Australia as had yet been seen in England (certainly a better one than had yet been seen at Lord's): short, fast 'leg-theory', to a field of four short legs. The results were very eloquent indeed: especially since Farnes, unlike Larwood and Voce in Australia, apparently felt no compunction about bowling it at the Oxford tail. Tindall, badly hit on the body, succumbed to a yorker next ball – the classic combination; Oldfield (name of ill omen!), the Oxford No. 11, was bowled off his neck; Townsend, the Oxford opening bat, was also hit on the neck, and fell on his wicket.

It is relevant, and yet on the whole beside the point, to say that there were still major differences between this onslaught and Larwood's bowling in Australia. There

244

were. Larwood, as we have seen, never bowled 'bodyline' at tailenders, and Farnes was a young, relatively inexperienced and considerably less controlled fast bowler bowling at young and relatively inexperienced batsmen. But it was all that Lord's had seen of 'bodyline'; and anyway, the point has been made that, once 'bodyline' had been used in Test Matches, its adoption in other grades of cricket sooner or later was inevitable. If 'bodyline' had been a deliberate, long-term strategy, and one that could moreover be (so to speak) patented, so that its further use remained under its original inventors' control, they would in all probability not have permitted its use in England in 1933 at all, but kept it under wraps for use against the Australians in 1934. Certainly they could have done nothing worse than permit its use in the Varsity Match. But whereas in Australia Jardine had, so to speak, had the genie of 'bodyline' safely bottled up, to be let out only as and where he pleased, now the cork was out of the bottle, and the genie was apt to turn up on the most unsuitable occasions. Together with Gentlemen and Players, and perhaps to a lesser extent Eton and Harrow, the Varsity Match was the holy of holies of traditional English amateur cricket and its values; and a lot of highly influential spectators who might – perhaps – have thought 'bodyline' an admissible method of attack against the Australians, were outraged by it when they saw it introduced into this pedigreed encounter.

Distaste for Farnes' methods of attack and denunciation of them were the universal tone of press comment: one highly significant reaction was the appearance of a letter, and the prominence given to it, in *The Times* from a prestigious group of signatories deploring Farnes' bowling and expressing strongly the hope and anxiety that nothing similar should be seen in the Eton and Harrow match, which immediately succeeded the Varsity match at Lord's. Both the *Cricketer* and (at the end of the season) *Wisden* expressed dislike of the Cambridge bowling: the comments of Frank Mitchell, the regular columnist of the *Cricketer* (under the pseudonym of 'Second Slip'), are moreover of interest for the way they express some of the confusions typical of English thinking about 'bodyline' at this time. Thus the use of the term 'leg theory' instead of 'bodyline' (which nowhere appears) made it possible to include under this category the bowling not only of Farnes but also of Jehangir Khan and R. S. Grant, both bowling off-breaks round the wicket: leg theory indeed in the traditional sense that it was bowled to a leg trap and a predominantly leg-side field, but utterly different in every other sense to what Farnes had to offer.

Frank Mitchell shared the general dislike of the Cambridge tactics, but argued not that they were intimidating but that they were dull, reducing cricket to a one-stroke game, and longing for 'a breed of leg-hitters' who would speedily clear away the short legs or would stand away at least from the medium-paced and slow bowling of this ilk and hit it on the off side. This of course is precisely what Bradman had done in Australia – but to Larwood! – and it would be interesting to know whether Mitchell was aware of it; but equally interesting is the implication that the objections to 'bodyline' are aesthetic rather than ethical (Mitchell specifically said that there was nothing *unfair* about the Cambridge tactics), and also that the proper remedy may lie with the batsmen themselves. Both lines of argument had been anticipated in Australia during the MCC tour, and it is easy to see their attraction to those Englishmen who had stoutly defended Jardine's tactics while the tour was in progress, but whose instinctive reactions were hostile when they saw something similar being enacted under their noses in England soon afterwards.

But the impact of Farnes' bowling in the Varsity Match on public opinion was small when compared with events at Old Trafford in the second Test against the West Indies a fortnight later. The first Test at Lord's had passed without major incident. Martindale there had had to carry the burden of the West Indies pace attack single-handed; but at

246

Old Trafford he had Constantine to share it with him, and, when England went in to reply to the West Indies first innings total of 375, the fur flew from the start. Both Martindale and Constantine bowled a great deal of fast leg theory – as the press still called it – to a packed leg-side field, in close imitation of Larwood's and Voce's bowling in Australia. Most of the English batsmen were obviously unhappy against it, especially Hammond, who had his chin laid open by one fierce bumper; but it was evident that the main target of the 'bodyline' was Jardine, again captaining England.

It was exactly this sort of direct challenge, however, that brought the best out of Jardine: whatever his weaknesses, his courage and his determination never failed him. Always a magnificent player of fast bowling, he played an unflinching innings of 127, using his height to the full to play the short balls down straight in front of him with a dead bat. Like the other two centuries scored against 'bodyline', McCabe's at Sydney and Bradman's at Melbourne, it was by any account a remarkable innings (though completely different from the other two in terms of technique), and as a personal riposte it could hardly be bettered. How far it really demonstrated the truth of Jardine's contention, that fast leg-theory could be mastered by a batsman of adequate temperament and technique, is more doubtful. Martindale and Constantine were genuinely fast bowlers, but neither possessed quite Larwood's speed nor his phenomenal accuracy. What is more relevant, they were bowling in conditions vastly different from those in Australia, on a wicket that had far less pace and bounce than those at Adelaide and Sydney.

Still Jardine's fine innings clearly *could* have been taken in England as a demonstration of the essential fairness of 'fast leg theory': the interesting thing is that the general reaction, as represented in the press, seems to have been quite otherwise. The match ended tamely in a draw, and the West Indies made no further use of 'bodyline' on the

247

tour;* but English observers, especially those among the cricketing Establishment, had not liked what they had seen. In the *Cricketer*, Frank Mitchell commented that 'it would seem that with the first suggestion of fast leg-theory the best batsmen can be made to perform knavish tricks'. Elsewhere in his account, the tell-tale term 'bodyline' once slips in (significantly, since the use of the word largely conceded the Australian case) and he concluded that 'it is a sorry thing'. As in his earlier comment on Farnes' bowling in the Varsity Match, Mitchell revealed by this choice of adjective his dislike of 'bodyline' when he saw it, coupled with his reluctance to say outright that it was unfair – an ambivalence that was to find its most perfect expression at the end of the season in *Wisden*'s account of the West Indies' bowling at Manchester, an account which wound up with the resounding conclusion that 'most of those who were watching it for the first time must have come to the conclusion that, while

* There has been much dark speculation about the origin of its use in the second Test. Fingleton, in *Cricket Crisis*, reports being told that the West Indies were put up to it by some leading members of the MCC – could this refer to the secret 'bodyline' sub-committee? – who wanted to see 'bodyline' in action so that they could form a better judgement of it. He adds that some of the West Indies side felt that, if it was to be used at all, it should have been kept for a faster wicket than Old Trafford. This seems far fetched, though it does indeed seem strange that it should have been used there, rather than at Lord's or the Oval, the venues for the other two Tests. The probable explanation, though, is that only at Old Trafford did Martindale have Constantine to bowl with him. This fact too is not without its obscurities. Macdonald reported, on one of his letters to the Australian Board of Control, that he had been informed that the West Indies had negotiated Constantine's release for the Oval Test also by the Lancashire League club to which he was contracted, on the understanding that Nichols, the Essex fast bowler, who had no county match on at the time, would replace him; but Jardine, getting wind of this, blocked the arrangement by insisting on the inclusion of Nichols in the England team for the Oval, in spite of the unanimous opposition of the rest of the MCC Selection Committee. I report this tale for what it is worth. Constantine did not play at the Oval and Nichols did, and it is true that Essex had no fixture that weekend; but it is also true that Macdonald was (as we have seen) bitterly hostile to Jardine.

strictly within the law, it was not *nice*' [my italics – what a sterling example of the use of the Great English Adjective!].

It seems true, therefore, that the sight of what 'fast leg theory' could mean in practice – even if it still fell well short of what the Australian batsman had had to face in Australia, as it probably did – during the 1933 season increasingly tilted English cricketing opinion against it, and that this reaction was brought to a point by its use in the Varsity Match and the second Test Match. The Test Match was played from 22–25 July, and by that time developments on the third 'front' – the negotiations between the MCC and the ABC on the new Australian Law 48(b) against 'bodyline', and on the forthcoming Australian tour of England in the following year – were also coming to a head. The Imperial Cricket Conference was to meet at Lord's on 31 July. At that meeting, the new Australian Law was due to be discussed; but before the meeting took place, Macdonald had been hard at work.

Macdonald had been startled and shocked by the unbending tone of the MCC's last cable, which he regarded as misrepresenting the general state of English cricketing opinion on the 'bodyline' issue. Whether he was right or wrong about that, it is clear that between the sending of the cable on 12 June, and the meeting of the Imperial Cricket Conference on 31 July, Macdonald had been doing some extremely effective lobbying, and, in particular, had succeeded in reaching a close understanding with a group of key members of the MCC Main Committee, and above all with the members of the secret 'bodyline' sub-committee, and that the grounds of that understanding were an agreement that 'bodyline' had to go. Unfortunately there is nothing to show what it was – what combination of instinctive dislike of 'bodyline' from the outset (Jackson in particular had been very reserved in his comments on it during the tour), abhorrence when they saw it practised in England, discreetly applied pressure from the Dominions Office and the Cabinet, and alarm at the prospect of the 1934 Australian tour being cancelled – that brought the MCC representatives to this frame of mind; but it is easy to see that the combined weight of these considerations must have been very formidable. At any rate, in mid-July Macdonald was assured in confidence by two members of the MCC Committee – one of them Jackson – that 'bodyline' would not be used against Australia in the forthcoming series. This, to Macdonald, was the main point gained; but two difficulties remained. One was the embarrassment of 48(b); the other, in effect, was the necessity of letting the MCC down as gently as possible.

48(b) was an embarrassment because the brusqueness of Australia's action in introducing it unilaterally alienated many even of those who were otherwise hostile to 'bodyline' methods, and also because there was widespread doubt, by no means confined to England, whether it was a satisfactory or even a practicable solution to the problem. Most of these doubts centred on the requirement placed by it on the umpires to determine the bowler's motives – whether he was in fact trying to injure or intimidate the batsman. The Laws as they stand today make a similar requirement; but in 1933, many agreed with the view stated by the MCC in their cable of 12 June that such a Law both asked too much of the umpire and placed too much power in his hands. Some (including Warner) thought that what was required was a more objective Law which would merely require the umpire to no-ball any delivery that pitched on the near side of a line about half-way down the wicket; others (including a critic of 'bodyline' as fierce as Alan Kippax) thought that what was required was not legislation at all, since this was a matter of cricketing ethics rather than the Laws of the game, but an official condemnation of 'bodyline' by the MCC, backed by an agreement among first-class captains not to countenance its use. The issue was urgent for Macdonald because, with the meeting of the Imperial Cricket Conference rapidly approaching, to which the MCC were intending to submit the Australian proposal, he soon discovered by dint of some careful lobbying among the delegates that, although there was almost universal condemnation of 'bodyline' (it would be interesting to know whether this was shared by the West Indies representatives), there was also a majority opposed to 48(b).

There was a flurry of intense diplomatic activity. It was largely Macdonald's influence, and his assurance that things in London were moving Australia's way, that had deterred the Board from sending a swift and intransigent answer to the MCC's unconciliatory cable of 12 June. Now, as the result of some deft and highly confidential negotiations with Jackson, Findlay and Hailsham (who, as President of the MCC, was to preside at the meeting of the Imperial Cricket Conference) and an exchange of cables with the Board in Australia, it was agreed to ask the ICC to defer consideration of 48(b) pending the conference of county captains to discuss 'bodyline' which the MCC had already announced (in its cable of 12 June) its intention of summoning at the end of the season – a suggestion which the ICC duly accepted without difficulty. The embarrassment of a public rejection of the Australian proposal was thus avoided, and Macdonald found himself working in intimate and confidential agreement with this group of men who controlled the levers of MCC policy to what was by now an end on which they were all agreed but which could not be publicly announced – the abandonment of 'bodyline'. It was a richly ironic situation, and one which less than two months earlier, at the time of the sending of the MCC's cable on 12 June, would have seemed to most observers not so much improbable as fantastic. It was there precisely that the second difficulty lay.

The awkward fact was that, in the exchanges with the ABC while the controversial series was in progress, the MCC had committed itself, to all appearances irretrievably, to a wholehearted defence of Jardine and his tactics in Australia; that it had reiterated this position as recently as 12 June; that in doing so it had the overwhelming support of English popular opinion; and that nothing it had yet said in public implied any weakening of that position. Even though, in the inner circle at Lord's where power lay, it had now come to be accepted that 'bodyline' must go, at least to the extent that it must not be used against Australia in 1934, it was uncertain whether the Main Committee as a whole accepted that view, still more uncertain whether the mass of the members at large did so, and almost certain that the great bulk of the English cricketing public did not. It was not so much that Macdonald's soundings of English opinion had been wrong, but that they seem to have been restricted to a very narrow, though certainly very important, group of leading players and administrators, whose views were very different from those of the mass of the uninformed public.

The notes of triumph and euphoria in retrospective comment on the past series continued to echo through the columns of the popular press throughout the summer: Jardine and Larwood remained the heroes of the moment, and if the assumption that they would again play the leading roles for England in 1934 (always providing that Larwood was fit) was for the most part unspoken, that was because it was almost unanimous. At the very least, the MCC had a very difficult problem of public relations on their hands if they were indeed to do a U-turn and abandon 'bodyline'. On top of that, there was the salving of their own pride to be borne in mind; and there was the still more awkward problem of what was to be done about Larwood, and about Jardine. What prospect was there of inducing either of them to eat humble pie, by abandoning the methods which had brought them both triumph and fame? And if the answer to that was 'none', how was it going to be possible to drop the two men who had been universally hailed as the heroes of the triumph in Australia?

Macdonald, and the small group of the MCC Committee with whom he was in close contact, were acutely aware of these difficulties. Macdonald appears never to have been very much interested in the general issue of 'bodyline' and

252

of whether and how it could be eliminated from the game – he was, after all, an agent of the Australian Board of Control, whose main function was the control of Australia's part in the game at international level, and his main concern throughout was with the 1934 series and with ensuring that 'bodyline' was excluded from it.

The basic issue was determined at a crucial discussion that took place at Lord's on the evening of 31 July, following the meeting of the Imperial Cricket Conference and a meeting of the full MCC Committee. Those present at this discussion were Macdonald, Hawke, Lewisham, Jackson and Findlay (this meeting in fact is the most suggestive piece of evidence that it was precisely these four who constituted the secret sub-committee). Hailsham alone, of those with whom Macdonald had been in closest contact during the past weeks, was absent (very probably called away by his political or ministerial duties), and Macdonald had had a private discussion with him in advance. On this occasion, all the cards were put flat on the table. The MCC representatives proposed leaving the issue of the use of 'bodyline' in the forthcoming Test series to be settled by discussions with the Australian management when the team arrived. It is probable that this was no more than a negotiating position, and that they were not surprised when Macdonald rejected it – he was, as he later said in his report to the Board, well aware that the Australian negotiating position would be weakened the moment the team left Australian shores, since from that moment onwards cancellation would become a less and less credible threat. He insisted that Australia had a right to know in advance whether or not 'bodyline' was to be used against them, as this would affect the selection of their team. If its use was not ruled out, Australia could select 'at least four fast bowlers to maintain a battery of shock attack at both ends in all the Test matches'. Shades of the West Indies attack of the 1980s!

In making such a suggestion, Macdonald went beyond his brief, for there is no evidence that the ABC had ever

253

considered such a move: the sanction they preferred (and that Macdonald had also preferred up to this moment) was cancellation, not retaliation – indeed, it is more than doubtful whether such a battery of fast bowlers could have been found in Australia at the time. But his judgement of the moment, and of the men he had to deal with, was sound. Hawke said, 'Reprisals, by God!'; Macdonald replied, 'No, I would call it reciprocity, merely mutual action and reaction.' At which, according to his letter to the ABC recounting the events of the meetings (from which all this account is derived), 'our happy relations enabled us to laugh over this sinister aspect of such a situation'. It is a cosy picture, and in its way a curious one, so widely was it at odds with the popular perception of relations between the MCC and the ABC at the time.

Macdonald went on to put the crucial question directly, but in tactfully veiled form: 'Whether the particular type of bowling to which exception was taken by Australia' – a roundabout form of wording which neatly avoided both 'bodyline' and 'fast leg theory', since both had partisan implications – 'would be used on the tour'. The MCC representatives presumably took a deep breath and looked at each other – and said they were prepared to give an assurance that it would not. Seeing his fish so nearly landed, Macdonald redoubled the delicacy with which he was playing it. Formally, the assurance would have to come from the full MCC Committee, a number of whom were not – so to speak – in the plot, and he appreciated the difficulties that this might present. How, he asked, would the MCC representatives like the ABC's official approach for the assurance to be phrased? The reply was a suggestion that the ABC should request 'an assurance that the type of bowling to which exception was taken in Australia would not be used against them in England in 1934, on the grounds that while they [Australia] recognized that it was in strict conformity with the laws of cricket, its practice and continuance were not in their opinion in the best interests of the game: inasmuch that it eliminated stroke-play and thereby seriously interfered with the interest and pleasure of the spectators'.

Thus, in the MCC's attempt to let down Jardine and Larwood, English public opinion, and its own pride, as lightly as possible, was aesthetics called in as catspaw to pull the MCC's chestnuts out of the fire and to save the burnt fingers of ethics. Its suitability for the role is a matter of very grave doubt: whatever effect 'bodyline' might have had on the crowds in Australia, it did not seem to have bored them. But what was required was, of course, a face-saving formula, not an accurate description of the real facts of the case: *homo diplomaticus* is a noble animal.

On this note, the discussion closed. Lewisham did make what in the circumstances can only have been a lame attempt to raise the barracking issue – the dying kick of the English contention that this, rather than the nature of the English bowling tactics, had been at the bottom of the troubles in Australia. But the course of events since the return of the touring side to England had irretrievably cut the ground from under this position, and left the rival Australian perception of events in a dominance which it has never since lost; and Macdonald needed to do no more than suggest that the behaviour of the Australian crowds was only to be expected in the circumstances, and to make the essentially anodyne promise to advise the ABC to take 'the very fullest measures of control in future tours'.

Macdonald had won his victory, and he was wise enough not to rub it in. In his report to the ABC, he strongly commended to them for their official reply to the MCC's cable of 12 June the formula which the MCC representatives themselves had suggested; he particularly emphasized the desirability of avoiding the use of the word 'bodyline', which was like a red rag to a bull to the MCC, though Macdonald himself thought it an entirely accurate description of the bowling in question. He added, not without malice, one feels, a reference to a surprising incident that had occurred a few days earlier: a public condemnation of 'bodyline' by, of all people, Arthur Carr, heretofore one of the most strenuous defenders of Larwood, Voce and all their works. It arose from a recent match between Notts and Leicestershire, in which Voce (Larwood was still out of the firing-line) had let fly at the Leicestershire batsmen in the first innings to their evident distress. Leicestershire in the 1930s were a very lowly side, but in H. A. Smith they had a fast bowler of some considerable pace, and when Notts came to bat, he retaliated in kind, concentrating his attentions particularly on Carr. Carr did not enjoy the experience, and the upshot was an agreement between the two captains that in future the fast bowlers should, to quote the decorous words of *Wisden*, 'refrain from attempts to make the ball rise unduly'.

It was, in its way, an excellent example of what could be achieved by controlled retaliation, and of how the excess of fast bowlers might indeed be curbed by agreement between captains; but, although consistency never much bothered Carr, his subsequent condemnation of what he called 'head-high bowling' occasioned some mirth to Macdonald and to the Australian opponents of 'bodyline'. It was indeed something new to hear Carr saying, 'Somebody is going to be killed if this sort of bowling continues ... Sooner or later something will have to be done, so why not now?'

The English season ended without further drama on the field. It was not until 21 September that the Australian Board of Control met to draft a reply to the MCC's cable of 12 June, in the light of all that had happened since then and of Macdonald's report of his negotiations in London. The cable they then sent is ample evidence of the extent of their justified confidence in their representative in London. It read:

We note that you consider that a form of bowling which amounted to a direct attack by the bowler on the batsman would be against the spirit of the game. We agree with you that Leg-theory Bowling as it has been generally practised for many years is not open to objection. On these matters there does not appear to be any real difference between our respective views.

We feel that while the type of bowling to which exception was taken in Australia, strictly was not in conflict with the laws of Cricket, yet its continued practice would not be in the best interests of the game. May we assume that you concur in this point of view and that the teams may thus take the field in 1934 with that knowledge?

We are giving consideration to the question of barracking and you may rely upon us using our best endeavours to have it controlled in future tours.

We are most anxious that the cordial relations which have so long existed between English and Australian cricket shall continue.

If read simply as a reply to the MCC's cable of 12 June, without any knowledge of what had been passing in the committee-rooms at Lord's in the meanwhile, this was an astonishingly forbearing response to what had been a remarkably harsh communication. It almost falls over backwards in its determination to find uncontroversial passages in the MCC's cable that it can agree with. But of course its real meaning can only be read in the light of Macdonald's negotiations. The ABC had followed his advice. They avoided the controversial word 'bodyline', and in making their request for an assurance that the offending thing itself should not be used against them in 1934, they used the MCC's proposed formula almost word for word, jibbing only when it came to the explanations that the MCC had suggested for the banning of 'bodyline'. It was really asking too much of Australians who had seen 'bodyline' to expect them to pretend that there was nothing wrong with it except that it made for dull strokeplay and bored spectators. At this point, presumably, frankness had had enough and felt that it could concede no more to hurt feelings in England than to omit explanations altogether. For the rest, those who drafted the cable knew, even if they

257

could not publicly say, that they had won their case, and could afford to be generous.

This was not quite the end of the matter as far as the battle of cables between the ABC and the MCC was concerned, because both the full Board of Control and the full MCC Committee contained a number of members who had not been fully party to all that was being said and done in their names during the summer's exchanges, and who did not share the confidence that by now existed between the leading figures of the two governing bodies. As far as the MCC were concerned, this was apparent from the reply that they sent on 9 October to the Australian cable, which read:

The MCC Committee appreciate the friendly tone of your cable and they heartily reciprocate your desire for the continuance of cordial relations.

In their view the difference between us seems to be rather on the question of fact than on any point of interpretation of the Laws of Cricket or of the spirit of the game. They agree and have always agreed that a form of bowling which is obviously a direct attack by the bowler upon the batsman would be an offence against the spirit of the game.

Your team can certainly take the field with the knowledge and with the full assurance that cricket will be played here in the same spirit as in the past and with the single desire to promote the best interests of the game in both countries.

The Committee much appreciate your promise to take the question of barracking into consideration with a view to ensuring that it shall be kept within reasonable bounds.

Your team can rely on a warm welcome from MCC and every effort will be made to make their visit enjoyable.

This exchange of cables gave rise to a *Times* leader

calculated to rejoice the heart of all connoisseurs of that great paper in the days of its glory. *The Times* congratulated both the MCC and the ABC on the exchange. It added that:

> There remains the question of tactics for next summer's matches. In this matter the MCC rightly make no formal pledge which would either limit the freedom of the captain of 1934 or imply a censure on the captain of 1933. But they will not resent an intelligent reading between the lines. It is clear then that Mr Jardine, who is once again leading a team on their behalf, retains their full confidence. On the other hand, the particular kind of fast leg bowling that has been the source of controversy is likely to be dropped. It will not be dropped because it is illegal; it will not even be dropped because it is against the spirit of the game. It will be dropped because it interferes with our Australian friends' enjoyment of cricket – and consequently with our own.

It is obvious that *The Times* leader-writer – as one would expect of a *Times* leader-writer of the 1930s – had inside information. It is more than possible that some of its readers at Lord's did not welcome a 'reading between the lines' as intelligent, or as well-informed, as this. But is this the height of hypocrisy, the height of diplomacy, the height of effrontery, or the height of a courtesy so supreme as to transcend all these distinctions? I confess that I do not know. One may note that it is only out of an acute sensitivity to the tender susceptibilities of the Australians that 'the particular kind of fast leg bowling that has been the source of controversy' is to be dropped: one may ask how real is 'the freedom of the captain of 1934' if the type of bowling with which his name is inseparably associated is banned in advance. But the message is clear: Jardine can captain England in 1934, but only on condition that he behaves himself.

In any case, it still remained to be seen whether the MCC's fine words would be enough to butter the ABC's parsnips. For a man like Jeanes, the Secretary of the Board of Control, who had been closely in touch throughout with Macdonald's negotiations in London, it might present no difficulty to read between the lines and see in the MCC's cable the concession of the assurance that the ABC had required. To more suspicious and less well-informed members of the Board, what necessarily stood out was that the MCC at no point of the cable of 9 October gave any specific assurance that 'the type of bowling to which exception was taken in Australia' would not be used against them in 1934, and this suspicion was only liable to be strengthtned by the clear implication in the second paragraph that the English attack in Australia had *not* amounted to 'a direct attack by the bowler upon the batsman'. It is in fact hard not to sympathize with them, and it is a great pity that the MCC archives contain no record of the discussions at the Committee meeting which drafted the cable. It may be that the dropping by the ABC, in their cable of 22 September, of the last part of the 'formula' which the MCC representatives had suggested to Macdonald, so irritated the Committee that they refused to give in so many words the assurance requested. But in the absence of a record, it is impossible to be sure whether the majority of those present at the meeting which drafted the 9 October cable thought they were giving a guarantee that 'bodyline' would not be used in 1934, or not, though the 'inner circle' of Hawke, Findlay, Jackson, Lewisham and Hailsham must have so intended.

The doubts of the ABC members can only have been reinforced by the coincidence of a new outburst by Larwood in the press a day or two after the MCC's cable, in which he said among other things that, if he was picked against the Australians next year, he would bowl leg theory, and he did not think the MCC would order him or anyone else not to bowl with a packed leg trap. From England, an alarmed Macdonald cabled that Larwood's statements were unofficial and unworthy of notice, and urged that the matter should be regarded as settled by a gentlemen's agreement; but the MCC cable had split the ABC almost down the middle. The Victorian and Queensland delegates rejected it as insufficient. Allen Robertson, the outgoing Chairman of the Board, wrote to Jeanes in Adelaide in strong terms to this effect, asking for an emergency meeting of the Board and a demand for a plain answer from the MCC on the 'bodyline' issue. But Macdonald, now about to sail for America again for the winter, anxiously urged the Board not to ruin his work by pressing the MCC for an outright surrender it could not deliver, and insisted that influential opinion in England was now overwhelmingly hostile to 'bodyline' and that there was no danger of its use in 1934; and when a special meeting of the Board was duly held on 16 November (now, it is worth noting, under the chairmanship of R. A. Oxlade, the leader of the New South Wales delegation, who had favoured conciliation throughout and regarded the MCC's cable as adequate), a compromise was reached. A further very brief cable was sent, but in tones far less militant than Robertson had suggested:

We appreciate the terms of your cablegram of October 9th and assume that such cable is intended to give the assurance asked for in our cablegram of September 22nd.

It is on this understanding that we are sending a team in 1934.

There, one feels, the MCC might well have let the matter rest; but they apparently felt that a further reply was necessary. When sent on 12 December, it read:

Reference your cable of November 16th, you must please accept our cable on October 9th, which speaks for itself [a very questionable assertion], as final.

We cannot go beyond the assurance therein given [and this was probably the literal truth]. We shall welcome Australian cricketers who come to play cricket with us next year. If, however, your Board of Control decide that such games should be deferred, we shall regret their decision.

Please let us know your Board's final decision as soon as possible and in any event before the end of the year.

It is some indication of the difficulties confronting what may be called the 'doves' on the MCC Committee, as well as their ABC counterparts, that even this guarded statement of intent was passed by only eight votes to five.

When Oxlade received the text of this cable from Jeanes, he apparently decided that the time had come for swift and decisive action. The Board was due to meet on 31 December, but Oxlade decided not to wait. He drafted a reply confirming the Australian acceptance of the MCC position and their intention to send a team to England next year as arranged, submitted it to the other members of the Board scattered across Australia by telegram for their approval, and as soon as he had the assent of a majority, sent his cable – ironically, and surely deliberately, exactly the same procedure as had been used in January for the sending of the original protest which Oxlade had so strenuously opposed.

The approval was no more unanimous than the support for the MCC's final cable had been – the vote appears to have been nine to five – and when the full Board met on the 31st, Oxlade had to survive a vote of censure which received the unanimous support of the Victorian and Queensland delegations. But the majority was nevertheless solid behind him: the cable had been sent on 14 December; and on the very same day the MCC cabled back its brief and relieved reply, looking forward to the arrival of the Australian team. There would be Test Matches in England in 1934 after all. With this drift of snowflakes, the blizzard of cables finally died away.

CHAPTER 9

The Controversy Resolved
(1934–1939)

The final exchange of cables in December 1933 marked the end of the war on what I have called the 'third front' – the dispute between the MCC and the ABC as to whether the Australian tour of 1934 should take place at all, and if so on what terms. On the other two fronts, the fighting was not yet over.

As far as the second front – the appearances of 'bodyline', or of something approximating to it, on English cricket grounds, and the English reactions to it – was concerned, this reached a climax with the meeting of county captains at Lord's on 23 November to consider what was by now (in England) coming to be called 'direct attack' (still avoiding 'bodyline', with all its awkward associations) in accordance with the undertaking made by the MCC in its cable of 12 June. Technically, this was held to consider the replies to a circular letter which the MCC had sent to all county captains asking their opinions on 'fast leg theory', and whether its development was such as to require official action to check it.

It is fairly clear from the terms of the cable that at the time it was sent the MCC were expecting the captains to support the view that there had been no such development, and that no action was needed. But by the end of the season, the situation was looking very different indeed, and the outcome goes far to justify Macdonald's estimate of English opinion on the issue. No minutes of the meeting at Lord's survive, but there is sufficient evidence to show that the majority of the county captains agreed that 'fast leg theory', as it had been bowled in the 1933 season, was a real threat to the game. They did not think that legislation was the right answer – to that extent they stood by the MCC's position – but instead looked for a solution along the lines suggested by Kippax in *Anti-Bodyline*, and foreshadowed by Arthur Carr and E. W. Dawson, the Leicestershire captain, in the Notts-Leicestershire match: an agreement between captains not to countenance its use.

At this point, there seems to have been a significant difference of opinion. The great majority of the captains apparently favoured an agreement that fast bowlers should not bowl to a leg trap; but – anyway according to Fingleton in *Cricket Crisis* – three of them, Jardine, Carr and V. W. C. Jupp of Northants, refused to go along with this, and would only consent to an alternative form of declaration which was finally drawn up, which stated that 'any form of bowling which is obviously a direct attack by the bowler upon the batsman would be an offence against the spirit of the game', and that the captains 'would not permit or countenance bowling of such type'. Fingleton does not state his sources, and his account must be to some extent suspect, since Jardine at least cannot have been at the meeting – he was at the time leading the MCC touring side in India, and must have been one of the three county captains recorded as being absent, but represented, on this occasion. However, his account makes sense to the extent that these three might very well have been expected to resist any attempt to forbid fast bowling to a leg trap – Jardine and Carr because of their well-known advocacy of 'fast leg theory', Jupp because the spearhead of an otherwise very unremarkable Northants attack was the fast left-hander E. W. Clark, who regularly bowled round the wicket to a leg trap in Hirst's and Foster's fashion (so too, of course, did Voce, which must have reinforced Carr's views).

In its final form, the declaration borrowed its language straight from the MCC's cables; but the alteration (as the ABC would have been quick to percieve) made a very great difference indeed. *'Would be'* – it was in the use of the conditional mood that the catch lay. It was the same point as the one implied by the MCC in their statement that their difference with the ABC was 'rather on the question of fact than on any point of interpretation of the Laws of Cricket or the spirit of the game'. The defenders of fast leg theory maintained, as Jardine and Larwood had both maintained in their books, that it did not amount to 'a direct attack by the bowler upon the batsman'. The majority of the county captains thought otherwise, and it is hardly surprising if, with the exception of Brian Sellers of Yorkshire, this majority was composed of those captains who did not possess fast bowlers with the talents or the disposition to exploit 'fast leg theory'. Whether or not it was dangerous, it could certainly be highly effective; and it is only human nature to strike an effective weapon from an opponent's hand if you can – the advocates of 'fast leg theory', of course, argued that it was precisely this that the Australians were attempting to do. But in its final form, the captains' joint declaration of November 1933 did not unequivocally denounce fast leg theory; and, although the inner councils of the MCC undoubtedly hoped that it would have this effect, as long as the gulf of interpretation yawned so wide it was never likely that it would suffice to provide a permanent settlement of the dispute.

'Bodyline wasn't pleasant,' I have heard Bill Bowes say; 'it was thrilling.' I suspect that this goes pretty close to the heart of the matter. By and large, it was obviously the players who found it unpleasant, the crowds who found it thrilling. In the long run, most first-class players were always going to come down against 'bodyline', because only a small minority of them could hope to profit from it, whereas any of them was liable to find himself facing it: this reaction had become increasingly clear during the English season of 1933. But, as Hobbs remarked, if 90% of the players were against it, 90% of the public were for it. As far as the English cricketing public was concerned, this might be explained by the fact that for them 'bodyline' meant victory over Australia, and in fact most discussions of 'fast leg theory' in the English popular press were confined to its use in the context of the Test Matches and the forthcoming Test series of 1934. But we have seen that Mailey, for one, thought that the Australian crowds were as much thrilled as angered by 'bodyline', and the experience of more recent Test series strongly suggests that highly aggressive fast bowling is something that will always draw the crowds in – it is significant that the wholly commercial enterprise of the Packer series in Australia laid great emphasis on it. No doubt they will enjoy it even more if it is being used by their own side against cowed opponents; but they will enjoy it anyway – there is, after all, even a pleasure to be got out of hating an opponent, as I suspect a lot of Australians enjoyed hating Jardine. The assertion often made by critics of 'bodyline' at the time, that it was intolerably boring to watch, was – I fear – wishful thinking. At most it was the reaction of the connoisseurs and the cognoscenti: Warner's *Cricketer*, which very fairly represented this class, after the Manchester Test against the West Indies quoted an unnamed authority on the game as saying that 'it eliminates every batting stroke except one, and that is a bad one'. There spoke the traditional voice of Lord's, but it was not the voice of the crowds and the popular press that reflected their passions and their tastes.

This was the problem that confronted the MCC as they contemplated the coming Test series of 1934. By the end of 1933, it was certain that the Australian tour would take place as planned; and it would take place on the strength of the private assurances that had been made to the ABC that 'bodyline' would not be used against them. Statesmen, the bulk of the cricketing Establishment and, so far as one can judge, a large majority of first-class cricketers were by then agreed – for reasons idealistic and mercenary, selfless and selfish, far-sighted and short-sighted – that 'bodyline' must be dropped; and some kind of vague validation had been given to this determination by the declaration of the county captains in November. But we have seen that their statement was equivocal, and stopped well short of an outright condemnation of 'fast leg theory'; and apart from it, there had been no official condemnation of 'bodyline', still less any official repudiation of Jardine's conduct of the Test series in Australia – on the contrary, officialdom had feted and flagged him and his victorious team as enthusiastically, on the face of it, as the common mass of English cricket followers. True, the tone of papers like the *Cricketer*, *The Times*, the *Telegraph* and the *Manchester Guardian* had been growing increasingly critical of 'bodyline' as 1933 went on, especially in view of its use in the Varsity Match and the Manchester Test; but in volume their voice was entirely drowned out by the continuing vociferous support for Jardine, Larwood and fast leg theory provided by papers like the *Express*, the *Mail* and the popular Sunday papers.

The attitude of the bulk of the public, as the 1934 season approached, was thus that the MCC had never condemned 'bodyline' as such, still less repudiated the captaincy of Jardine and the bowling of Larwood and Voce in Australia; that it was that captaincy and that bowling that had won the series for England; and that it was therefore to be assumed that the selectors would turn to them again for the 1934 series in England. In the circumstances, it is hard to blame the public for seeing things in this light: especially as the MCC had apparently shown their continuing confidence in Jardine by appointing him to captain England at home in 1933, and in India for the 1933–34 tour.

It is clear that at the very least the MCC were going to have a major public relations problem on their hands in 1934. So they did; and whereas it is very arguable that the elitist structure and secretive habits of the MCC had on the whole served it well in the long and devious negotiations with the ABC, these characteristics were far less well suited to the task of communicating with, or conciliating, a mass public opinion that, as 1934 went on, became increasingly heated, frustrated and suspicious.

The MCC had in fact changed front almost diametrically on 'bodyline'; but the conversion did not extend even to all the members of the Main Committee, and it had happened abruptly and very late in the day – apparently between 12 June, when they sent their unbending cable to the ABC, and the end of July, when the harmony between Macdonald and the inner councils of the MCC, represented by Hailsham, Lewisham, Hawke, Jackson and Findlay, seems to have been complete. By then, of course, Jardine was already leading England against the West Indies, and it was far too late to seek a plausible replacement of him for the forthcoming tour of India – a tour for which in any case Jardine was, on the face of it, particularly well qualified by the Indian background of his own childhood. There is, nevertheless, an entry in the reticent minutes of the Main Committee for a meeting on 10 July which, between the lines, says a great deal: 'After prolonged discussion it was decided to invite Mr D. R. Jardine [to captain the team to India] and to ask the President and Treasurer of the MCC to have a talk with Mr D. R. Jardine when the official invitation is extended to him.' I would give a good deal for a transcript of that 'prolonged discussion', or of the 'talk' which followed it. The President and Treasurer were Hailsham and Hawke; and it is quite impossible not to believe that the main theme of the talk was the desirability of eschewing the use of 'fast leg theory' in India and of avoiding anything like the uproar out there that had marked the tour in Australia. Nationalism, after all, was a red-hot issue in India in 1933 (during the Australian tour, Pataudi had got fed up with being hailed by barrackers as 'Gandhi'), and a full-blooded use of 'bodyline' by the MCC side might all too easily fan it to a still hotter flame.

It may well be relevant that, according to Fender, Jardine hesitated to accept the captaincy of the Indian tour, and was only persuaded to do so by Fender's argument that it committed the MCC to a public demonstration of continuing confidence in him. In any case, the MCC's fears were – in the main – not realized. Neither Larwood nor Voce went to India. The English fast bowlers were Nichols and Clark, neither of whom was in Larwood's class for pace and neither of whom attempted anything like systematic 'bodyline' as it had been seen in Australia; but the tour had a lot of abrasive moments nevertheless. Clark, a left-hander, commonly bowled round the wicket to a leg trap, as we have already seen; on top of that, both he and Nichols made pretty free use of the bumper, as did some of the Indian pace bowlers. In the Test at Calcutta Clark hit one of the Indian openers, Dilwar Hussain, on the head and knocked him out, and at the end of the tour the umpire, Frank Tarrant, who had played cricket for both Victoria and Middlesex, submitted a highly critical report of his bowling to the MCC. Major scandal was avoided, but the reports of the Indian tour that reached Lord's cannot have done much to reassure the MCC when they considered the prospects of Jardine captaining England against Australia in the coming series.

It was this that in many ways was emerging as the key problem for the MCC in the spring of 1934 – what was to be done about Jardine and Larwood? They had been the architects of victory in Australia, and Jardine had gone on to lead England to victory in four successive Test series; while it was becoming apparent that Larwood had recovered from his troubles with his feet, as had at one time seemed unlikely, and was likely to be fit to bowl again in the forthcoming season. Yet if they were selected, what would the Australian reaction be, and what security could the MCC have that there would be no recurrence of 'bodyline'? And if they were omitted, how could their omission be justified to the public?

The crucial figure was Jardine, in the sense that Larwood had never been personally unpopular in Australia, and had never been regarded as the true author of 'bodyline': he could revert to orthodox off theory methods without loss

269

of face, and most Australians would welcome his reappearance in the England side if he did so. But Jardine was a different matter. Macdonald was only one of many Australians who felt that the selection of him to captain England in 1934 would in itself come close to making a resumption of Test cricket between England and Australia on the old friendly terms impossible. He was (he told Jeanes in a letter dated 1 January 1934) completely satisfied that the MCC would honour implicitly their undertaking that 'bodyline' would not be bowled, but in Jardine he had no faith at all. He had told Findlay, before sailing for America in October, that 'if Jardine was made captain in 1934, the contests would be, not England v Australia, or Australia v England, but Jardine v Australia, or Australia v Jardine, and that under his captaincy there would be a veiled vendetta', and had expressed to him his 'fervent and pious hope that after the strenuous Indian tour Mr Jardine might feel he was entitled to a relief from cricket responsibilities in order to devote himself *exclusively* to civic and personal matters!' And when the Australian team finally sailed for England at the end of March, the matter was put even more pithily by W. L. Kelly, one of the authors of the original cable and one of the most unrepentantly militant members of the Board: 'If cricket in 1934 is played as it was in the old days, you will regain the Ashes. If cricket or alleged cricket is played under the captaincy of a man named Jardine, I will strike that out and simply say that I wish you every success.'

What *was* to be done about Jardine? It was not only the Australians who felt that he must go if the ruptured cricketing relations between England and Australia were ever to be properly restored. Warner, in the centre of the controversy by reason alike of his experiences in Australia and his membership of the MCC Committee, felt the problem especially acutely – the problem of how (to quote a letter to Rockley Wilson from his brother) 'bodyline' was to be safely excluded 'without letting Jardine down too badly'. Early in January, Warner wrote a worried letter to Hore-Ruthven in Adelaide:

The real trouble is Jardine. Is he to be Captain? At present I say 'No' unless he makes a most generous gesture of friendliness and then I am not sure I would trust him. He is a queer fellow. When he sees a cricket ground with an Australian on it he goes mad! He rose to his present position on my shoulders, and of his attitude to me I do not care to speak. It is hoped he may retire at the end of the Indian Tour, but in many quarters here – where they do not know the truth – he is a bit of a hero. If he is captain in the First Test and is not friendly he will not captain in the 2nd, but I would not have him at all …

Hore-Ruthven, sensitive to the currents of Australian opinion, replied anxiously and bluntly: 'If you want the game to be played in the proper spirit and the whole controversy buried once and for all, keep Jardine out of the picture on any plea you can find.'

Warner's position was particularly sensitive because, together with Percy Perrin and T. A. Higson, the Chairman of Lancashire CCC, he had been on the Selection Committee for the 1932–33 tour, and the question arose of whether he should continue to serve on it in 1934. In view of his – by now – widely known hostility to Jardine's conduct of the Australian tour, the difficulties, as long as the question of the England captaincy remained unresolved, were obvious. In February, he wrote to Findlay on the subject:

Of course if DRJ were captain it might be awkward, but your conversation the other day led me to understand that DRJ would be required by MCC to give certain guarantees which would appreciably ease the situation … I do not consider DRJ – in his Australian form – can produce the friendly relations and happy spirit which MCC so urgently desire in the coming Test matches – and which are so very vital for the good of the game.

In the end he stood down: the 1934 Selection Committee

consisted of Perrin and Higson, under the statesmanlike chairmanship of Sir Stanley Jackson, whose quiet influence behind the scenes the previous year had evidently been a powerful force in bringing the MCC Committee round to the conviction that the Australian demands for the relinquishment of 'bodyline' must be met. With Higson also by this time a determined opponent of 'bodyline' – so much so that we find Macdonald, in America, suggesting to the ABC that Higson might well act as his proxy at a forthcoming meeting of the Imperial Cricket Conference at which the issue was going to be discussed – there could be little doubt that the selectors would ensure the observance of the MCC's pledge to the ABC, even if this meant an unpleasant confrontation with Jardine.

In the end there was no confrontation – or at least no public one. What is lacking in this story, most unfortunately, is anything from Jardine's side. Jardine is long dead, and no relevant papers of his have yet emerged to throw light on his thinking or his intentions during the winter of 1933–34, while he was leading the MCC side in India. He stayed on in India – where he had of course many personal contacts – for some weeks after the side returned home in early March, and as far as public knowledge went, the next that was heard of him was a thunderbolt in the form of an announcement by him published in the *Evening Standard* of 31 March. It was curt and extremely to the point: 'I have neither the intention nor the desire to play cricket against Australia this summer.' Thus were the MCC let off the hook by the victorious captain they were trying to summon up the nerve to drop.

This sequence of events could well give grounds for suspicion that pressure had been brought to bear on Jardine from the MCC, perhaps in the form of an intimation that he would not be asked to lead England in 1934 unless he was prepared to give an undertaking that he would not resort to 'bodyline' tactics against the Australians. His announcement in the *Evening Standard* could then be read as a curt rejection of such a degrading requirement, a rejection entirely in keeping with Jardine's character. An explanation of this sort would account for what otherwise appears as the suspiciously convenient nature (from the MCC's point of view) of the announcement; and, as we shall see, it would be much in line with the way the MCC appear to have handled Larwood in similar circumstances. I do not rule out the possibility that something of the sort actually happened; but on the whole the weight of the evidence appears to favour a more innocent explanation. During his Indian tour, Jardine had been impatiently looking forward to his engagement and marriage: his bride-to-be's parents had forbidden a public engagement until after his return. The engagement was in fact announced very shortly after his return to England, and he was married later in the summer; and he apparently played no more first-class cricket after this. Add the fact that Jardine had already led England for four successive Test series which, taken together, meant that he had been playing cricket more or less continuously for nearly two years, and that he might well feel that he needed a rest and that his professional commitments demanded it, and it is probably unnecessary to look any further for the explanation of his decision not to play in the forthcoming series against Australia.*

Larwood was a different matter: he was less committed to 'bodyline' than Jardine had been, no doubt, but in early 1934 he was still the great hero of the English cricketing public – the man who had tamed Bradman, and was expected to do so again – and that public would take a lot of satisfying if he was omitted from the Test side, or if he was included, but seen to be bowling on a leash, forbidden to

* Though it must be admitted that it remains curious that he should not have let the MCC know all this in advance privately, which would certainly have been more courteous than leaving them to find it out by reading it in the papers, as he apparently did. The most likely explanation is that he had heard that the MCC had already sold the pass to the Australians – which is undoubtedly the light in which he would have regarded the matter – and felt that in these circumstances courtesy was not called for.

repeat the methods which had been so successful in Australia and which the MCC had still never openly repudiated.

The nearest thing to an official verdict ever issued on 'bodyline' was the special article on 'The Bowling Controversy' which appeared in the 1934 *Wisden* by the editor, S. J. Southerton. Such is the unique authority of *Wisden* that it has generally been taken as a sounding-board for official opinion at Lord's; and if so, this article left no doubt where Lord's stood by the spring of 1934. It printed in full and without comment the text of all the cables exchanged between the ABC and the MCC, after which Southerton went on to give his own measured verdict on the affair. He saw the 1932–33 series as the climax of a tendency which he deplored, reaching back over several Test series, for Anglo-Australian Tests to become 'battles rather than pleasurable struggles' – 'the *result* of the contests was given a prominence out of keeping even with the importance of Test Matches'. He blamed the Australian papers for their introduction of the inflammatory term 'bodyline'; he condemned the ABC's original cable as 'petulant'; he defended the MCC's handling of the controversy, and their defence of Jardine while the tour was in progress; but, all that said, his verdict was unequivocal. Southerton could not believe that the near-unanimous voice of Australian opinion was wrong when it condemned Larwood's and Voce's bowling as deliberately intimidatory, and as constituting a direct attack on the batsman; he refused to accept that what had been bowled in Australia was no more than 'leg theory' as it had been bowled years before by Root and others. He referred to the demonstration of fast leg theory by Constantine and Martindale in the Manchester Test as sufficient evidence that it amounted to an attempt to drive the batsman into playing false strokes by endangering his life and limb. And in his last paragraph he stated his opinion very plainly indeed:

I hope that we shall never see fast leg-theory bowling as used during the last tour in Australia exploited in this country. I think that (1) it is definitely dangerous; (2) it creates ill-feeling between the rival teams; (3) it invites reprisals; (4) it has a bad influence on our great game of cricket; and (5) it eliminates practically all the best strokes in batting.

It was a sweeping condemnation.

But although this might be the voice of Lord's, it was not the voice of the sports columns of the mass circulation dailies, nor of the mass of their readers, who wanted nothing better than to see Larwood repeat in England the feats he had wrought in Australia. It would, of course, in a sense have made life easier for the MCC if Larwood had been unfit to bowl in 1934 as he had been in 1933; but in fact he had made a remarkable recovery and, although he was never again nearly as fast as he had been in Australia, it was evident from early in the season that on merit it would be very difficult to find another fast bowler who could credibly replace him in an England side. But if he were included – what then? It is small wonder if the Australians were nervous at the prospect – in view of the doubts and heart-searchings over the adequacy of the MCC assurances that had preceded the decision to send the team; in view too of the assertions that Larwood had made in the press in the previous autumn, that if he was picked he would bowl leg-theory, and he did not think the MCC would stop him. Macdonald at the time had brushed those statements aside; but in the early weeks of the 1934 season in England, with all the popular press cheering Larwood on, it was not easy for the Australians to be so sure that they could safely be ignored.

1934 was to be an unhappy season. It was poisoned by suspicion from the start: popular (and justified) English suspicion that some kind of secret deal had been made between Australia and the English cricketing Establishment that Larwood should be dropped, or at least should

275

not be allowed to bowl 'bodyline';* Australian suspicions that the deal would not be observed. Crowds were apt to be less well disposed towards the Australians than they had been in the past; the Australians were apt to scent 'bodyline' on very little provocation, and to react demonstratively. For this they had at least the justification that it soon became apparent that the county captains' declaration of the previous November was not in practice stopping some fast fast bowlers – notably Bowes and Voce – from continuing to make very free use of the bouncer; and that, however scrupulously the MCC might abide by the terms of their undertaking to the ABC in the Tests, the Australians also had to play all the counties, over whose captains the MCC had no direct authority. It was, in particular, clear from the start that Nottinghamshire v the Australians was likely to be an explosive fixture, in which the Australians might have to face both Larwood and Voce, not indeed under the captaincy of Jardine, but under that of Carr, which was very little if at all better. Whether or not for this reason I cannot say, but it is a fact that when the Australian's itinerary was fixed, their match against Notts was put in mid-August, very late in the tour.

Larwood made no attempt to revert to the methods he had used in Australia in any of the county matches in which he played; but the public demand that he should be selected for the Tests, and the expectation that, if he was, he would again use fast leg theory (as indeed he had said he would), continued unabated. It was, consequently, a cause of great disappointment when, on the eve of the selection of the team for the first Test, he announced that he was unfit and did not wish to be considered.

There are some grounds for thinking that this unfitness

*Jardine summed up the popular suspicions well in the book that he wrote about the 1934 tour from the press box, *Ashes and Dust*: the abandonment of fast leg theory, he said, was due to the fact that the counties were not prepared to face the financial consequences of the abandonment of the tour. This was indeed an important part of the truth – but not the whole truth.

was diplomatic. Larwood played in both the county matches in which Notts were involved during the first Test, and bowled with effect, and in *The Larwood Story* he himself says that he declared himself unavailable for the Test on Carr's advice in the hope that public demand would then force his inclusion on his own terms for the second Test. There is no doubt that Larwood was aware of the MCC's anxiety to avoid any reversion to 'bodyline' in the Tests. In April, before the season began, Sir Stanley Jackson, the chairman of the selectors, had invited him to a private meeting to discuss the whole issue. We have seen that Jackson had maintained a remarkably open-minded attitude on the 'bodyline' issue throughout the controversy, and this was Larwood's impression at the meeting; but although nothing conclusive came out of it, he can have been left in no doubt that the selectors were not keen to see 'bodyline' used in 1934. He may also of course have had some intimation from Jardine of the MCC's attitude: more certainly, according to his own later account, he had been made aware of it unmistakably by Sir Julien Cahn in a pre-season game in April on Cahn's private ground.

The reappearance of Cahn in this story is interesting. Although not a member of the MCC Committee, he was a munificent private patron of the game and an influential member of the Notts CCC. He was, therefore, a natural intermediary, and it would not be surprising if he was asked to take advantage of the forthcoming game to approach Larwood (such an approach would, of course, normally have come more naturally from his county captain; but Lord's were hardly likely to regard Carr as a suitable intermediary on this occasion). According to Larwood, Cahn took him aside during the game and told him that, if he wanted to be considered for the Tests, he would have to apologize to the MCC for his bowling in Australia and promise to bowl 'legitimately' in future. Presumably this message emanated from Lord's; but it is possible that even more august sources were involved, for Larwood also reports hearing indirectly later in the season that J. H. Thomas had said that Larwood must not represent England again unless he was prepared to apologize for what had happened in Australia.

There must be some element of doubt about this evidence, which is indirect, and dates from thirty years after the events described. Nevertheless, it is hard to suppose that Larwood imagined it, or made it up; and it does make sense – given the pressures under which the MCC were working, they might well have made such an approach to him. Ideally, the Selection Committee no doubt *wanted* Larwood to play – if they could be sure he would not bowl 'bodyline'; for pretty certainly he *was* the best fast bowler they had, and in any case the best demonstration the Australians could have that 'bodyline' was over and done with would be the spectacle of Larwood back in the England side and bowling conventional off theory like a good boy. But there was never any prospect of persuading Larwood to apologize for something which seemed to him to call for no apology – indeed, for a bowling achievement for which he had received the MCC's own support and congratulations. It is not surprising if he came to feel that he had been used as long as he was wanted, and cast aside when he became an embarrassment, and if a note of bitterness increasingly crept into his published comments. He would not play in the Tests on the MCC's terms, and the reason for this was not only pride. He could well remember how Bradman had treated him on English wickets in 1930, and he knew that he had never recovered his full pace after his breakdown in Australia. He cannot have relished the idea of giving Bradman and the other Australian batsmen an ideal opportunity for taking revenge for the humiliations he had inflicted upon them in Australia: from that point of view too, there was much to be said for a bout of diplomatic unfitness before the first Test.

There was not much luck about for the MCC in 1934. Jardine's withdrawal might count as one stroke of good fortune, perhaps; but if so, it never struck again that

278

summer. Ideally, they would have wished Larwood to have played, to have bowled orthodox off theory, and to have proved himself as effective in that mode as he had been in Australia; and even if only the first two of these conditions were fulfilled, that would have been something. Failing that, if he refused to play at all unless he was allowed to exploit fast leg theory, they would have liked to have found a team which could have beaten Australia without him – the only way in which the press and public clamour at his non-selection could have been stilled. Neither happened. England went into the first Test at Trent Bridge – the home ground of Larwood and Voce – with only one fast bowler (Farnes) and under a makeshift captain. Following Jardine's withdrawal, the selectors had turned, no doubt with relief, to Wyatt, the obvious next choice, whose personal opposition to 'bodyline' was an additional recommendation, as his successor; but an injury forced Wyatt to withdraw at short notice, and C. F. Walters, the Worcestershire amateur and opening bat, led the team instead. Australia won by 238 runs, and press and public alike went up in a united shout of 'I told you so'. Farnes – who seems never to have reverted to 'bodyline' after 1933 – had in fact done well on his Test debut, taking 10 for 179 in the match, but the pressure on the selectors to include Larwood in the side for Lord's was intense; and they had already decided to invite him to play when events over the weekend of 17–18 June transformed the whole situation.

Lancashire were playing Notts at Trent Bridge: it will be remembered that the Lancashire chairman was the selector T. A. Higson, and their side included Duckworth, who had been one of the strongest supporters of Jardine and Larwood in Australia. On the first morning, on a most unusually lively wicket for Trent Bridge, Larwood and Voce played havoc with the Lancashire batting, Larwood at one stage taking six wickets in twenty-nine balls for one run. He did this without resorting to 'bodyline', but he nevertheless made anything short of a length rise sharply and most unpleasantly, as he always did, while at the other

279

end Voce made still freer use of the short-pitched ball. Several of the Lancashire batsmen were painfully hit, including Duckworth, who underwent an immediate and radical conversion in his attitude to 'bodyline'. At the end of the innings the Lancashire management protested about the methods of the Notts fast bowlers, and at the end of the match protested officially to Lord's and let it be known that they would refuse to play Notts the following year.

This was the first open complaint that had reached the MCC that the county captains' agreement of November 1933 was not being observed, and it gave rise to heated argument. To Nottinghamshire, it was a flagrant case of 'Give a dog a bad name ...' Carr, their captain, was to write soon afterwards in his memoirs that he knew even before the match began that Lancashire intended to stage a protest against Larwood and Voce. Where he heard it he does not say, but he does say that both the Lancashire captain, Eckersley, and the senior Lancashire professionals (presumably excluding Duckworth) said that it was nothing to do with them and that *they* had no intention of objecting. The inference is very strong that Higson was the real author of the protest, and scarcely less strong that the real object was to stage a demonstration of the dangers of 'bodyline' which would justify the MCC in demanding undertakings from Larwood that he would not bowl it in the forthcoming Test, and in introducing legislation to ban it altogether: further back still lies the remoter inference that this was all the result of behind-the-scenes pressure by the Australians to which the MCC were cravenly giving way (for good measure, Carr adds elsewhere in the book that he had been told by Perrin, another of the selectors, before the season began that, if Larwood played for England in the forthcoming series, he would not be allowed to set his own field – i.e., would not be allowed to bowl leg theory).

This was certainly what Larwood himself, and a large proportion of the English cricketing public, came to believe. We have seen already what measure of truth there is in it, as far as the MCC's general attitude, and the part played in determining it by Australian pressure, are concerned. But Carr was never a very exact or reliable witness, and I cannot credit the Machiavellian implications of his version: though it is likely enough that Higson, whose hostility to 'bodyline' and anything resembling it is beyond question, was the force behind the protest, and seized the opportunity of the injuries inflicted on the Lancashire batsmen to force the issue to a crisis. There is not much doubt that in doing so he would have had the warm support of the majority of county captains, who considered that Notts (and Yorkshire) had been flagrantly defying the intention of the condemnation of 'direct attack' bowling that the captains had issued at the end of the previous season. But for Larwood it was the last straw – especially as he was perfectly clear that he had bowled nothing aginst Lancashire that fast bowlers given the bonus of a lively wicket had not been accustomed to bowl for years. It was not his fault if he bowled it better than most, and was a nastier proposition for batsmen to face in consequence. Up to that point, there seems to be no doubt that he was prepared to play in the second Test if he was invited. Whether he was prepared to do so even if he was forbidden to bowl 'leg theory/bodyline' is perhaps less clear. It is quite certain that neither the selectors nor Wyatt (now restored to the captaincy) would have been prepared to have him in the side on any other terms, and it would seem that by mid-June there had been plenty of indications to make that sufficiently clear to Larwood himself: maybe he had simply not faced up to the issue in his own mind. But after the events at Trent Bridge on the Saturday, he was convinced, not merely that he would be forbidden to bowl 'leg theory' if he played at Lord's, but that that ban was the product of an official conspiracy, to which the MCC were party, but which originated with the determination of the Australians to block a form of attack which they knew they could not master; and in this belief he had the support of both Carr and Voce.

On the following day, 17 June, both Larwood and Voce went on public record to this effect in the Sunday papers. In a front-page article in the *Sunday Dispatch*, Larwood said that he had 'definitely made up his mind not to play against Australia in this or any of the Tests', and stated his conviction that the MCC 'had given way to political or other influences determined at all costs to placate Australia'. He went on to state the elements of his position in a series of trenchant sentences – which, it must be admitted, the MCC, if they had ever tried, would not have found it easy to answer:

> They [i.e., the MCC] have never admitted that my bowling is directed at the body of the batsman.
> They have not discovered anything in the rules to prevent it.
> They have not had the courage to alter the rules.
> If I was right in Australia, I must be right now.

There was a supporting article by Arthur Carr, and Voce wrote a similar article in support of Larwood for the *Sunday Express*.

The Nottingham trio had gone overboard: they had declared their own lack of faith in the MCC, and in the process destroyed any prospect of either Larwood or Voce being selected for any of the remaining Tests against Australia. The selectors did nothing to mollify Larwood's resentment by naming Bowes in his place to partner Farnes at Lord's – Bowes, who was well known for his deliberate exploitation of the bumper, and who, in Larwood's mind, was allowed to get away with it by the same selectors who were down on him, Larwood, like a ton of bricks on far smaller provocation – whether because Bowes did not normally bowl to a leg trap (which was true), or because the Australians were less frightened of him than they were of Larwood. Bowes bowled a fair ration of bouncers at Lord's, but he too – according to his own account – soon discovered that the ground rules were not what they had been. After tea on the second day, when he had just bowled Woodfull and Bradman was coming to the wicket, his captain, Wyatt, came up to him, and said, 'Bill, I've just had a message from the pavilion – "Ask Bowes not to bowl short."' 'And what do you say as captain?' 'Well, if they want it friendly, perhaps they'd better have it that way.' It is the sort of conversation which is apt to be remembered very differently by the two participants: Wyatt has no recollection of it at all, and thinks it very unlikely that it took place. But, whether it actually took place or not, it is at least superbly *ben trovato*, so perfectly does it sum up the popular version of the MCC's attitude to the 1934 Test series – 'Well, if they want it friendly, perhaps they'd better have it that way.'

And if that was the way they were going to have it, there was not much doubt who was going to win it – and more than there had been in Australia. True, the fates were kind to the MCC at Lord's – they got their victory without the aid of Larwood. It was 'Verity's match', the match in which the Yorkshire slow left-hander took fourteen wickets in a day on the Monday after overnight rain, and England won by an innings. But after that it was back to 1930. Bradman resumed his inexorable succession of multi-centuries (304 at Leeds, 244 at the Oval) as the England selectors vainly rang the changes on a variety of other fast bowlers – Bowes, Farnes, Allen, Clark – all but Larwood and Voce; and although the third and fourth Tests were draws, at the oval Australia finally clinched the series and regained the Ashes in overwhelming fashion, winning by an innings and 562 runs, one of the biggest margins in the whole of Test cricket. Throughout the series the MCC's promise that 'bodyline' would not be bowled was scrupulously observed – in the eyes of many of the English public, all too scrupulously. Only in the last Test was there one minute final flare of controversy.

For that game, the England selectors included E. W. Clark, of Northamptonshire, who, as we have seen, regularly bowled round the wicket for his county to a ring

283

of short legs. This was not, by any strict definition, 'bodyline', for Clark normally pitched the ball well up and relied on swing to do his work for him. Nevertheless, it was near enough to it for Wyatt to avoid this field setting early in the Australian innings, and to set a slip field for him instead. This was presumably a concession to Australian sensibilities: it is not very suprising if Wyatt, bringing Clark on for a new spell when Australia had reached 365 for 1, felt that the time had come for drawing the concessions a little narrower, and gave Clark his normal leg trap. Clark still for the most part bowled an orthodox length, and was not notably more successful in this mode than he had been in his previous one; but the incident made an impression on the Australians none the less. It was also noted, with very different emotions, by Jardine and Carr, who, not required on the field, had in the fashion of the 1930s promptly been commissioned to report the game for the press instead. Jardine's acidulous presence there can certainly have done nothing to make the Selection Committee sleep easier at nights.

So the MCC's promise was honoured, and good relationships between the cricketing communities of England and Australia were, officially and tentatively, restored: the price was the loss of Jardine, Larwood and (for the time being) Voce to Test cricket, and the embittering of a great weight of English public opinion. His feelings fanned by the sporting columns of the popular press, the average occupant of the free seats was left at the end of the season with an uneasy sense of grievance, a sense that the MCC had somehow sold the national cause down the river. It was in many ways a narrow, one-sided and unfair view of the issue; but it was a widely held one for all that, and it is easy to see how it came to be so. The MCC had shown itself much less than adept in its handling of its public relations problem; and the resentment bred came to a head at the point where trouble was obviously to be expected – in Nottinghamshire's match against the Australians just before the last Test.

Only one of the English principals in the 'bodyline' controversy played in that game in the end. Carr did not play again during the season after a breakdown in mid-June; and Larwood, who was again having trouble with his feet and had not bowled in Nottinghamshire's three previous matches, was left out of the side at his own request. But Voce played, and the match took place in front of a large and keenly partisan crowd who were convinced almost to a man that their local heroes, Larwood and Voce, had been betrayed by the MCC and unfairly omitted from the England side as a result of behind-the-scenes pressure from the Australian side whom they now saw before them – and the omission of Larwood probably did nothing to pacify them. It is no wonder if the Australians themselves approached the game with a degree of trepidation – the more so since they had already been given a fairly rough ride by Voce in the same fixture on their last tour. Batting first, they were bowled out for 237 (Bradman, incidentally, did not play), Voce taking 8 for 66, and no less than five of these fell to catches in his four-man leg trap. The 1935 *Wisden*, which had made up its mind on the 'bodyline' issue by this time, in its description of the match openly described his methods as 'direct attack', but according to most accounts, Voce in this innings bowled very much as he had been bowling for most of the past five years, left arm inswingers, bowled over the wicket to a leg trap and including a more than average ration of short stuff, but hardly 'bodyline'. It is significant that, according to *Wisden*, for most of the time he was bowling to no more than five men on the leg side all told, whereas in Australia he and Larwood had frequently bowled to seven. The Australians, however, were demonstratively unhappy with his bowling, and the atmosphere was made worse by repeated spells of retaliation in another mode, barracking by the Trent Bridge crowd.

The climax, however, was still to come. On the second day, Notts in their turn were uneventfully bowled out for 183, and after tea the Australians went in for their second innings. Only four overs were bowled before bad light stopped play; but of those four, Voce's two consisted of a barrage of head-high bumpers. Next morning he did not appear on the field, and it was officially put out that he would play no further part in the match because of 'sore shins'. This was altogether too much for the crowd, who immediately scented further kow-towing to the Australians: the visiting team played throughout the day to a barrage of boos and catcalls from the ring, and it must have been a great relief to all concerned when the match petered out in a draw. The Australian management protested officially to the MCC.* There seems in fact to be no doubt that they had made it clear after the second day's play that if Voce bowled on the Tuesday as he had done on the Monday evening – perhaps even if he was not withdrawn from the game – the Australians would refuse to continue with the match, and that Voce's indisposition on the last day was indeed essentially diplomatic, as the crowd suspected and as Voce himself shortly confirmed in the press.

If any further demonstration was required that there was still anything but universal agreement as to what constituted 'direct attack' and what fast bowlers might and might not be permitted to get away with, it was provided by Nottinghamshire's last match of the season, staged, most undiplomatically, against Middlesex at Lord's. In that match Voce hit Muncer, one of the lower order Middlesex batsmen, so badly on the head that he had to be carried off and was unconscious for twenty minutes: another Middlesex batsman was also badly hit, and the Middlesex management were so angry that they announced that they would follow Lancashire's example and refuse to renew fixtures with Notts for the 1935 season. Time was proving true what many Australians had always said: that when England had seen enough of what 'bodyline' really meant,

* Against Voce's bowling, not against the crowd's behaviour, which is understandable: to have done that might have laid themselves open to irony.

286

it would take action itself to stop it. The difference was that, whereas in Australia the pressure had come largely from the crowds, in England it came overwhelmingly from the players and the administrators.

The MCC, anyway, had by the end of the season had more than enough of 'bodyline', and of complaints against Notts, and having seen the ineffectualness of the declaration of the county captains against 'direct attack' at the end of the previous season, were determined now to take action which should be genuinely effective. No doubt to some extent this was harsh on Notts. The Committee of the Notts CCC, confronted with the complaints about their side's bowling by Lancashire, Middlesex and the Australians, rejected Lancashire's complaints as wholly unjustified, and also rejected the Australian complaints except insofar as they referred to the two overs Voce had bowled on the Monday evening, and on both points the umpires involved supported them. They added that, as far as Larwood was concerned, the Committee had 'never had reason to question' the fairness of his bowling. People – the Australians and others – were apt to sniff 'bodyline' in every ball bowled by Nottinghamshire fast bowlers in 1934, and no doubt there was justice in Larwood's complaint that Bowes and others were allowed to get away with bowling that would have had the wires to Lord's humming red-hot if he or Voce had attempted anything similar. But there is little doubt that by the end of the season the MCC had the great bulk of the English cricket-*playing* community behind them – for reasons worthy or unworthy – when they decided to act against 'bodyline'.

On 20 September a specially appointed sub-committee met to discuss the whole issue with Australian representatives (H. Bushby, the Manager, and W. C. Bull, the Treasurer of the touring party, together with Macdonald). There was discussion of the exact definition of what constituted 'direct attack' bowling. It is fairly clear that there was some feeling on the MCC side of the table that the Australians had on some occasions made a lot of fuss about very little during the 1934 tour. They complained not only about the Notts match, but also about Clark's bowling at the Oval in the final Test, and the note of exasperation is discernible, through the formal working of the minute, in Jackson's reply that there was 'no justification for any complaint whatever' about it. But the MCC affirmed their intention of taking firm action against 'fast leg theory' as soon as they had had time to consult the Advisory County Cricket Committee at the end of the season. When this meeting took place, Nottinghamshire found themselves alone in the dock, the attack upon them being led with vigour by Allen; and when Carr claimed that it was ridiculous to suppose that he would ever let a bowler bowl at a batsman, Allen's reply, 'Gentlemen, now we've heard everything,' was received with general applause. Nottinghamshire were left to count the cost of defying the rest of the English cricketing community, and on 8 October the MCC appointed a new sub-committee to define direct attack and recommend how to eliminate it. But this was not all: the sub-committee was also commissioned, most significantly, to consider amending the existing LBW Law.

Thus did two streams which had flowed on parallel courses for many years at last come together. We have seen the previous history of this: the gradual growth of pad-play, and in the way in which its deliberate exploitation by batsmen in the 1920s had been one of the factors driving fast bowlers in the direction of deliberate intimidation. For years there had been a party, led with great persistence by R. H. Lyttelton, in favour of widening the terms of the existing Law in favour of the bowler – indeed, as I have already shown, attempts to do this reached back as far as the 1880s. If, therefore, steps were now to be taken to put an effective ban on the deliberate use of intimidation, there was a logic in revising the LBW Law at the same time, and in thus giving back to fast bowlers with one hand something of what was taken away from them with the other. From one point of view, no doubt, this was a

288

nostalgic attempt to get back to the 'Golden Age' before 1914, when supposedly no batsman made deliberate defensive use of his pads, and no fast bowler tried to intimidate a batsman; but from another, it was a thoroughly realistic adaptation of the Laws to the developments that had taken place in the game over the past twenty years. It is not the least remarkable example of Bradman's shrewdness that he, who had been so early in urging the Board of Control to take action to check the English use of 'fast leg theory' in Australia, was almost equally early in seeing the logic of this and in following it up by suggesting a revision of the LBW Law. He wrote to the MCC in the summer of 1933 with such a proposal, and indeed a wider one than that finally adopted, for he suggested that under certain circumstances a batsman might be liable to be given out LBW even if the ball pitched outside the *leg* stump.

The sub-committee of the MCC would not go this far; but they did propose the revision of the Law to permit LBW decisions in the case of balls pitching outside the off stump (but still striking the batsman between wicket and wicket) which, tried experimentally for the first time in the 1935 season, has since become an accepted part of the Laws of the game, and it is obvious that it was this concession that had most relevance to the lot of the fast bowler. There is no question that the sub-committee were aware of the intimate connection between this issue and the other issue they were commissioned to investigate, that of 'direct attack'. On this, they took evidence from the Secretary and Assistant Secretary of the MCC and from seven leading first-class umpires, who were unanimous in their statement that 'direct attack' was on the increase in England and ought to be eliminated; but as to how this should be done, there was considerable difference of opinion – though the failure of the 'captains' agreement' of the previous year had at least eliminated one possibility.

One member of the sub-committee, Wyatt, favoured the suggestion of no-balling all deliveries that pitched short of a line drawn across the wicket: most of the umpires consulted favoured this solution (and in view of the direction the development of the game has taken in the last twenty years, one may regret that it was not adopted). But Jackson was outspokenly hostile to it (why he was does not appear from the record), and brought most of the rest of the sub-committee round to his opinion. In the end, it was resolved simply that fast short-pitched bowling directed at the batsman was unfair, and that umpires should be encouraged to act against it under Law 43 – the 'fair and unfair play' Law.

It was this solution that the MCC Committee finally adopted, at a meeting at the end of October. No alteration was made to the Laws themselves, but in due course an addition was made to the accompanying 'Instructions to Umpires', directing them to intervene in the case of 'systematic bowling of fast short pitched balls at the batsman standing clear of his wicket'. This – it may fairly be said – was a very minimal interpretation of 'bodyline' or 'direct attack': in particular, in the phrase 'standing clear of his wicket' it showed clear traces of recent controversies, for it had always been the English contention that the troubles of the Australian batsmen against Larwood and Voce were due in large measure to their practice of moving across the stumps to play the ball, and the new Instruction would have afforded no protection to batsmen indulging in such a practice. Bowes indeed is on record as saying that it made no difference to his bowling in practice, since in his experience batsmen never did stand clear of their wickets to play the ball: indeed, the form of the Instruction left it technically still open to the MCC to argue that the English bowling in Australia had been perfectly fair, and presumably therefore also to recall Larwood and Voce (and Jardine!) to the England team, to bowl as they had bowled then. But this is fantasy: nobody at the MCC showed any disposition to argue in this fashion, and, although it was tacitly agreed by all concerned that the question of whether the English bowling in the 1932–33 series had been fair or not should be interred in decent silence, undoubtedly most of them by now accepted in their heart of hearts that it had not. In any case, the new Instruction was as much a symbol as a piece of precise legislation. What it meant was that there was now a general resolve, in England as well as Australia, that intimidatory fast bowling had increased beyond all tolerable limits, and that it would be eliminated, by calling in the Laws of the game if necessary – and because that will was now firm and clear, it was, at least for a long time to come, observed without any need actually to invoke the Instruction. In those circumstances it did no harm to insert a phrase that did something to salve the wounded pride of the MCC, and that was unlikely ever to be strictly interpreted in practice.

Thus the issuing of the revised 'Instructions to Umpires' in the spring of 1935 may be taken to mark the point at which 'bodyline' was officially outlawed in cricket – and to that extent also to mark the point at which this book should draw to a conclusion. Things, of course, were not quite that tidy in practice. In Nottinghamshire, there was an epic row when it became known that the Committee of the Notts CCC, following the match against the Australians, had written to the MCC apologizing for Voce's bowling at the beginning of the Australians' second innings (not, it should be noted, during their first innings) and undertaking to prevent a recurrence, and had also agreed that this letter might be forwarded to the ABC. To a great many zealous Nottinghamshire men, this meant truckling to the Australians who were the true authors of the trouble. A special general meeting of the Club was requisitioned at which 2500 members attended, and after long, noisy and embittered proceedings (much concerned with the real state of Voce's shins), a motion of no confidence in the Committee was carried. This came close to an implicit approval of the type of bowling which had just been condemned by the MCC and the Advisory County Cricket Committee, and for several weeks there seemed to be a strong prospect of Nottinghamshire going its own way in outright defiance of the rest of the English cricketing Establishment, and finding itself excluded from the County Championship in 1935 in consequence. But as the prospects of this outcome sank in, heads cooled in Nottinghamshire. The motion of no confidence was rescinded, the county promised to abide by the new ruling against 'direct attack' bowling, and Carr was replaced as captain by S. D. Rhodes and G. F. H. Heane.

So far as my information goes, the new 'Instruction' to umpires was never in fact resorted to in England before the War: there was no need for it. Consensus had been reached, and from then on county captains and fast bowlers (consoled to some extent by the revision of the LBW Law) avoided 'direct attack', sufficiently at least to keep out of trouble with the umpires. Certainly nothing more was seen of systematic short-pitched bowling directed to a leg trap. In the continuing Test series with Australia, the embers still took a time to cool. A delicate point, clearly, was the next visit of an English side to Australia, in 1936–37. That side was captained by G. O. Allen. Allen was an obvious candidate for the post on grounds of both character and all-round ability; but there can be no doubt that his appointment was also likely to provide the maximum reassurance to the Australians that nothing more would be seen of 'bodyline'. Larwood – who had headed the national bowling averages again in 1936 – was not considered for it, and would doubtless have refused to go. But Voce, who had swallowed his pride the previous summer, and indicated to the MCC his readiness to play for England if selected, had been chosen for the last Test against the touring Indians in 1936, and was included in the party for Australia. This might alone have been enough to raise hackles in Australia, had not Allen insisted on Voce putting his name to an apology for his bowling on the previous tour. This was, one may think, rather hard on Voce; but it was a price which was essential if his inclusion in the side was to be accepted without trouble in Australia, and it was one which he was prepared to pay. As it was, he bowled superbly, and his bowling gave rise to no controversy at all,* in a thrilling series which Australia won 3–2.

It was this series which marks the real return to mutual confidence in cricketing relations between England and Australia; and even in that there was a flurry of anxiety before the last Test, when the score stood at 2-all and tension and excitement were running high, at the news that the Australian selectors had included the fast bowler Nash, whose bowling in Victoria's match against the MCC had aroused some critical English comment. Nothing came of it: the affair was smoothed out at a conference, summoned by the chairman of the ABC, between the captains and the umpires before the game began (it was one of the great assets of the 1936–37, as contrasted with the 1932–33, series that good relations between the captains, Bradman and Allen, were maintained throughout). The visit of the 1938 Australian side to England was the first series since 1930 in which nothing whatever was heard of the 'bodyline' issue; and soon after that, all cricketing controversies were stilled by the greater controversies of a wider world.

* Indeed, he was to go to Australia yet again, at the age of thirty-seven, with the 1946–47 tour.

Epilogue

We can, and we often do, look back on the 'bodyline' episode as something entire in itself, something closed and finished in the history of cricket – like, shall we say, the throwing controversy in the 1890s – and perhaps the temptation to do so in a golden jubilee retrospect like this one, written fifty years after the event, is particularly strong. But I tried to show in an earlier chapter that to view 'bodyline' fairly, we have to see it as a natural development at the particular stage of evolution that first-class cricket had then reached; and an awareness of that should suggest that, if 'bodyline' had a past, it probably had a continuing future too.

And so it has had: though there is something to be said for the other view as well. 'Bodyline' received so severe a check, and was finally so firmly rejected by the ruling authorities of the game in both England and Australia in 1933–35, that it was something like a quarter of a century before fast bowling broke through its inhibitions and resumed its natural line of development; and even then, the memory of 'bodyline', and the issuing of formal instructions to umpires to prevent its recurrence, ensured that some features of it as it was bowled in Australia in 1932–33 have never reappeared, and probably never will. In particular, the more recent limitation of the number of leg-side fielders, although introduced with a different object, has made impossible the setting of the kind of field that Larwood and Voce bowled to in 1932–33 – the packed leg-trap that was the hallmark of Jardine's tactics with the two (or more) long legs out behind them.

There seems to be no doubt that after the winter of

1934–35, a general consensus reigned that the deliberate and systematic exploitation of short-pitched bowling by fast bowlers with the aim of intimidation had been banned from the game. This did not exclude traditional – full-length – leg theory, which was exploited by large numbers of fast-medium inswingers before and after the Second World War. It also did not exclude the occasional use of the bumper; but for a quarter of a century after 1935, no fast bowler was bowling three or four short balls an over, or bowling to a field specifically set on the assumption that he would be doing so. As far as England and Australia were concerned, the fast bowling boot was firmly on the other foot after the War: it was Australia now which had the monopoly of really fast bowlers, in Lindwall and Miller. In the 1932–33 series Lindwall, then a schoolboy, had worshipped Larwood from afar, and deliberately modelled his own action and method on him, as he readily acknowledged. When, during the 1948 tour, a spectator called out to him, 'Lindwall, you've copied Larwood,' his reply was immediate and direct: 'And why shouldn't I copy the master?'

In the same situation as Gregory and McDonald had been in 1920–21 – of knowing that they had the means of intimidation, and that England did not have the means of retaliation – Lindwall and Miller, feeling the same temptations, reacted in much the same way: they bowled a lot of bumpers, and were indeed sometimes accused of bowling too many, but never based their attack on them, and bowled not to leg traps, but to 'umbrella fields' of slips and gullies. Lindwall, like Larwood, is on record as saying that he never in his life tried to hit a batsman. The same was true of their successors of the 1950s, the Englishmen Trueman, Statham and Tyson, the Australian Davidson, the South Africans McCarthy, Heine and Adcock, and others.

In the 1960s this began to change. After a generation, the inhibitions imposed by the 'bodyline' affair began to wear off, especially as it was realized how weak the restraints imposed upon fast bowlers by the Laws really were, and how reluctant umpires were to invoke them. Most people would probably say that the real pioneers this time were the West Indians Griffith and Hall, but the example, once set, was widely and swiftly followed. It is true that this was still not 'bodyline', inasmuch as it was not bowled to a leg trap; but no regular watcher of cricket in the late 1960s and throughout the 1970s could fail to be aware of the increasing exploitation by fast bowlers of the period of deliberate intimidation as one of their main weapons. Larwood, watching Test cricket 1970s-style, said without hesitation that there was far more use of the bumper in it than he would ever have attempted; and at least some of its practitioners left no doubt of what their objectives were. Denis Lillee, in his book *Back To The Mark*, has said outright, 'I try to hit a batsman in the rib-cage when I bowl a purposeful bouncer, and I want it to hurt so much that the batsman doesn't want to face me any more.'

In the 1930s, 'bodyline' aroused intense and widespread indignation, and within two years was – at least supposedly – legislated out of existence. In the 1980s the regular, deliberate and aggressive use of the bouncer has come to be regarded as so much part of the natural order of things that it is possible to hear commentators on radio and television discriminating nicely between 'good' and 'bad' bouncers, the 'good' bouncer being not, as the innocent might expect, the one that threatens no harm to the batsman, but the one that it is difficult for him to avoid. Typically, the response to the increasing aggressiveness of modern fast bowling has been, not to check the aggression, but to devise new and far more elaborate forms of protective gear for the batsman exposed to it, notably of course the helmet. The violence itself is taken for granted.

To all this, the Laws of the game – considerably altered now since the new 'Instruction to Umpires' was first drafted in 1935 – have been a wholly inadequate barrier: the most they have achieved has been to channel intimidation and to ration it. Their essential failure is explicit in Lillee's remark quoted above: if a modern fast bowler can profess that creed and practise it without serious interference by the umpires, it is clear that the attempt to exclude intimidation from the game by Law has failed, and largely been abandoned. To some extent this is because a perfectly satisfactory definition of what it is intended to ban has continued to elude the legislators, and umpires have shrunk from trying to apply a law which rests so much on a subjective judgement, and which different umpires would be likely to apply widely differently if they tried to enforce it. Their task has been made harder by the fact that modern intimidation is much more diffuse than 'bodyline'. It is typical of the absolute-ness of Jardine's mind that 'bodyline' was an affair of blacks and whites: it was, at any given moment, being bowled or it was not, and if it was, the element of intimidation was continuous; there was the field specially set for it, and you could expect four or five balls short of a length each over. It was therefore something easy for umpires to recognize, and correspondingly easy to ban. But modern intimidatory fast bowling – which typically originates more with the bowler than the captain – is less systematic than that, and correspondingly harder to isolate and define. It is a matter of a couple of bumpers an over, or whatever the umpire will allow, thrown in unpredictably, without alteration of field, in the midst of balls of more orthodox length and direction. There is a great deal to be said for Larwood's contention that, because it is less predictable, it is also actually more dangerous than 'bodyline' – witness the near-fatal accidents to the Indian batsman Contractor in the West Indies in 1962, and to the New Zealander Ewan Chatfield against Peter Lever in 1975 – or if it is not, it is only because batsmen have learned to wear helmets.*

* Helmets, indeed, are in the same position today as pads were a hundred years ago, protective clothing pure and simple. It is fascinating to speculate whether the use of them will develop in the same way, and whether in fifty years or so Lord's will be anxiously scratching its head over the increasing vogue of deliberate helmet-play.

I think umpires have been more passive than they might have been in face of the recurrence of intimidatory fast bowling in the last generation, and that they have something to answer for here. But umpires have always been the servants of the game rather than its masters: ultimately, they take their lead from what the players, the public and the administrators want, and they have rarely acted strongly without a strong lead from one or more of these (usually the administrators). In the end, I would argue, they have come to accept the permanent presence of the element of deliberate intimidation in the game because, on balance, it is something which the media and the public find thrilling, and such is the dependence of the modern first-class game on the media and the public that, that being so, there is no more to be said.* I do not claim that this is a total explanation. I think there is probably also a sense in which any game, played professionally under the intense pressures of public and media attention, tends to develop in the direction of violence whether the public and the media actually desire it or not (modern rugger is quite a good example, even in the absence of professionalism).

That the element of intimidation in the game has increased so much is not surprising when one considers the immensely increased role and respectability of violence in our society, compared to the society of the 1930s in which 'bodyline' appeared; and especially the way in which it has gained ground in the media, the entertainments industry and mass spectator sport. There is a sense in which

---

*It is only the first-class game I am speaking of here. But it may be significant – though I hope not – and it is certainly ominous if so, that in the last two years I have, for the first time in my life, twice seen bumpers deliberately used in schools cricket. I have seen a batsman felled by one, I have seen the impact this has on the confidence of those who have to follow him, and I have seen the immediate raising of the temperature among both players and spectators that resulted from it. I have also experienced for myself the dilemmas and difficulties the umpire faces in trying to apply a Law which rests in part on his guess about the bowler's intentions. It was on the miniature scale a very instructive experience for an author of a book on 'bodyline'.

298

'bodyline' was ahead of its time. I am inclined to think that the deepest insight into it was that of Mailey and Bowes, both of whom sensed that, for all the uproar on the field, the crowds in some sense enjoyed it. It was, no doubt, an illegitimate and a shameful enjoyment, and in the 1930s that was still enough to condemn it; but the spectacle of violence *is* exciting, dreadfully exciting, and neither illegitimacy nor shame deter much any more. It is, of course, also true that whereas in 1932–33 the game was still largely run by an elite who could impose their own standards on it, it is today frankly a part of the entertainments industry, which has to pay its way or go under, and the standards of the crowds and the television companies dominate all. If a demonstration of this is required, one has to look no further afield than the story of the 'Packer series' in Australia, the Suez Crisis of traditional cricket, where the media interests confronted the cricketing Establishment and won by weight of money – a victory whose repercussions have been felt far outside Australia, where it took place. It scarcely needs emphasizing again that the 'Packer tests' made a more conscious use of the spectator appeal of violence than had ever been attempted in cricket before.

There is, therefore, a way in which 'bodyline' anticipated what can be seen as the central tendency of the game in the last generation: the irony of it is that it did so almost entirely accidentally. I do not think that 'bodyline' was envisaged as clearly, or worked out as fully in advance, by Jardine as has often been supposed; but Jardine will always, and rightly, be thought of as its mastermind. Jardine, though, adopted it for reasons which had nothing to do with the fact that the underlying drift of mass spectator sport was setting in this same direction. That 'bodyline' might have a profound appeal to the crowds who watched it would never have occurred to Jardine, who despised the crowds and denied their right to exert any influence on the way the game was played – if it had occurred to him, it would probably have tended to deter him from using it.

The attraction of 'fast leg theory' – or 'bodyline', as it became – for him was that it satisfied an immediate tactical need: that he found in it a means of beating Australia. I have argued already that, if there is a sense in which the ruthlessness of Jardine's approach reflected the values of a world which had been through the First World War, yet his view of cricket was in many ways deeply traditional and old-fashioned, above all in this refusal to recognize the presence of the crowd and the legitimacy of its desires. It is not the least odd feature of the 'bodyline' controversy that he should nevertheless, accidentally, have anticipated so much of the sort of cricket that the crowds of the next fifty years were going to want to see.

I suppose there is, finally, some obligation on the writer of an account of the 'bodyline' controversy to attempt some judgement on the rights and the wrongs of it all.

It will have been readily gathered from what I have written that I think cricket is a better game without intimidation. It will also have been gathered that I think 'bodyline' was a natural development in the early 1930s, given the way fast bowling had been evolving over the years and the pressures of Test Match cricket at the time: indeed, to some extent I even think it was a natural development in the course of the 1932–33 series itself. But there was an element of deliberate intent – Jardine's – in it from the start, and that element hardened as the series went on and as 'bodyline' itself became more clearly defined, in the minds of the players on both sides and of the public. That something went very seriously wrong with the series is certain; how to distribute the blame for it is more difficult.

Much of it – very probably the greater portion of it – does not belong to individuals at all. Some of it must be attributed to wholly impersonal forces, like the mood of the public in the aftermath of the First World War and in the shadow of the Depression. Some of it rests on the anonymous masses of the cricket-following public in both countries, whose intense thirst for victory and resentment at defeat put pressures on the game which it was ill fitted to resist. A great deal of it, to my mind, rests on the popular press, both English and Australian, which revelled in the opportunities for sensation which the affair provided, and in consequence played it up for all it was worth and a great deal more, enlisting a weight of public emotion on both sides that greatly prolonged the controversy and made it much harder to settle than would otherwise have been the case.

When it comes to individuals, the central figure, inevitably, is Jardine. It is very difficult to be fair to this complex, proud and unbending man. The easy thing to say is that he was a magnificent captain and a magnificent cricket thinker, but a disastrous leader of an England tour of Australia. Jardine's greatest weakness, paradoxically, was also one of his greatest talents – the ability to abstract, to consider a problem in isolation: in this instance, to consider the practical problem of how best to win the Test series against Australia, perhaps without reference to the broader assumptions that underlie the Laws of the game, and certainly without reference to the social context in which Test Matches take place. For all the rhetoric that was uttered during the tour about cricket as a builder of the bonds of Empire (not that Jardine himself ever lent himself to this kind of thing, as far as I know), in practice Jardine simply ignored what I have called the diplomatic aspect of an MCC tour abroad: in Australia at least, he went out to win the Test Matches and to settle his personal accounts with the Australians, and for very little else at all. This was an unreal abstraction. Test Matches by the 1930s were a very great deal more than contests between teams of cricketers representing England and Australia. They were occasions on which the hopes, the fears and the intense emotions of hundreds of thousands, even of millions, hung; and they could not be properly conducted by a man who simply shut his eyes to the fact. The belief that the crowd were there, if at all, on sufferance – like the spectators at the practice session at Adelaide! – and that the press ought not to be there at all, was in itself a very serious disqualification indeed for the leader of an English side in Australia. It became a fatal one when united with the positive antipathy for Australian crowds, if not for Australian cricketers, that Jardine seems to have derived from his experiences of them in 1928–29, and which the 1932–33 tour immensely reinforced.*

I do therefore think that Jardine bears the heaviest responsibility for what went wrong with the 1932–33 tour, in the sense that another captain – almost any other English captain of the last fifty years – would have handled the situation that arose, in the Adelaide Test and thereafter, very differently and more happily. But I also think that, Jardine being Jardine, the outcome was practically inevitable: that he had not got it in him to behave otherwise than as he did, and indeed that when the storm broke he conducted himself with great moral courage and an impressive degree of dignity and restraint. If, in the whole affair, one has to look for somebody who is to blame in the sense that he really *ought* to have known better, I am more and more inclined, the more I think of it, to look in the

---

*The comparison with Michael Brearley, which has occurred to me repeatedly while I have been writing this book, is very interesting. Both were typical Oxbridge men of their generations: both were captains in the English amateur tradition. Both were batsmen of very high talent – both, incidentally, greatly distinguished themselves batting for their universities against visiting Australian teams, and both, one might add, failed afterwards to reproduce their finest batting form in Test cricket (neither of them ever scored a century against Australia). Both had extremely successful records as Test Match captains. Both knew what it was to fall foul of Australian crowds (though certainly with a great difference in degree). Both, above all, were examples of the captain as thinker. But here the parallels end. The intellects were differently directed: Jardine was, above all, a theorist of techniques and tactics on the field, Brearley above all a theorist of team leadership. Moreover, harshly treated though he often was by the Australian press and public, Brearley never disdained them, as Jardine did, or failed to appreciate the importance of the public relations side of his position. The criticism I have made above of Jardine's leadership in Australia makes no sense at all applied to Brearley.

direction of the selectors who appointed Jardine captain; and, ironically, especially in the direction of Warner, for, by his own account, it was Warner who more than anyone was responsible for the appointment.

Poor Warner paid dearly for his error if ever man did, for nobody suffered as much on the tour as he was to do; but surely he *should* have known Jardine well enough to sense something of his attitudes towards Australia and Australians, and to realize that they ruled him out as a candidate for the job. Warner, it is true, had not been in Australia with the 1928–29 tour, and had therefore seen nothing of Jardine's encounters with the Australian crowds; nor, to the best of my knowledge, had any of the other members of the Selection Committee.

But if they could not recognize Jardine's disqualifications for the job through their own knowledge of him, the MCC of all bodies should surely have had the means of information at hand to supply the defect. Rockley Wilson surely cannot have been the only one of those who knew Jardine to have spotted the danger: indeed, even Crutchley did so, at a time when he scarcely knew Jardine at all. What about Fender, who had both been in Australia to cover the 1928–29 series for the press, and was a close personal friend of Jardine? If he was too much of *persona ingrata* at Lord's to be consulted by the selectors, what about Chapman, Jardine's captain in Australia in 1928–29? Or what about Jardine's own father? One way or another it should have been possible for the selectors to know that Jardine, for all his talents, was not the man for *this* job. I suspect that they too, after the hammering England had taken from Australia in 1930, narrowed their vision dangerously in looking solely for a captain who could avenge that defeat; and that, if blame is to be handed out, a fair share of it in consequence belongs by rights to them.

For the rest, I think that the Australian Board of Control, admittedly acting under very great pressure, undeniably made a hash of their handling of the original protest at Adelaide – certainly in its wording and its immediate release to the press, very probably in its timing, arguably in the decision to send it at all. In the Australian phase of the 'battle of the cables', while the tour was still in progress, the MCC squarely outplayed the ABC. In the English phase during the summer and autumn of 1933, the verdict was reversed. The ABC, admirably advised by Macdonald in London, had decisively the better of this, the final phase of the controversy – the phase that has determined the way in which the affair has been interpreted ever since. It was not, of course, a simple trial of strength of will and diplomatic finesse between the two governing bodies: each in turn was favoured by the fitful winds of public and professional opinion, changing circumstances and government influence, and these largely determined the outcome.

The MCC, at its best in the world of diplomatic exchanges and words quietly exchanged in club-rooms and well-carpeted corridors, did not show up to advantage in 1933–34 when it came to the handling of a sensation-seeking press and a suspicious public; nor was its handling of individuals always above reproach. Jardine himself perhaps played too active a part in the course of events throughout, right up to his final withdrawal from the scene, to deserve a sympathy which he would certainly never have solicited. But Larwood is a different matter. He was not the author of 'bodyline' but its executant, even if its willing executant. He did what he was asked to do: he broke the back of the Australian batting, he found the answer to Bradman, he won the series for England, and was officially congratulated for it by the MCC. A year later all this was held against him. He found himself in the position of the accused, who would be allowed into the England team only, if at all, on sufferance. In 1934, he became the whipping-boy for bowling in ways which others had followed with impunity for years, and were still following. I think he sometimes said things in public which would have been better unsaid, and which he may have regretted since; but he behaved like a man of decent pride, and I think he had reason to feel harshly treated. He deserved better of English cricket than it has ever publicly recognized.

This brings me to my final point. The last, and greatest, question is whether 'bodyline' deserved the condemnation it finally received; whether the hostility of the Australian reaction to it was justified. That the reaction was inflamed by partisanship I have no doubt at all: it was not all pure moral indignation. Nothing struck me more forcefully when I was in Australia recently gathering material for this book than the number of people I met who had seen the 'bodyline' Tests – including the Adelaide one – and who felt, then as now, that Larwood's attack had been perfectly fair. I remember one friend in particular who, as a schoolboy, saw the whole game at the Adelaide Oval, and still recalled his sense of shame at the behaviour of his countrymen.

I did not myself see those games; and all that I know about first-class cricket is what I have watched, what I have read about, what I have seen on television, and what I have been told by the small number of first-class cricketers I have talked to. These are formidable disqualifications, and I have good reason to hesitate before passing any judgement at all. If one is nevertheless demanded of me, I would say that I think the case against 'bodyline' has gone largely by default, and that its unfairness was a good deal less obvious than is commonly assumed. It was based squarely on intimidation, and I do not like intimidation in the game; but I think it is too late in the day to hope to keep it out.

If a convincing technical answer could have been found for 'bodyline' – if the batsmen could have solved the problem for themselves (as, thirty years earlier, they had worked out a technical solution to the googly) – 'bodyline' might still have been regarded as rough, as unpleasant, as ethically marginal, but I doubt if it would have been condemned as unfair. To stick that badge on it was in a way an admission of despair on the part of the batsmen. I think it could, and probably would, have been technically solved (I think in particular that Bradman would have mastered it), if only it had not been put in execution by a captain of

305

ruthless consistency and a fast bowler of genius. Given Larwood, the problem *was* unmanageable within the existing Laws of the game. It is harsh to condemn a man for his genius, but it is that that brings me in the end to the conclusion that 'bodyline' was indeed unfair.

'Larwood –' as Arthur Mailey said '– that was different.'

Notes on sources

Unpublished Material
The two obvious sources of information on the 'bodyline'
controversy are the records of the two governing bodies,
the MCC and the ABC (now the ACB), and I have been
fortunate enough to have access to both. The records of
the MCC, however, are gravely defective – possibly due to
salvage drives during the Second World War. Very little
appears to survive beyond the printed committee minutes
for the period, which are on the whole unrevealing. There
are, for instance, no minutes of the sub-committee which
handled the dispute with the ABC throughout its most
delicate stage between May 1933 and the end of the year –
though in this case, given the secrecy with which the sub-
committee carried on its business, it may be that no
minutes were taken. But there are also no minutes for the
meeting of county captains at Lord's in November 1933 to
discuss 'direct attack', nor apparently for meetings of the
Advisory County Cricket Committee for the period,
although these must have existed. More seriously, the
reports on the 1932–33 tour which Jardine, Warner and
Palairet delivered to the MCC after their return to England
have also vanished. Apart from the printed committee
minutes, the only relevant materials now surviving are
three files, two containing copies of outgoing correspondence for January and February 1933, which are useful
mainly as illustrating the very limited understanding of
what was happening in Australia that then prevailed at
Lord's, and a single file of incoming correspondence for the
period which contains one or two scraps relevant to the
'bodyline' affair. A file of what may well be very valuable

correspondence on the subject was left to the MCC by the Earl of Gowrie (the former Sir Alexander Hore-Ruthven), but this is not at present available for inspection (though the letters mentioned below as published by E. W. Swanton may well be included in it).

The records of the ACB in Melbourne, by contrast, are complete and highly informative, though inevitably limited by the fact that it was the MCC, and not the ABC, whose team was using 'bodyline'. They consist of minutes, supporting material, incoming letters and copies of outgoing correspondence, for the entire period of the dispute. Further limitations arise from the fact that meetings of the ABC were few and far between, and that much business while the controversy was at its height was clearly conducted verbally, often by telephone; but the Board's records are by far the most valuable unpublished source of material on the controversy now existing, so far as my knowledge goes. In particular, Macdonald's letters from London during 1933 throw a flood of light on what has up to now been one of the darkest corners of the affair, the process by which the MCC came to reverse its original stand on 'bodyline' in the course of that year.

Government records in both countries would also seem worth investigating, since both governments were involved in the affair to some degree; but my enquiries at the Public Record Office in London and the Australian National Archives in Canberra were wholly unrewarding, though not due to any lack of courtesy or helpfulness on the part of the staff. I could trace no references to the affair in the indexes (though anyone who knows the maze-like nature of public records will understand me when I say that I am not absolutely certain that this means that no relevant records exist). As I have mentioned in the text, there is independent evidence for the destruction of the Dominions Office files dealing with the matter.

Finally, I have been able to use a copy of the very valuable diary of E. T. Crutchley, the British Representative in

Australia in 1932–33, which is in the possession of his son, Mr Brooke Crutchley.

Newspapers and Periodicals

The amount of newspaper material dealing with the events of the tour and its aftermath, particularly the more controversial episodes, is of course enormous, and I make no pretence to having done more than scrape the surface of it during the limited time I have been able to spend in the newspaper section of the British Library at Colindale and in the State Libraries of South Australia and New South Wales. As far as Britain is concerned, the actual reports of events in Australia can be narrowed down to only three or four sources, as I have explained in Chapter 3, but the quantity of comment and correspondence arising from them was vast, and would certainly repay fuller research. This is probably even more true of Australia, where all the major dailies were represented during the tour by their own correspondents.

Periodical discussion of the rights and wrongs of 'bodyline' was also extensive, and of particular interest here are the files of the leading cricket periodicals of the two countries, the *Cricketer* and the *Australian Cricketer*, for the period.

Books

I have already given some account in Chapter 8 of the flood of books published in both countries in the immediate aftermath of the tour: from the English side, Jardine's *In Quest of the Ashes*, Larwood's *Body-Line?*, Hobbs' *Fight For The Ashes*, and Bruce Harris' *Jardine Justified*, from the Australian side. R. W. E. Wilmot's *Defending the Ashes*, Alan Kippax' *Anti-Bodyline*, and Arthur Mailey's *And Then Came Larwood*. Over the years since 1933, at least five more books which may be considered to be substantially about the famous tour have appeared: Jack Fingleton's *Cricket Crisis* (1946), Larwood and Kevin Perkins' *The Larwood Story* (1965), R. S. Whitington's

Bodyline Umpire (1974), E. W. Docker's *Bradman and the Bodyline Series* (1978), and most recently Ronald Mason's *Ashes in the Mouth*, which I have not yet read at the time of going to press.

Many other books contain briefer references to the affair, some of them highly illuminating. Fingleton, in particular, referred to it over the years in almost every one of the numerous books he wrote. P. F. Warner's account of the tour in *Cricket Between the Wars* is especially valuable; and also worth consulting are A. W. Carr's *Cricket With the Lid Off*, Bill Bowes' *Express Deliveries*, Ray Robinson's *Between Wickets* and *The Wildest Tests*, David Frith's *The Fast Men* and V. Y. Richardson's *Vic Richardson Story*. Biographies and autobiographies of varying degrees of interest also exist for several of the other players involved in the affair. Outstanding among them are two recent biographies: Irving Rosenwater's *Sir Donald Bradman* and Richard Streeton's *P. G. H. Fender*. In a category of their own are E. W. Swanton's *Follow On* and *Sort of a Cricket Person*, both of which contain chapters on the 'bodyline' tour which are particularly valuable for their quotations in full of some of the letters about the affair exchanged between Warner and Hore-Ruthven – letters which are otherwise unavailable.

Two recent essays of some interest on the whole 'bodyline' episode are Derek Birley's in his book *The Willow Wand* and, from a more sociological angle, Brian Stoddart's 'Cricket's Imperial Crisis' in the collection *Sport in History* edited by R. Cashman and M. McKernan.

The basic importance of *Wisden* for the relevant years is so obvious that it seems scarcely necessary to mention it; but it is perhaps worth saying that the 1934 volume is as important as the 1933 one, especially for its reprinting of all the cables exchanged between the ABC and the MCC in the course of the controversy and for the magisterial summing-up of the whole 'bodyline' issue by the editor, S. J. Southerton.

Index

Love, H. S. 167
Lyons, J. A. (Prime Minister of Australia) 93, 95, 118
Lyttelton, R. H. 143, 288

Macaulay, G. G. 154, 162
McCabe, S. J. 18, 28, 33, 36, 44, 103, 104, 111, 115, 149, 153, 168, 178, 201–2, 204, 247
McCarthy, C. N. 295
McDonald, E. A. 17, 21, 26, 38, 40, 63, 69, 75, 76, 137–9, 145, 147, 148, 152, 156, 164, 209
Macdonald, R. 220, 222–3, 227–8, 233, 239, 243, 247, 249–61 *passim*, 263, 268, 270, 272, 275, 287, 304
Mailey, A. A. 68, 103, 106, 107, 137, 148, 224, 266, 299, 306
Mant, G. 66–7
Martindale, E. A. 238, 247, 274
Marylebone Cricket Club (MCC): 14, 54, 55, 57–60, 64, 68, 78, 79, 88, 90, 91, 135, 136, 143, 161, 179, 215–93 *passim*, 304; annual general meeting (1933) 228; Main Committee 79–81, 94–5, 100, 220, 221, 233, 239–40, 242, 243, 244, 249–50, 252–3, 254, 258, 260, 262, 268, 290; selection committees: (1931) 161–2; (1932) 166, 170, 179, 270–1, 303; (1933) 247; (1934) 270–2, 277–9, 281, 283–4; 'bodyline' sub-committee 227–8, 235–7, 239–44, 247, 249, 253; calls conference to discuss 'bodyline' 241–2, 251, 263–5, 267, 276, 280, 287; sub-committee to ban 'bodyline' 287–9, 294–5; reactions to ABC cables 78–81, 96; cables to ABC 80–1, 85, 94–5, 189, 218, 235, 236–7, 249, 250, 251, 255, 256, 257, 258–61, 262, 263, 265, 268, 274; changes position in 1933–34 233–5 244, 249–51, 268, 269,

270, 272, 273, 274, 277–9, 280–4, 287–92; attitude to Jardine 79, 166, 179, 235, 251–2, 259, 267, 268–73, 274, 303; treatment of Larwood 252, 273–82, 304; public resentment of 275–6, 284–5
Mead, C. P. 142
Melbourne (see also Test Matches and England Tour of Australia, 1932–33) 25
Middlesex 286–7
Middleton, R. F. 55, 57
Miller, K. R. 137, 139, 295
Mitchell, F. see 'Second Slip'
Mitchell, T. B. 19, 102, 109, 110, 168
Muncer, L. 286

Nagel, L. E. 29
Nash, L. J.
New South Wales (see also England Tour of Australia, 1932–33): 22, 27, 90; governor of 118–20
New South Wales Cricket Association 88, 219
New Zealand: 18, 54, 121; England team in (1933) 123–6
Newspapers: influence and activities of 9–10, 82–4, 93, 95, 97, 107, 215–16, 220–1, 226–7, 298, 301; on third Test 45–7, 48–9, 53, 56, 58–9; on fourth Test 97–8; Australian, on 'bodyline' 25–6, 62, 86–7, 117–18, 182–3, 231, 274; English, on 'bodyline' 26, 62–9, 74–8, 88–9, 189, 209, 235, 245, 266, 267; on Jardine 107, 110; individual papers (London, except where otherwise stated): *Advertiser* (Adelaide) 36, 53; *Argus* (Melbourne) 26; *Australasian* (Melbourne) 24; *Australian Cricketer* 42; *Bulletin* (Sydney) 70; *Cricketer* 155–6, 224, 245, 248, 266, 267; *Daily Herald* 74; *Daily Mail* 89, 267; *Daily*

Wales 27, 180–1, 182, 205; in first Test 28, 201; in second Test 32; in third Test 50; misses fourth Test 102; in fifth Test 114–15; in England, 1933–34, 235, 236, 237, 238, 256, 264, 276, 279, 280, 281–3, 285–7, 291; after 1934, 293; descriptions of his bowling 195–200

Wall, T. 17, 36, 38, 116, 201
Walters, C. F. 279
Warner, P. F.: 7, 20–1, 61, 64, 67, 73, 78, 79, 93–4, 99, 109–10, 120, 136, 141, 154, 155, 156, 161, 166, 179, 207, 303; at third Test 45–8, 56–7, 58; relations with Jardine 48, 84, 163, 271, 303; in England, 1933–34, 236, 240, 271; love of Australia 20, 47; attitude to 'bodyline' 47–8, 84, 110, 182, 236, 250
Watson, F. 239
Western Australia (see also England Tour of Australia, 1932–33) 19, 97
West Indies (see also Test Matches): 13, 251; in England (1933) 224, 238–9, 244, 246–9

Wickets, pace of 31, 33, 36–7, 102, 110, 200–1, 202, 247
Williams, R. G. 210
Wilmot, R. W. E. 224
Wilson, E. R. 163, 270, 303
Wisden 132, 138, 148–9, 159–60, 245, 248–9, 274–5, 285
Woodfull, W. M.: 17–18, 22, 27, 61, 63, 67, 102, 164, 165, 166, 168, 192, 203, 204, 205–6, 207, 210–11, 221, 283; hit in 'Australian XI' match 25, 182; hit in third Test 40–4, 184, 194, 206, 208; in third Test, 44, 45–50, 53, 55, 56, 58; in fourth Test 103–7; in fifth Test 113, 114, 115, 117
Woods, S. M. J. 136
Woolley, F. E. 18
World War One, impact on cricket 7–9
Wyatt, R. E. S.: 18, 36, 37, 84, 109, 147, 175–6, 178, 180; in England, 1933–34, 236, 279, 281, 283, 284, 289–90; attitude to 'bodyline' 84, 122, 188, 279

Yorkshire: 153–5, 156, 227, 281; *v.* Surrey (1932) 154–5